D0081295

Latin America

Bankers, Generals, and the
Struggle for Social Justice

James F. Petras

Howard Brill
Dennis Engbarth
Edward S. Herman
Morris H. Morley

Rowman & Littlefield
PUBLISHERS

ROWMAN & LITTLEFIELD

Published in the United States of America in 1986
by Rowman & Littlefield, Publishers
(a division of Littlefield, Adams & Company)
81 Adams Drive, Totowa, New Jersey 07512.

Copyright © 1986 by James Petras

Library of Congress Cataloging-in-Publication Data

Petras, James F., 1937–
    Latin America: bankers; generals, and the
struggle for social justice.

    Bibliography
    Includes index.
    1. Latin America—Economic conditions—1945–
—Addresses, essays, lectures. 2. Latin America—
Relations—United States—Addresses, essays, lectures.
3. United States—Relations—Latin America—Addresses,
essays, lectures. 4. Debts, External—Latin America—
Addresses, essays, lectures. 5. Military government—
Latin America—Addresses, essays, lectures.
6. Social justice—Addresses, essays, lectures.
I. Brill, Howard. II. Title.
HC 125.P4643   1986   337.8   86-1885
ISBN 0-8476-7505-X
ISBN 0-8476-7515-7 (pbk.)

86 87 88 / 10 9 8 7 6 5 4 3 2 1

Printed in the United States of America

Contents

Tables

Preface

During the last two decades, investigation of the world-wide expansion of capital and the concomitant growth of global political and economic organizations has come into sharp relief in Third World Development studies. This was a useful corrective to the narrow-focus approach rooted in modernization theory, which examined the stages of growth of isolated nation-states. Yet the world economy has evolved over time: configuration characteristics of one period are outmoded in the next.

In the 1950s and 1960s paramount importance was correctly attributed to the United States in shaping and controlling Third World development. In the 1980s there are strong grounds for challenging this assumption: the emergence of newly industrializing countries, Western and Eastern competitors, and new economic structures (such as OPEC and ASEAN) indicate a *tendency* toward increasing dispersion of power within the world economy. New trading networks and sources for technological transfers within the Third World mark alternative possibilities. Many of these changes, however, are not fully exploited by Third World countries, in part because they are still influenced by "globalist" conceptions of the world economy. New interstices for investment and regional opportunities for trade are not seized because there remains the idea that dependency on the United States is unavoidable—an economic fact of life that may be struggled against but must be endured. In the opening essay "The Tyranny of Globalism," we subject the various globalist approaches to criticism both at the theoretical and empirical level, pointing to globalist misconceptions concerning the nature of "power" in the world economy as well as their failure to grasp the empirical changes in the world economy. Globalism, which appears to be a "radical approach," ultimately is described as a prescription for passivity and conformity as it imputes overwhelming importance to world market determination. In contrast, by examining power as a set of conditional class relations, we point to the possibilities of reversing and overcoming existing forms of imperial domination.

While global domination is not fixed and irreversible, imperial power persists even as its forms are changing. If the 1960s were the era of the expansion of multinational corporations, and the 1970s the period of financial expansion abroad, the 1980s are characterized by the increasing importance of the multilateral banks. As the world economic crises of 1980–1981 deepened, both multinational corporations and commercial banks were placed in a vulnerable position: their overseas holdings and loans were threatened by unpayable debt payments and declining markets. The multilateral banks (such as the International Monetary Fund and the World Bank) stepped into this delicate situation. Our essay "the International Monetary Fund, Austerity, and the State in Latin America" situates the role of the IMF in a complex matrix: it is neither an omnipotent power nor a technical financial institution but rather a political actor utilizing economic instruments to refashion the economic and social structure of vulnerable Third World countries. The major point of the essay, however, is to emphasize the interplay between the IMF, the metropolitan states, private banking, Third World states, and the class forces within the targeted countries in shaping the impact of IMF policy. The growth of IMF influence in the debt crisis is not absolute. It takes place in the context of countries which have increasingly industrialized and created important "pressure groups" and class institutions capable of resisting the radical free market dogma espoused by the IMF and its clientele.

The third essay, "Third World Industrialization: Implications for Trade Unions," describes the uneven process of industrial expansion and the varying strategies open to labor movements confronted with political and economic challenges from local regimes as well as from the IMF and international corporations. Capitalist industrialization is not a linear process smoothing out the incongruities of Third World societies: growth and crises, increased income, and the extension of wage relations have combined with the current draconian measures prescribed by the IMF to create greater class and national polarization. Complex and flexible alliance strategies are discussed as mechanisms through which trade unions could more effectively intervene in the political process.

In this context, the economic crises and IMF-led offensive promoting "free market" prescriptions to solve the world crises have dashed hopes for international economic reform expressed by Third World leaders in the early 1970s. The essay "Reagan's Policy and the New International Economic Order: Epitaph for an Unsuccessful Movement" discusses this development and the shift in emphasis from reform to increase national development to "reforms" to increase metropolitan penetration.

In Latin America two contradictory processes have emerged in response to the economic and political crises: a return to democracy and heightened militarization of U.S. policy. In South America the 1980s have witnessed the demise of free-market economic policies, accompanied by burgeoning social movements, and the increasing isolation of

U.S.-backed military regimes. The possibilities of continuing the autocratic, export-oriented regimes were overwhelmed by skyrocketing debts and declining markets. The military and their U.S. backers yielded governance to traditional civilian politicians on condition that they retain existing military structures and prerogatives and respect debt obligations. The essay "Resurgent Democracy in Latin America?" describes the constraints and contradictions inherent in this negotiated transition to democracy, its fragile foundations, and its limitations as an instrument for overcoming the current economic crises.

In Central America the demise of the free-market regimes and the growth of social movements have not led to democracy but to increased militarization of the region under the direction and financing of the U.S. government. The growth of terror and violence as instruments of control, the centrality of the military, and the all-purpose use of anticommunist ideology define U.S. political intervention. Washington's political perspective is described in our essay "Anticommunism: Washington's Alliance with Death Squads and Generals." The possibility of alternatives to military definitions of relations with the region are presented in our comparison between Canadian and U.S. policy: "United States and Canada: State Policy and Strategic Perspectives in Central America."

The struggle for social justice in Latin America goes on *within* and *against* the boundaries established by the bankers and generals. The correspondence between the increasingly bellicose policy of the Reagan administration and the massive financial commitments of U.S. banks underlines their reciprocal influence in shaping U.S. policy. The emerging democratic and socialist movements attempting to improve living standards in Latin America confront these two major institutions shaping U.S. policy. The decay of civilian democratic regimes in this difficult context would open the door to a new period of militant confrontation between the military and revolutionaries. Ultimately the solution to the crises is not to be found in liberal political reforms but in a democratic socialist transformation. In the final essay "Authoritarianism, Democracy, and the Transition to Socialism," the possibilities and problems involved in the transition to socialism are discussed, focusing on the twin problems of democratic vulnerability and authoritarian proclivities. The politics of transition must consider the external dangers of destabilization and great-power intervention, which require measures to safeguard the security of the regime as well as the establishment of conditions for the reconstruction of democratic institutions. The essay concludes by reconceptualizing the notion of "socialist pluralism" and offering a critique and alternative to "market socialism."

Part I

Perspectives on Development

1 / *The Tyranny of Globalism*

JAMES PETRAS and HOWARD BRILL

> [The] U.S. cannot hope to compete successfully with an
> old-established manufacturing country such as Britain.
> —J. R. McCulloch, as cited by Engels (1968: 333)

Introduction

The tendency to look to the explanation of development or underdevelopment as a product of determinations by the advanced capitalist countries, or as simply a reflection of the operations of the world market, was an influential paradigm among many Third World analysts in the 1970s.[1] In this paper we specify several basic theoretical and empirical shortcomings in globalist approaches to the study of world economy. Our approach emphasizes changes in the world economy in the 1970s and 1980s which create a new set of relationships and networks of exchange that cannot be encapsulated in a simple dichotomous or trichotomous descriptive stratification approach.

We begin our discussion by focusing on the links between global theorizing and Weberian conceptions of power, neoclassical and Ricardian economic theory, and modes of analysis based on deductivism. We elaborate a relational class conflict approach to the world economy and emphasize the regulation and transformation of capitalist relations at the subsystem (national-class) level.

In the second part we examine empirical patterns that are characteristic of new directions and tendencies in the world economy. In particular we point to the emergence of alternative resources for development which provide Third World countries with opportunities to reduce dependency on advanced capitalist countries. New resources that exist within and between Third World countries provide Third World regimes with the opportunity to select and exploit new markets and redefine their relations with advanced capitalist countries.

Definition of Globalism

The failure of globalist theories to account for changes in the world economy during the 1970s and 1980s led to numerous reappraisals of development theory and attempts to reject or reformulate theories of development.[2] But generally these reformulations merely reproduce the same theoretical problems, replacing a bipolar static conception of the world economy with tripartite or multipolar static conceptions. In addition to a "core" and "periphery" we encounter a "semi-periphery" and, when this new category becomes inadequate, a "permieter of the core" and "perimeter of the periphery" are invented (see Arrighi 1985, 7). The changes in the world economy are explained on an ad hoc basis; the concept of "blocked development" is replaced by the notion of "dependent development," the traditional international division of labor is replaced by a "new" international division of labor, new labels are created to categorize changes that cannot be explained by existing theoretical constructions. These reformulations are inadequate because the basic assumptions about the organization of power and the conception of the world economy do not change.

Underlying different theories and formulations of Third World development is the particular perspective, known as "globalism." While not constituting a unified or coherent theory and methodology, this approach consists of a set of assumptions and modes of reasoning which are embedded in a disparate group of theories concerned with the world economy. Globalism can be described by a set of four characteristics (although particular theories which are a product of this perspective may utilize only a partial set of these characteristics). First, domination is conceived in terms of institutionalized power. Power is an attribute of a position within a compulsory organization, in this case the interstate system. Second, the position of an actor within the interstate system is determined by an analysis based on a static-equilibrium theorization of the market. Third, the social totality is an expressive totality—the parts of the whole express the essential nature of the whole. The institutional structure of the world economy is reproduced in the internal characteristics of the nation-states which are its members. The analysis of the social totality proceeds by the assimilation of all its constituent elements into a unitary scheme which attempts to subsume all the system's characteristics at the same level of abstraction, thus leading to essentialism and the raising of empirical generalizations to systemic axioms. Fourth, arguments are developed by means of deductive or axiomatic reasoning. The attributes of the actors are deduced from postulates that presume a particular systemic organization. These characteristics of globalist thought have become embodied in the categories of "core" and "periphery," which serve both to describe and classify countries according to representative attributes and to analyze those attributes in terms of deduced "relations" arising from particular models of social and economic action.

The Weberian Roots of Globalism

Conceptions of institutionalized power involve the identification of a hierarchy of organization and the attribution of power to the upper levels of the "structure." For Weber (1978) an organization constitues a set of rules and expectations (the "order"), which governs the social activity of its members. The "order" of an institution is enforced by a specific order (the "chief") or a group of actors (the "administrative staff") whose position in the organization gives them the ability to "influence" or "command" other members. Transferred to the world economy, this perspective identifies "power" as residing in the "core" nations. For globalists the world economy constitutes a system with a set of rules and expectations, organized by the "core," which governs the economic activity of the other member states. The order of the world economy is enforced by a specific group of actors ("core" states) whose position in the global system gives them the ability to command other members. The problem with this approach is that it can never account for change except ex post facto. Whenever there is an alternation in power, the new institutional configuration is described and categorized.

Power is not a "thing" derived from institutional position but rather a *relation* of domination and subordination between social actors (such as classes or nations). The two-sidedness of a power relation requires that one consider the capacities within both "core" and "Third World" social formations and states. A subordinated actor is never absolutely controlled—there is always a potential for resistance within the relation. The globalist perspective paints a picture of domination based on a passive-receptacle notion of the Third World, in which the internal class forces are nonactors or even blank surfaces ready to be shaped and exploited by the "core."

The institutional conception of power has no place for class struggle. An unequal distribution of power is assumed as given, and modifications in that distribution are understood to be limited. The problem of domination is reduced to tracing out flows of influence, capital, commercial exchanges, and processes of production. A relational approach to power begins by identifying the sources of strength and weakness in both the dominant and subordinate, and recognizing that there are different sets of resources that shape the capacity to act. While the "core" may have disproportionate capital, the "periphery" may have a mobilized and organized labor force. The conflicts and compromises that are the concrete manifestation of a particular relation will be molded by the different resources defining the context in which relations exist.

Institutional configurations and market forces derive from, rather than being determined by, the contextual basis of a relation.

Deductive Logic and Neoclassical Paradigms

Globalist theories frequently, but not always, utilize a deductive logic to organize their theoretical statements. These statements can vary considerably in form and content, although three common forms can be identified. One form is analogous to the economic theory of comparative advantage. Certain abstract actors are identified as possessing the most resources (of a particular kind one might note) a priori, and the exercise of power is then derived from this general level. This "structural advantage" is then mapped onto particular countries or regions. Roemer (1983) uses this approach in a critique of comparative advantage theory, ironically allowing us to see the virtual identity of these nominally opposed theories. While neoclassicists see the differential distribution of capital as value-neutral, globalists identify it as the source of power in an ethically unjust world. Another form taken by this approach is to use particular abstract formulations or extensions of formulations from classical Marxist texts as ideal-typical representations of concrete historical activity (see Marcussen and Torp 1982, and Marcussen 1982 on the work of S. Amin). Thus capital flows from Western countries are merely representations of the "tendency of the rate of profit to decline" despite the varied reasons and different forms that capital flows can take. The abstract logic of capitalist accumulation is confused with concrete processes and patterns. A third variation, empirical generalizations, are valid and even useful for particular conjunctures, but are here raised to abstract postulates or axioms. These axioms then become the basis for demonstrating "laws" that "prove" the inevitability of the axioms from which they were derived. Thus the characteristics of "extraverted growth," instead of being understood in terms of historically specific relations and the processes that determined them, become an eternally self-replicating set of conditions.

Ironically, while theoretical formulations employing the globalist perspective are commonly situated in a discourse explicitly criticizing neoclassical ideologies of development, they implicitly adopt many of the same assumptions and methods. Both neoclassicists and globalists conclude that the creative, constructive (in terms of the expansion of the whole system) forces of the world economy are transmitted from the "core" of that economy to its "periphery." Despite different political orientations, both perpectives arrive at similar conclusions because at a certain level they embody the same set of assumptions. The extent to which a theorist working within a similar set of assumptions utilizes an axiomatic or deductive form of reasoning will govern the consistency with which conclusions will match the assumptions. For example, Roemer (1983) utilizes neoclassical assumptions and methods to analyze unequal exchange. The concept of unequal exchange is given a formal definition apparently related to Marx's concept of surplus labor and is shown to occur in the model Roemer constructs. But this leads Roemer to question the ethical justice of the original distribution of means of production rather than to examine the nature of relations between actors and the contradictory tensions inherent in those relations. Roemer, by formalizing this approach with extreme rigor and precision, unintentionally shows us its limits.

There is little question that there are inequalities in the world. This is not an extraordinary fact; it is not a radical conclusion. Is anyone surprised that there are "winners" and "losers" in a capitalist world economy? The ideologists of capitalism do not claim otherwise. The thrust of neoclassicism is to demonstrate that inequalities, by the miracle of the market, result in the maximization of social wealth. It is possible to analyze social inequalities, to categorize them, develop orderings and ranks, seek the rules and expectations governing economic orderings, and perhaps even attempt to understand the historical conditions which limit, reproduce, or extend inequalities. This is the problematic developed by Weber and is one of the major intellectual heritages of globalism. This framework can successfully describe the set of rules and expectations which helps sustain inequalities. But as a means of understanding and predicting social change in capitalism, it is strictly limited, as it excludes the central role of class struggle from the analysis.

The Weberian approach accepts the neoclassical conception of the market as the starting point of the theoretical analysis of capitalism. The neoclassical market is an abstract concept, not an empirical category; it is a particular way of apprehending reality. The market is the point of exchange between actors who enter it formally equal but often unequally endowed with exchangeable resources. At the empirical level it is possible to introduce formal inequalities, so-called "distortions," but the theoretical strucure is based on a certain abstract conception of the market. The market results in the formation of a temporary relation between two actors and the exchange between those individuals of equivalent resources. If, after a series of exchanges are consummated, the actors are endowed with unequal resources, it is because they entered the point of exchange unequal. Market relations merely reproduce the preceding unequal distribution of resources. The existence of unequal actors precedes the relation between the actors, which is equal and qualitatively uniform. While Weber argues that the market is not a universal, ahistorical entity but something rooted in the accidents and determinations of human history, he accepts the concept of the market as an abstract point where actors come to relate under formally equal conditions. Although globalist theories frequently, if not always, include some critique of neoclassical economics, neoclassical conceptions creep into globalist theories because those theories accept conceptions of power implicitly based on the neoclassical market. This "back-door neoclassicism" is even more evident in theories that develop abstract notions of unequal exchange on the world market (see Dostaler 1982, for a discussion of the influence of neoclassicism on post-Saffra Marxist theoreticians).

The "Iron Cage" of Globalism

The neoclassical and globalist conception of the market is a static-equilibrium model.[3] Neoclassicists express this in terms of a program that constrains social actors to maximize their utility. Globalists express this in terms of the conditions required to reproduce the "system." Both models lead to the same result—the distribution of the social product after exchange is the same as before exchange. It is possible to add a concept of accumulation to static-equilibrium models, but this results in a larger "pie" being sliced in the same way as the previous "pie." Because relations are conceived of as temporary, uniform, and formally equal, there is no theoretical space for change in the relations between actors.

Weber's inability to transcend theoretically the concept of the market is reproduced in his metaphor of the "iron cage." Capitalism becomes an inescapable social reality except through the appeal of a mystical charismatic leader, who by altering the values of people destroys the iron cage. It is remarkable that a similar formulation is prevalent in globalist conceptions. The iron cage is replaced by the "system," which is also inescapable except in toto. For Amin, the charismatic leader takes the the form of a universal ideological transformation, or for others a world war (see Sutcliffe 1972; 192). Prospects for the former are extremely unlikely and for the latter likely but surely unwelcomed.

Actors do not form purely economic relations under formally equal conditions. Relations are comprised of different levels of interaction; political, economic, ideological, and social—combined, unequal, and in contradiction. These relations are not static—as they are extended and reproduced they are also transformed. The transformative processes can be understood in terms of an abstract logic, but the concrete patterns that manifest them are historically specific. The reality of inequalities should not blind us to the possibility of changing the relations of domination on which those inequalities are based. The question is then the manner in which relations are changed and the historical possibilities available at any particular conjuncture.

In contrast to the globalist perspective in dependency theories is a relational approach to the problems of development. The world economy cannot be understood as merely the aggregate of the parts that comprise it. But neither can nation-states, regions, or classes be reduced to an expression of the whole. Nation-states, regions, or classes can only be understood in terms of their own specific logic. The existence of a world economy does not in any sense imply its homogeneity. The expansion of capitalism occurs through combined and uneven development. Since social relations in a capitalist world economy are viewed as being contradictory—that is, in tension—change cannot be conceptualized as an exogenous force that shifts a system in equilibrium but as endogenous to the system.

The relational approach argues inductively that domination is a consequence of the particular relations that evolve between states and classes within and between regions. What becomes critical in this approach is the changing capacities within Third World countries—the emerging of new class forces and the forging of new class alliances capable of redefining the nation's role in the world market and its relations within the Third World. The process of altering relations at the global level begins through changes within the national class and state structure.[4]. The changing structure of the world market and economy presents varying opportunities, risks, and constraints over time. The ability to maximize opportunities and to minimize the effects of limitations and exposure to dangers is largely a function of local state and class capacities. This does not mean that the global context is unimportant, since opportunities may be very limited and constraints very extensive and strict. Nor should foreign intervention be ignored. The ability, for example, of foreign intelligence services to penetrate state apparatuses is a real danger; but as the Cuban experience shows, the success of interventions is not inevitable.

New Developments in the World Economy

There are several sets of changes that provide openings for Third World countries to minimize the impact of relations with "center" nations as a controlling factor. First, there has been a *dispersal of controlling resources* among a variety of countries, as opposed to their concentration in one or two dominant countries. The United States no longer "monopolizes" industrial, technological, financial, or commercial activity in the world economy. East and West Germany, Hungary and Sweden, South Korea and North Korea, Japan and the Soviet Union (among many others) offer opportunities for obtaining advanced technology and modern machine goods at competitive prices (Berrios 1983, figs. 1 and 2; and Sabolo 1983). Trade is increasing between Third World countries (so-called South–South trade)—developing an intraregional pattern that is beginning to supplant traditional North–South trade (Shinohara 1983). The proliferation of new banking centers and local multinationals (both public and private) within Third World countries provides the organizational capacity for joint ventures between Third World countries and smaller advanced countries (Kumar 1982, 418).

Growth in East–South trade has increased both absolutely and relatively. In addition, trade relations between Socialist countries and the Third World have been based on long-term agreements which offer greater trade stability (Berrios 1983, 242). The positive features of East–South trade must, however, be balanced by a number of negative aspects (ibid., 241). First, Socialist countries generally export capital goods to Third World countries and import primary products. Nor has this trade remedied the continued deterioration of the prices of primary products relative to capital goods. East–South trade has tended to be concentrated, affecting only a few of the developing countries—the so-called newly industrializing countries (NICs) and countries located in strategic geopolitical locations. A substantial part of Soviet trade with developing countries has consisted of arms transfers. In addition, growth in East–South trade has occurred simultaneously with growth in East–West trade, and therefore both Socialist and developing countries are competing for the same markets in the West. Socialist countries export primary products to and import capital goods from the West.

Economic assistance by Socialist countries to developing countries is considerably smaller than aid from the West (ibid., 243–44). Soviet aid to developing countries amounted to only 1 percent of all assistance. The fact that Soviet assistance has, however, tended to be long-term has enabled Third World countries to develop some long-term plans. Technical assistance, consisting of technicians and educational training, has been much more significant (ibid., 245). The number of technicians sent to developing countries has increased from 15,900 in 1970 to 72,655 in 1978. Technology agreements are also increasing (ibid., 248). Socialist assistance generally takes the form of payments-in-kind rather than financial aid, because of the chronic shortages of exchangable currencies in Socialist countries.

Joint ventures between Socialist and local enterprises are increasing (ibid., 247). An interesting feature of this trend is that these joint ventures are frequently composed of a combination of Western, Eastern, and local enterprises. Investment in new productive facilities throughout the world seems to be conducted by complex consortiums drawing capital from a multiplicity of sources.

Trade between Third World countries has grown. In 1963 intra-Third World exports from non-petroleum-exporting countries amounted to 17.4 percent of their exports, but in 1983 South–South exports grew to 30.2 percent of their exports (Sabalo 1983, 595). The size of Third World trade remains relatively small, but the aggregate data indicates a change in how that trade is divided between Third World and industrialized countries. Relative to all world trade, intra-Third World trade is small and the absolute rate of increase compared to the rate of increase for world trade has been considerably less (ibid., fig. 3). By focusing on the size of world trade, however, the significance of South–South trade can be lost.

In a number of countries and in certain regions, major shifts to manufactured goods and even capital goods is occurring although most Third World exports are still primary products. These shifts are seen most dramatically in Southeast Asia (see table 1.1). Capital goods exports grew from less than 5 percent to over 25 percent since 1960 in South Korea, Singapore, and Hong Kong (Shinohara 1983, 66). Southeast Asian exports shifted from Great Britain and the United States to Japan (Shinohara 1983; 66). Singapore's exports to Japan accounted for 10.9 percent of its total exports, while exports to Malaysia, Hong Kong, and Thailand accounted for 29.9 percent of its exports in 1982 (U.N. 1984). Although the importance of Japan in Southeast Asian trade must not be underestimated, this trade is qualitatively different from neo-colonial trade and is occurring within the context of a matrix of trade relations that includes other industrialized countries and other Third World countries.

The quantitative importance of Third World multinationals cannot be presently determined with precision (Kumar 1982, 398), but some figures are available. South Korean overseas investment "exceeds $248 million;" Brazilian foreign investment reached $60 million in 1978; and Taiwan, Hong Kong, India, and Argentina are also engaged in major foreign investment activity (ibid., 399–400). Most foreign investment

Table 1.1. Shift in Export Commodities

	Year	Share of manufactured goods in total exports (percent)
South Korea and	early 1960s	approx. 15
Taiwan	1980	almost 90
Malaysia	1960	0–5
	1980	27
Philippines	1960	0–5
	1980	24
Thailand	1960	0–5
	1980	35

Source: Shinohara 1983, 66.

"has gone to developing countries" (ibid., 400). Third World multinationals tend to use technology adapted to Third World conditions and have lower overhead and expatriate costs than multinationals from "core" countries (ibid., 404, 406). Third World multinationals improve the bargaining strength of host countries (ibid., 414) and can provide alternative sources of investment, technology, and managerial capacities. But Third World multinationals do not inherently reduce dependency or foreign domination. Third World multinationals are motivated by profit, not solidarity. The development of economic relations between Third World countries does not exclude the possibility that these relations may represent new forms of exploitation.

The second factor that is important is the growth of productive forces within the Third World and their capacity to *disaggregate the "investment" and "technological purchase" packages to select, adopt, and harness elements favorable to national development*. Parallel to the increasing poliferation of sites of production, there exist a variety of sources and methods of collaboration. The simple dependence on direct investment to obtain technology is no longer the only approach or the most desirable one. Time-bound contracts, with training and fade-out formulas, are one alternative. The development of institutional structures to facilitate the acquisition of new technical skills and promote innovation is essential. The successful use of alternative opportunities depends upon the development by the state of an institutional and entrepreneurial framework capable of absorbing the investments and advancing on the basis of the borrowed technology.

The development of linkages between Third World countries and the growth of productive forces within the Third World still remains quantitatively limited (Kumar 1982; 419). What is crucial is not only the degree of dependence at any given moment *but the direction of movement*. The basic issue is whether dependency provides resources to create autonomous growth or becomes a chronic condition, reproducing itself through relations and forces incapable of transcending the initial stages of "dependence." The potentialities for "conversion" from dependency to autonomous development then are not linked to autarkic development but to the capacity to exploit market opportunities selectively and to harness them to dynamic internal forces.

Dialectics of Growth: Class and State Capabilities

Our approach emphasizes *choices by internal state and class forces* over against the globalist determination by the world market or "core" countries. This is not a voluntarist exercise in will which overlooks differential power and resources. We argue that it is possible for Third

World countries to *avoid deep structural links* and reduce the negative consequences of subsequent confrontations with "core" countries through multiple relations with a variety of non-"core" nations offering competitive opportunities. Of course the focus on state activity and internal class forces does not exist in isolation from the world economy. The expansion of the economic activities of the dominant capitalist nations during the 1960s clearly played a facilitating role in the industrialization of the NICs. It is also important to recognize that dependency can be transformed into more subtle forms. The control of marketing channels by multinationals can limit the access of Third World enterprises to export markets. This approach does not ignore the power of "advanced capitalism" but rejects the conception of domination as a static condition and the neglect of political activity as a category in the analysis of domination.

Abstract notions of "the market" obscure the plurality of points of access, as well as the variety of terms and possible associations that have emerged over the past decade. The term "the market's power" mystifies the various arenas of commercial transactions and the political rather than economic considerations frequently involved in those transactions. Even in high technology product areas, such as semiconductors, micro-computers, and biotechnology, it is possible for Third World countries to develop very specialized products and find outlets within the interstices of the market. The selective use of tariffs and trade barriers or the threat of these barriers can force multinationals to move some high-technology processes to Third World countries.

In certain sectors involving moderate advances in technology, the ability of Third World countries to progress is established. In the heavy machinery and tool industries of Brazil, Korea, Mexico, and Taiwan, "significant progress" has occurred (Kumar 1982, 406). Evans (1979, 172–94) argues that nationalist pressure in Brazil forced the foreign-owned pharmaceutical industry to engage in local research and development, although those activities were limited and were initiated only after considerable pressure was exerted. The threat of protectionist measures in Mexico and Brazil in support of a fledgling microcomputer industry in those countries resulted in a flurry of negotiations and threats by the U.S. computer industry and the U.S. State Department, respectively. The Singapore consumer electronics industry is being encouraged, through a variety of incentives by the state, to move from labor-intensive goods to high-technology items (U.S. Department of Commerce 1983b, 2–3). Production is being shifted from semiconductors to "hybrid circuits and memory devices." The development of an integrated electronics industry is being fostered, but through the substantial movement of multinational production into Singapore. In Hong Kong most computers are imported, but a small volume of local production is being established in the minicomputer areas (U.S. Department of Commerce 1983a, 3, 8–9).

The most advanced technology, the "fifth generation" projects in artifial intelligence, is overwhelmingly dominated by the U.S. and Japan. It is not merely the Third World that is dependent here but also Western Europe. The extent to which developments in this area will affect economic activities is presently unknown, although the massive resources being allocated for research suggests that it will be significant. The prospects for Third World countries in acquiring these technologies seems limited. But a distinction needs to be made between the development of new scientific and technical knowledge and its assimilation into production. If the assimilation of knowledge was purely an additive process, Great Britain should be the most technologically advanced in the world and a latecomer like Japan relatively backward.

Third World countries face the problem of advancing beyond the initial stages of industrial diversification, overcoming local vested interests, and developing more technologically sophisticated products. The alternative is to fall victim to not only the advanced capitalist countries but to the new wave of industrializing countries who are just emerging in the marketplace. As Kumar (1982, 420) notes, "Economic domination is not an exclusive trait of industrialized states. Japan's imperialism towards other Asian countries during the 1930s and 1940s, with its creation of the "Asian Co-prosperity Sphere," is perhaps the most extreme example of this possibility. South Africa's economic dominance over the southern African region has deeply affected regional development and limited both the political and economic choices of neighboring countries. In South America the relatively rapid growth and large size of the Brazilian economy compared to other South American countries opens the possibility of its domination of those countries.

The "expansion and differentiation" (see Marcussen and Torp 1982) of the international division of labor cannot be understood purely in terms of redeployment strategies organized by the "core," but rather as the result of deliberate political-economic choices taken by relatively autonomous state regimes in conjunction with local segments of the capitalist class in different regions. While multinational corporations in advanced capitalist countries may plan to redeploy in Third World countries, redeployment itself requires a set of compromises and alliances between foreign capital, local capital, and state regimes (Evans 1979). In addition, the need for multinational corporations to redeploy may be a result of the increasing development of Third World countries, their increased capacity to select between different sources of primary and intermediate products, and the ability of Third World countries to retain greater control over their resources. For example, in the aluminum industry, the long-term growth in demand will probably come from the major industrializing countries; currently Brazil, Mexico, South Korea, and Argentina account for 10 percent of world aluminum consumption (Holman et al. 1985). This movement in demand, combined with higher costs for energy and bauxite, has led production and investment in the United States, Western Europe, and Japan to be reduced. New investment in Third World aluminum production is conducted not only by multinationals from advanced capitalist countries but also by Taiwanese and South Korean corporations (Tanzer 1982, 78–79; and Kerns 1982, 79). New investment in aluminum production characteristically involves complex consortiums of foreign capitalists, foreign states (such as Japan in Venezuela and Malaysia), and local state regimes.

State regimes do not merely represent the dominant classes but can formulate policies for the most dynamic segment of the ruling class, namely the industrialists. Thus industrialization in the Third World has to be understood as being "due to a significant extent to the political decision of domestic economic and social agents which came together in the definition of the strategy formulated by the State" (Fajnzylber 1981, 121).

The transformation of the international division of labor provides the greatest difficulties for theories dependent on static conceptualizations of the relations between regions of the world economy. Once a certain degree of infrastructural, transport, and communication capacity is developed, capital can move freely between different geographic areas. It is not surprising that capital moves, since a multiplicity of factors may result in higher profits in one region as opposed to another. But when capital moves into a new region, it must be assimilated into a preexisting matrix of relations which in turn is altered by the intrusion of foreign capital. Politically this translates into designing policies and constructing alliances which foster relations that promote development, limit dependency, and control the formation of classes or strata with a vested interest in dependent relations.

The state plays a central role in the "upgrading" of industrial production, as with other aspects of Third World development, by regulating the inflow of imports, investments, and loans and by promoting the formation of markets, innovative activity, and ventures into new product lines. A constructive policy is based on the harnessing of external inputs to the development of locally based production rather than the reverse. Dependency, foreign takeovers, imperial intervention, and the permeation of the political structure by foreign interests are real dangers and a frequent occurrence. The dangers of integrating into the world economy must, however, be viewed in conjunction with the opportunities. Also the adequacy of autarky as a reasonable strategy for many small countries must be seriously questioned. Internal resources are frequently too limited to support the diverse needs of a human population existing at even minimal living standards. For large countries, access to foreign exchange, capital goods markets, and advanced technology provide means for the expansion of industry greater than possible for policies based on self-reliance through autarky.

Contrary to popular opinion, the states in the NICs of Southeast Asia follow interventionalist strategies. Fajnzylber (1981, 127) summarizes these strategies:

> the subordination of the financial sphere to the objective of industrial growth; the definition of sectoral priorities and integral economic policies in support of selected branches; the clear articulation with an entrepreneurial sector [; . . . the political repression of the labor force]; and the design and clear utilization of a massive policy of training labour.

Similarly Brazil has identified priority sectors which are then subjected to a combination of selective protectionist measures, subsidies, state investment, and requirements for local content in the raw materials and instruments of production (Teubal 1984). The political repression of the working class is another component of this strategy. A weakness of Brazil's strategy during the 1970s was the failure to control the financial sector, and the resulting debt crisis forced Brazil to acquiesce to the intrusion of the IMF. The ability of the IMF to reshape a country's development strategy is an illustration of the dangers involved in indiscriminate integration into the world economy.

The dangers resulting from insertion in the world market can be contained through a closely coordinated strategy worked out by the state and productive sectors. The recent debt crisis affecting several major industrializing Third World countries is an example of the *lack* of state regulation of borrowing, and the weakness of local efforts at disciplining capital to enforce savings and investment. The subsequent intervention of the IMF in all aspects of Third World development agendas and the resulting massive outflow of service payments is fair warning to those countries that engage in indiscriminate insertion into the world market exchanges and borrowing. In contrast, the capacity of the Southeast Asian countries, except for the Phillipines (see Cline 1984, for projection on debt-servicing difficulties), to rebound from the economic crisis and recapture their rhythm of growth indicates that the economic crisis did *not have a uniform impact* on all countries involved in the world market. The nature of the set of relations between a country and the world economy and the mediation of those relations by the state—not the mere fact of their existence—is the central issue. The openness of the Asian countries to trade was matched by a carefully calibrated borrowing policy linked to the growth of export industries and capable of coping with debt payments. Local financing, supplemented by selective foreign investments, allowed these countries to avoid the debt trap. In Latin America, the opportunity to borrow from external sources became a *substitute* rather than a supplement from local savings and investment by the public and private entrepreneurial groups. While foreign investment can be used to achieve internal development goals, it can also serve to link local development to the needs of multinational banks.

Conclusion

The globalist perspective fails to explain adequately the combined and uneven development of an expanding world economy characterized by the increasing differentiation of the Third World. Globalism does not provide a useful basis for constructing development policies. Prescriptions based on the total transformation of the world economy are completely unrealistic at the present time. The denigration of local development efforts as hopeless or as the mere reshuffling of a zero-sum game is an invitation to passivity or to autarkic experiments, with devastating results in both cases. Globalism blocks an understanding of the cumulative dispersion of economic power and the establishment of new networks of relations through the representation of the world economy as a unified and expressive totality rather than a structured totality composed of a set of transactions, exchanges, and associations involving discrete and localized actors transforming and transformed by the development of capitalism. The focus on institutions rather than relations and the unilinear conception of the flow of power distorts the dialectical interaction between regions and countries and denies the significance of action and change within state and social structures. The notion of dependency as a static condition instead of a relation leads to theories which fail to examine the role of class struggle in altering and redefining a country's insertion in the world economy and role in the international division of labor.

There is no inevitable path of development in the Third World, no formula or model that can be simply practiced or copied without concern with concrete political realities. Because of class strata with objective interests in the continuation of dependent relations, many countries will be unable to alter external relations or sustain new relations without first restructuring internal social and political relations. Particular geopolitical contingencies, such as proximity to imperialist states actively engaging in military interventionism, can limit available choices. There should be no illusions concerning many of the regimes capable of promoting and sustaining development in the Third World: these regimes are frequently repressive and inegalitarian. Development has not been the antithesis of exploitation: it has been a historical process that changes the form of exploitation and transforms the forces which reproduce and struggle against exploitation. Relations of domination continue. What is in question is the terms under which domination continues, the changes in the capacities of the dominant and the subordinate, and the transformations in the contradictions defining a relation of domination.

The walls of the globalist cage—the notions of dependency and development shaped by static conceptions of social and economic organization—are being breached by the emergence of several developing countries engaged in relatively successful strategies for autonomous growth. New networks and centers are proliferating outside the bipolar "core" and "periphery" framework. By moving beyond globalist dogma, the way is open for a more realistic, activist, and open approach to the possibilities of development.

Notes

1. Some of the most important texts within the globalist paradigm are Amin (1974), Emmanuel (1972), Frank (1978), Frobel et al. (1977), and Wallerstein (1979). This paper is not intended as a balanced critique of these specific works but rather as a criticism of a particular approach to understanding the world economy. The insights of these authors are, of course, significant and valuable.

2. For criticisms see Bernstein (1982), Henriquez (1983), Marcussen (1982), Petras (1983), and Petras and Trachte (1978). This list is by no means exhaustive, and the quality of the cited papers varies widely. Note also that the position of Petras (1983) on the NICs is considerably different from the interpretation presented here.

3. See Roemer 1983, and Marcussen and Torp 1982, 142–43 on S. Amin. Note that what Amin and Marcussen and Torp describe as a dynamic equilibrium we are calling a static equilibrium. "Static" does not exclude change but implies that endogenous change is directed towards an equilibrium. A "dynamic" model focuses attention on the time-path of a variable; whether a "dynamic" model tends towards equilibrium is an open question. This is the conventional usage in economics. The distinction, for our purposes, is not that important. A relational approach requires a mathematical description that not only includes change in variables but reflects the fact that the relations between variables also change. These models do exist, but the question of their usefulness for explaining social change is beyond the scope of this chapter.

4. Relational approaches based on different units of analysis are possible, but the unit of analysis chosen is largely determined by the type of questions being asked. The distance between New York and Paris is measured in kilometers, not millimeters. If the question is concerned with how to *alter* existing global relations, the most appropriate unit of analysis appears to be the state and social classes. If the problem is why change is limited and slow (in terms of the length of a human life), other units of analysis may be more appropriate.

Bibliography

Amin, S. 1974. *Accumulation on a World Scale*. New York: Monthly Review Press.
Arrighi, G. 1985. "Fascism to Democratic Socialism: Logic and Limits of a

Transition." In *Semiperipheral Development: The Politics of Southern Europe in the Twentieth Century* (from manuscript), edited by G. Arrighi. Beverly Hills: Sage.

Bernstein, H. 1982. "Industrialization, Development, and Dependence." In *Introduction to the Sociology of "Developing Societies,"* edited by H. Alavi and T. Shanin, 218–35. New York: Monthly Review Press.

Berrios, R. 1983. "The Political Economy of East-South Relations." *Journal of Peace Research* 20 (3): 239–52.

Cline, W. R. 1984. *International Debt: Systemic Risk and Policy Response.* Cambridge, Mass.: MIT Press.

Dostaler, G. 1982. "The Transformation Problem." *Studies in Political Economy* 9 (Fall): 77–101.

Emmanuel, A. 1972. *Unequal Exchange: A Study of the Imperialism of Trade.* New York: Monthly Review Press.

Engels, F. 1968. *The Condition of the Working Class in England.* Translated and edited by W. O. Henderson and W. H. Chaloner. Stanford, Calif.: Stanford Univ. Press.

Evans, P. 1979. *Dependent Development: The Alliance of Multinational, State, and Local Capital in Brazil.* Princeton, N.J.: Princeton Univ. Press.

Fajnzylber, F. 1981. "Some Reflections on South-East Asian Export Industrialization." *CEPAL* [Economic Commission for Latin America] *Review* 15 (Dec.): 111–32.

Frank, A. G. 1978. *Dependent Accumulation and Underdevelopment.* New York: Monthly Review Press.

Frobel, F., et al. 1977. "The Tendency Towards a New International Division of Labor: The Utilization of a Worldwide Labor Force for Manufacturing Oriented to the World Market." *Review* 1 (1): 73–88.

Henriquez, P. 1983. "Beyond Dependency Theory." *International Social Science Journal* 96 (2): 391–400.

Holman, R. A., et al. 1985. "Aluminum Industry." *The Wall Street Transcript* 87 (7) (Feb. 16): 76, 936–76, 944.

Kerns, H. 1982. "South Korea's Strategic Loss." *Far Eastern Economic Review* 119 (Feb. 5): 82.

Kumar, K. 1982. "Third World Multinationals: A Growing Force in International Relations." *International Studies Quarterly* 26 (3): 397–424.

Marcussen, H. S. 1982. "Changes in the International Division of Labour: Theoretical Implications." *Acta Sociologica* 25 (supplement): 67–78.

Marcussen, H. S., and J. E. Torp. 1982. *The Internationalization of Capital: The Prospects for the Third World.* London: Zed Press.

O'Neill, H. 1984. "HICs, MICs, NICs, and LICs: Some Elements in the Political Economy of Graduation and Differentiation." *World Development* 12 (7): 693–712.

Petras, J. 1983. "The 'Peripheral State': Continuity and Change in the International Divison of Labour." In *Capitalist and Socialist Crises in the Late Twentieth Century,* edited by J. Petras, 116–35. Totowa, N.J.: Rowman & Allanheld.

Petras, J., and K. Trachte. 1978. "Liberal, Structural, and Radical Approaches to Political Economy: An Assessment and an Alternative." In *Critical Perspectives on Imperialism and Social Class in the Third World,* edited by J. Petras, 13–62. New York: Monthly Review Press.

Roemer, J. E. 1983. "Unequal Exchange, Labor Migration, and International Capital Flows: A Theoretical Synthesis." In *Marxism, Central Planning and the Soviet Economy,* edited by P. Desei, 34–60. Cambridge, Mass.: MIT Press.

Sabalo, Y. 1983. "Trade Between Developing Countries, Technology Transfers and Employment." *International Labour Review* 122 (5): 593–608.

Shinohara, M. 1983. "More NICs in time . . ." *Far Eastern Economic Review* 120 (Apr. 28): 66–67.

Synder, D., and E. L. Kick. 1979. "Structural Position in the World System and Economic Growth, 1955–1970: A Multiple-Network Analysis of Transnational Interactions." *American Journal of Sociology* 84 (5): 1096–1126.

Sutcliffe, R. 1972. "Imperialism and Industrialization in the Third World." In *Studies in the Theory of Imperialism,* edited by R. Owen and B. Sutcliffe, 171–92. London: Longman.

Tanzer, A. 1982. "Taiwan Looks Abroad After Drastic Cuts in Production." *Far Eastern Economic Review* 119 (Feb. 5): 78, 83.

Teubal, M. 1984. "The Role of Technological Learning in the Export of Manufactured Goods: The Case of Selected Capital Goods in Brazil." *World Development* 12 (8): 849–65.

United Nations. 1984. *1982 Yearbook of International Trade Statistics.* New York.

U.S. Department of Commerce, International Trade Administration. 1983a. *Country Market Survey: Computers and Peripheral Equipment: Hong Kong.*

U.S. Department of Commerce, International Trade Administration. 1983b. *Country Market Survey: Electronic Components: Singapore.*

Wallerstein, I. 1979. *The Capitalist World Economy.* Cambridge: Cambridge Univ. Press.

Weber, M. 1978. *Economy and Society.* Edited by G. Roth and C. Wittich. Berkeley: Univ. of California Press.

2 / *The International Monetary Fund, Austerity, and the State in Latin America*

JAMES PETRAS and HOWARD BRILL

Introduction: Overview

IMF interventions during the past ten years have attracted considerable attention from critics on both the Left and Right. These criticisms have tended to focus on the perceived harshness or softness of the adjustment process forced on countries facing a balance of payments crisis. The debate over IMF policies has typically centered on the alleged merits or deficiencies of monetarist versus structuralist analyses of the balance of payments problem in developing countries. While this debate is important, it has resulted in a neglect of other issues.

Regardless of the severity of the adjustment process, or its success or failure, the implementation of IMF-sponsored policies has reshaped the economic and social relationships within national economies and between the local and world economy. IMF intervention and accompanying incentives and constraints have altered the economic behavior of social actors to favor local and international finance capital at the expense of local productive classes.

As an integral part of Western capitalism, the IMF has contributed toward *restructuring* Third World economies, opening them to exports and flows of capital in periods of world expansion; *extracting and transferring* surplus from the Third World to the West in times of debt crisis; and *enforcing* economic obligations in times of declining income and world-wide economic contraction. The IMF does not act independently—nor does its symbolic representation as an international body signify that it is anything less than a political-economic instrument for Western captial. The IMF is a significant actor, but its effectiveness is based on the economic interests it represents and its capacity to fashion a policy that defends those interests. It is important neither to exaggerate nor underestimate the specific role of the IMF. It is neither an omnipotent force nor a technical agency: its power is anchored in the changing relations of power between capitalist countries (the internal divisions of capital within a country), as well as evolving West–South relations. The global repercussions of IMF intervention—implicit in its wide-ranging role as regulator and enforcer of global economic relations—have provoked global resistance. These reactions have at different times led to rejection and modification of IMF policies (and subsequently weakened its effectiveness in its various roles) and at other times exacerbated the worst effects that those policies sought to ameliorate (deepening debt, chronic balance of payments problems, hyperinflation, and so on).

It is our contention that IMF intervention and efforts to regulate capitalist development have not eliminated or ameliorated economic instability and depression but *transferred it from one set of actors to another;* from the West to the South, from bankers to producers, from capital to the popular classes. What is called *stabilization* by the IMF, bankers and the business press *de*stabilize (a) the economies of the South (through transfer of surplus), (b) the lives of workers (through unemployment and declining income), and (c) local capital (through credit squeezes and resulting bankruptcies). The particular tunnel vision that accompanies the discussion of IMF stabilization leaves out everyone who is not part of the narrow social base that promotes and benefits from IMF policies. If stabilization is put into a broader context, it is clear that the purpose of IMF policy is *not* stabilization of "the economy" but the regulation of a particular set of economic relations and the consolidation of a particular set of financial interests. It is these interests that establish the parameters of IMF policy and define its ideology—it is the pursuit of these interests that frequently leads to the unbridgeable gap between IMF stabilization rhetoric and the generalized instability that these same policies provoke.

As a source of liquidity, the IMF plays an important institutional role in the reproduction of the international circulation of capital and commodities. During periods of crisis, the task of reproducing international circulation becomes especially difficult since at these times states tend to erect barriers to the movement of commodities and capital. In addition, the concentration and centralization of international capital in transnational banks tends to amplify liquidity crises and has increased the threat of substantial systemic disintegration. In recent years IMF interventions have been directed at buffering and regulating massive movements of capital, especially those associated with the oil shocks and the debt crises of some Third World states. One component of IMF regulation has resulted in the alteration of the structures through which the costs of economic instability are allocated among social classes and between states.

The intensity and direction of IMF interventions are limited and mediated by local class and state structures. During periods of crisis, states have few options. Usually the alternatives to the IMF are either cessation of foreign trade or a severe contraction of demand to relieve pressure on foreign reserves. The threat of forced autarky gives the IMF considerable leverage over states with declining reserves of exchangeable foreign currencies, but this leverage is limited. The particular model of accumulation operating in a country, the capacities of a state to design and implement autonomous policies, the duration and frequency of balance of payment crises, class alliances and cleavages, and the state's means of regulating class conflict affect the ability of the IMF to restructure relationships. Since it is the local state which must implement any IMF-inspired policy, its capacities and the particular class interests which shape it are of particular importance.

The implementation of IMF policies alters class alliances and frequently results in declining income, which strains the local reproduction of capitalist relations. Strikes, riots, and mass movements are frequently results of the adjustment process and occasionally lead to changes in regimes. However, there have been few, if any, instances of social revolutionary changes. Since the effects of IMF policies strike across class lines, they have tended to produce cycles of authoritarian and populist regimes based on multi-class movements usually hegemonized under local business or middle-class groups.

In order to focus on the current impact of the IMF in Latin America, it is necessary to review the history of IMF involvement with Western capital and its subsequent relationships with the Third World, as well as the changing nature of IMF policies. We will then develop a typology of IMF-state relationships and explore the theoretical implications of that typology. The impact of contemporary policies will be examined in terms of changes in economic relations and social conflict. Finally we will outline a course of future investigation.

The IMF: Changing Role and Policies from 1950s to 1970s

The IMF shifted from a primarily European to a global orientation with the growth of international capitalism. Accompanying its geographic expansion was the widening of its policy activity—from promotion of trade liberalization to active regulation of multiple types of capital between regions of the world economy. While the IMF was developing its own agenda, its effectiveness in realizing its policies was based on a parallel development of converging economic interests within Latin America: the growth of export-oriented national-state and private capital and the establishment of multinational subsidiaries. This convergence of IMF and local capital in the 1960s was part of the process of the internationalization of capital—a process that however was resisted in certain countries, particularly where popular movements and regimes were in ascendance (as in Chile in 1970–1973).

The relative importance of the IMF has waxed and waned depending on the relative dynamics of other capitalist institutions, the degree of popular mobilization, and the overall strength of its international backers. In summary, the matrix of factors shaping the role of the IMF in Latin America includes: The stage in the growth of world capitalism; the increasing demands of multiple forms of capital expansion; the existence of collaborating groups with convergent interests within Latin America; and the overall expansion and contraction of the world economy.

The IMF was founded as part of the package of institutions and agreements that emerged from the Bretton Woods Conference. During the late 1940s and early 1950s, IMF activity was largely confined to Western Europe (Bird 1978, 16). During this period IMF activity in the Third World was limited to educational and advisory missions, although membership in the Fund restricted state activities which would interfere with movements of international payments (ibid., 16–17). During the late 1950s and the 1960s the IMF took a more activist role toward Third World countries through increased credit drawings tied to the implementation of austerity programs (Lichtensztejn 1983, 212). IMF intervention linked monetary stabilization with development and with financial schemes specifically designed to aid "primary-product exporting countries through agencies such as the Compensatory Financing Facility and the Buffer Stock Financing Facility (Bird 1978, 18–19).

The policy formula of the IMF during the 1950s and 1960s was limited to the liberalization of trading relationships (Lichtensztejn 1983, 213). The "opening up" of Third World countries involved the reduction of barriers to commodities and foreign capital. But as Lechtensztejn states, the implementation of this formula by Latin American countries was not uniform. The populist regime of Brazil resisted these policies until it was overthrown by the military and replaced by an authoritarian regime. In addition, the form of foreign capital flows varied: Uruguay and Chile favored finance capital while Brazil, Mexico, and Argentina "encouraged" direct investment. (ibid., 213–215). Lichtensztejn further argues that the implementation of trade liberalization represented not so much an "imposition" as an "implantation" that resulted from the "convergence" of local and international capitalist interests (ibid.).

The case of Brazil is particularly interesting. During the 1960s, drawings on the Fund were fairly limited (Marshall et al. 1983, 300). IMF stand-by agreements served mainly as a "seal of approval" for other forms of financial flows and for private investment. The limited role of the IMF suggests that it was the military regime and its backers who were responsible for implementing the extremely severe wage policy as part of its stabilization program (Bacha 1983, 324–25). For Brazil in the 1960s the IMF did not initiate, but legitimatized a policy already decided on by the regime.

In the late 1960s and early 1970s the IMF's influence in Latin America declined (Lichtensztejn 1983, 213). During this period the Bretton Woods international monetary system collapsed due to the weakness of the U.S. economy, which was strained by the American commitments in Vietnam. In Latin America, increased labor unrest led to the establishment of populist regimes or the strengthening of existing programs of redistribution. The growth of the transnational banking system and the exponential growth of international trade during this period provided alternative sources of finance for regimes embarking on growth-oriented macroeconomic policies.

The growth of international trade set the stage for the debt and balance of payments crisis that began in 1973–1974 and which has continued with only brief respites to the present. The scale, intergration, and concentration of capital and commodity flows have produced a system which is extraordinarily sensitive to minor failures in liquidity. For example, in recent months a failure of a small savings and loan bank in Ohio resulted in a run on the dollar in foreign exchange markets. In the late 1970s spiralling interest rates led to massive capital transfers from Third World to Western bankers. The decline in commodity prices relative to capital imports, the restrictions on trade, the increasing cost of invisible payments, the export of dollars to Europe by local capital, and investment in nonproductive activities and luxuries by the middle classes all contributed to declining productive capacity relative to the growing size of the debt. The oil shocks of 1973–1974 and 1979–1980 resulted in a massive transfer of value from oil importers to the oil exporters. All of these factors posed a major balance of payments problem for many Third World countries.* During the second oil shock, the overextended international financial markets suffered a loss of confidence, which resulted in a cutback in the flow of capital to Third World countries. The number of "multilateral debt renegotiations" per year rose from two countries in 1975–1976 to eight in 1981 (Killick et al. 1984, 27). The combination of these factors and the inability of regimes to reduce internal demand provided the circumstances in which the IMF could play an enlarged role in regulating capitalist relations. Between 1979 and 1981, IMF high-conditionality lending "surged" (Williamson 1983, 642–45; and Killick et al. 1984, 151-52). After 1981 IMF lending was

---

*The "terms of trade of non-oil LDCs deteriorated by 15 percent," according to Killick et al. (1984, 2) between 1974 and 1982.

reduced "perversely" (Williamson 1983, 647) at the onset of a major world recession. IMF lending was so sharply curtailed that net new commitments were negative (Helleiner 1983, 13). Williamson (1983, 648) suggests that the arrival of the Reagan administration played a role in reduced IMF lending and that this regime was "markedly less support-ive of a major role for the Fund" than the Carter administration.

IMF Agreements: Preconditions, Performance Criteria, and Stabilization Program

The main lever through which IMF regulation of national economies takes place is agreements with recipient countries. It is precisely through credit mechanisms and the conditions tied to them that the IMF has been able to enforce the restructuring of the internal relations of produc-tion and the flows of capital between the Northern banks and Latin American economies. It is crucial to note, however, that IMF leverage is nowhere or at any time the same: maximum leverage is exhibited in those cases where countries have exhausted their easy credit terms and have the greatest need for refinancing. The ubiquitous role of the IMF is tempered by the level of internal discipline of the recipient country: the greater its prior dependence on outside financing, the greater its vulner-ability to the IMF stabilization program. IMF regulation is thus condi-tional on the prior penetration of international capital, the incapacity of the local state to contain the adverse effects, and the existence of internal political and social forces willing to pursue IMF stabilization measures in order to reestablish the status quo ante—a dubious course given the counterproductive outcomes resulting from IMF policies.

IMF agreements with recipient countries, while differing in important specifics, do share some general characteristics. Before identifying those general characteristics it will be useful to introduce some terminology used by the Fund (see Williamson 1983, 662–67 and Killick et al. 1984, 133–41). The *reserve tranche* consists of up to 100 per cent of a member's quota to the IMF and can be withdrawn unconditionally. The *first credit tranche* consists of the next 25 percent of the quota and is practically unconditional, although the recipient must formally show that a need for this financing exists and that some plan has been developed to resolve the balance of payments deficit. Other low-conditionality loans include the compensatory financing facility, the buffer stock financing facility, the oil facilities, and the trust fund. These facilities are provided under special circumstances to developing countries. High-conditional-ity loans are composed of the *upper credit tranches* and the *extended facility*. The upper credit tranches consist of one-year loans payable over a maximum of five years. The extended facility provides loans in support of three-year adjustment, payable over a maximum of ten years. The conditionality of the upper credit tranches takes the following form: the recipient and the IMF negotiate a stand-by agreement which consists of preconditions, performance criteria, and a letter of intent specifying a stabilization program.

Since IMF negotiations are conducted in secret, it is extremely difficult to determine what has been agreed to except in some exceptional cases (Jamaica, for example, has published its agreements; see Killick et al. 1984, 141–44). Fortunately, unpublished IMF documents reviewing stabilization programs (Killick et al. 1984, 190–99, 223 endnote 1) allow us a glimpse into the results of some secret negotiations. A review of thirteen IMF programs indicated that "exchange rate actions" (devaluations) and an "interest rate policy" (raising interest rates) were the two most common preconditions (ibid., 191).

A country is required by the agreements only to meet the performance criteria. At least formally, the recipient is free to ignore the IMF stabilization program. However, by establishing unattainable performance criteria, the IMF can force a recalcitrant recipient to implement a stabilization program. For example, the 1977 stand-by agreement with Jamaica involved reductions in payments deficits and the domestic money supply "clearly out of proportion to the size of resources directly available from the Fund" (Sharpley 1983, 244; see also Bernal 1984). According to Sharpley the 1977 agreement was apparently "a test of the general willingness of the Jamaican authorities to undertake a stabilization program" (1983: 245). Formally, the performance criteria are fairly limited. In addition to "standard clauses" prohibiting prepayment and new import restrictions, "bilateral trading agreements," and "new multiple currency arrangements," the agreements set ceilings on the expansion of credit (Killick et al. 1984, 191). In recent years agreements have also included "restrictions on new external debt," "minimum levels for foreign exchange reserves," and in a few cases a "reduction in current payments arrears" (ibid., 192). Devaluations, while not formally specified in recent agreements, are common, although the exact incidence is difficult to determine (ibid., 195–96). Contrary to popular belief, the performance criteria of IMF agreements are fairly limited, generally consisting of restraints on credit expansion.

The stabilization programs specified in letters of intent contain the provisions most often associated with controversies over IMF programs. The letters of intent have typically included taxation increases, reductions in the public sector, reductions of "consumer goods subsidies," wage policies, and other policies directed at pricing and publicly owned corporations (Killick et al. 1984, 196–97). The letters of intent are not binding on recipient countries, but our understanding of these programs should not be reduced to a consideration of their formal characteristics. Some regimes use letters of intent as a means of exerting leverage over other social actors. Killick et al. cite Panama and Uruguay as examples of countries which negotiated stand-by agreements without apparently needing credit (ibid., 197). The letters of intent can serve as weapons in ideological battles since they have the appearance of technically objective programs sanctioned by an important international institution.

The Ascendancy of the IMF—Mid-1970s to the Present: State IMF Relations

The majority of developing countries have utilized IMF credit; and the mid-1970s marked the period of greatest use (Killick et al. 1984, 153). Historically, developing countries in the Western Hemisphere have been the greatest users of IMF credit, but in recent years usage has shifted to Africa and Asia (ibid., 154–55). In absolute terms the largest users of IMF credit (as of 1979) have been "India, Argentina, the Phillipines, Chile and Pakistan [which have] accounted for 29 percent of total drawings by developing countries." (Killick et al 1984: 155). In terms of usage as a percentage of quota the "largest users" have been (as of 1979) "Nicaragua, the Philippines, Jamaica, Sri Lanka, Sudan, Chile, and Peru . . ." (ibid., 155). Later we will examine the experiences of Chile and Argentina more closely. It is perhaps worth noting that all of these major users of IMF credit have been sites of considerable social conflict. Since 1979 Thailand, Turkey, Yugoslavia, several African states, Brazil, and Mexico (since 1983) have emerged as major users of IMF credit (see Statistical Appendix to this chapter, Table 2A).

Although the majority of Third World countries have used Fund credit, the scale and the duration of IMF-supported programs vary greatly. It is extremely misleading to generalize about the use of Fund credit when the experiences vary so widely, as for example between Zaire and Yugoslavia. There is a broad continuum between countries where IMF personnel actually participate in significant ways in the day-to-day functioning of government and those whose involvement with the IMF has been limited and short term.

To understand the different impacts that the IMF has on different states, it is useful to distinguish three types of IMF-state relations. Based on the degree of IMF control and regulation of the local economy, we can identify:

1. Subordination: Direct control by the IMF of critical positions in the local state apparatus to sustain payments in disintegrating economies;
2. Convergence and Subordinate Agreement: IMF programs of stabilization were introduced and implemented by local state and entrepreneurial groups who share a common politico-economic perspective with

the IMF for overcoming the structural crises of relatively developed economies; and,

3. Negotiation and Resistance: IMF negotiates with the potential recipient, but terms are either rejected or significantly modified either by the regime or subsequently as a result of popular protest, resulting in the withdrawal of credit.

Certain countries, usually African, have been persistent users of high-conditionality credit and have accepted significant intrusions into their sovereignty. For example, Zaire has been a persistent user of IMF credit and has allowed IMF officials to occupy key positions "in the Bank of Zaire, the Finance Ministry, the Customs Office, and [the Planning agency]" (Callaghy 1984, 23). These states, according to Gruhn (1983), moved from colonialism to bilateral dependency with the former colonial state, to bilateral dependency with a major world power, to dependency with an international organization. In each case the new relationship appeared as an alternative to the earlier condition of dependency but substantially reproduced dependent structures. It is somewhat debatable whether this scheme can be generalized to all countries in this category. For Zaire, the Mobutu regime has followed a fairly classical course of comprador rule, with the state serving as the means of extracting surplus and redistributing it to nonproductive dominant groups locally and internationally. The change in dependent relationships has evolved more in response to systemic changes than from a search by the Mobutu regime for alternatives.

A second category, which includes Mexico, Brazil, Tanzania, and Kenya, consists of those states which have accepted IMF credit in response to structural crises resulting in short-term liquidity emergencies. Initially, local economic and state power centers developed and implemented IMF economic policies through a seemingly "autonomous" apparatus. The prolonged duration of crises in these countries, however, and the deep structural contradictions underlying them magnified the leverage of the IMF and reduced the autonomy of local actors who were oriented to "the outside." The IMF played an increasingly direct role in setting the terms of participation. For Mexico and Brazil the existence of alternative sources of foreign financing in the mid 1970s was a dual-edged sword; it provided immediate autonomy but eventually led to the current debt crisis, which has forced these countries to go to the IMF in the context of increased IMF regulatory power. The important distinction for us is that these countries have moved from having developed and implemented economic policies autonomously, with limited involvement from the IMF, to a situation of power-sharing. Our explanation must consequently emphasize the IMF's changing role in those states. While the IMF has not always played an important part in shaping the development agenda, in times of profound structural crisis even the larger countries with substantial state and local entrepreneurial groups must share the designing of macroeconomic practices with the IMF.

The third category is composed of those states which have resisted IMF conditionality and attempted to forge alternative strategies. Jamaica under Manley (in the last year of his regime) and Chile under Allende, were two cases. In the recent period Bolivia, under massive pressure from labor and peasant unions, has resisted implementing IMF terms—however, the opposition has no clear or coherent alternative and resistance is leading to hyperinflation. In the case of the Alfonsin regime in Argentina, initial resistance provoked IMF-enforced bank boycotts, which eventually forced the government to accept an IMF-style austerity program—resulting in increasing labor discontent over declining living standards.

IMF-state relations are shaped by the degree of labor mobilization, the linkages between state and labor, and, more fundamentally, by the direction of the flow of influence. Where the flow goes from the bottom to the top, the lateral influence of the IMF is limited; where the flow is reversed, IMF influence is maximized. Moreover, the more developed an economy and state structure, the less likely is direct intervention of the IMF and subordination of the recipient country. On the other hand, even highly dynamic countries with previous records of "relatively autonomous" growth are subject to the indirect influence of the IMF over major development agenda items. Negotiations between the state and the IMF in periods of crisis are asymmetrical—bringing increasing leverage to the IMF and greater vulnerability for the bargaining Latin country.

Third, regimes devoid of labor influence and with links to "export-oriented groups" and local financial centers are more likely to collaborate with IMF programs than are those with nationally based productive sectors oriented toward local markets. It should be realized that these are not hard and fast lines since, to the degree that local national capital finances its production from foreign capital sources and imports its technology, it is in a weak position to break off external financial ties. (What is most tempting in these circumstances is for productive classes to adapt to the new externally oriented model of accumulation and shift the costs of adjustment to local wage and salaried groups.)

The IMF and the Monetarist–Structuralist Debate

Theoretical justifications and criticisms of the IMF practices and monetarist theory are extensive. Despite the breadth and technical nature of this literature, the essential arguments can be summarized briefly. The monetarists argue that balance of payments problems arise from excess local aggregate demand relative to local supply and to foreign demand of local tradable goods. The short-term solution to excess local aggregate demand is contractive monetary and fiscal policies. Long-term economic growth requires stabilization as a precondition and is facilitated by the liberalization of internal and external trade. Some monetarists also call for expansion of demand in balance of payment surplus countries (De Larosiere 1984, 139). Critics usually adopt some type of structuralist position. They argue that monetarists tend to separate the problems of development from balance of payments crises. Development in the Third World has led to certain microeconomic patterns, including trading relationships between countries, which create long-term imbalances made manifest by balance of payment crises. Contractive policies, while necessary in some cases, generally solve the short-term balance of payments problems at the cost of restricting development and further exacerbating the contradictions underlying the crises. The assumptions of monetarism are overly simplistic, in this view, because they ignore the historical and systemic contexts of underdevelopment. On the other hand, some of the structuralists may be accused of the same kind of over-generalization and simplification as their monetarist adversaries.

To illustrate this point let us look at the case of Jamaica. Bernal (1984, 53–54) argues that controlling integration into the world economy and an expanded state role in production and distribution is a useful strategy for increasing capital accumulation in underdeveloped countries. One way Jamaica controlled integration was through quantitative import restrictions. The IMF argues that it is best to let the market control the amount of imports, that trade liberalization plus devaluation of the local currency will accomplish the dual goals of reducing imports while allowing the free flow of goods. Such a policy can, however, lead to shifts in resources of trading activities—to the importation of luxury goods.

Controlling integration into the world economy is not, by itself, a good thing, however. Import restrictions may serve to benefit local capitalists who use their profits for nonproductive purposes, or it may serve a state development plan that reserves foreign exchange resources for the purchase of capital goods. We should not forgot that some of the beneficiaries of import substitution in South America and the Caribbean have been multinationals which used near-monopoly conditions to extract surpluses in excess of what would have been available at international prices. Therefore, in the case of Jamaica we have to know which imports were restricted, where resources were used alternatively, and to whose benefit.

So in addition to analyzing the "fine structure of a productive system, we need to know the "gross anatomy" of the distribution of economic activity, surpluses and of social wealth in general. What is the distribution of economic activty into productive and nonproductive sectors, between private and public sectors, and between foreign and local owners? What does state economic policy consist of—what are its levels of financing and direct investment into production? What are the wage levels, and their pattern of distribution, and how is social wealth divided between labor and capital, and between consumption and accumulation? What proportion of state spending is diverted into collective consumption, infrastructure, income to bureaucrats, and to the support of the coercive apparatus? Given this data and some understanding of the path of change due to accumulation, we can then compare this historical alternative to the actual results of trade liberalization and devaluation.

Structural Impact of IMF Policies

IMF policies have a profound impact on the political institutions, levels of political mobilization, and social relations of a recipient nation, as well as upon the structure of production and insertion of the nation's economy into the world economy. There is a pronounced tendency of IMF policies to heighten social tension and depress local industry, while increasing the level of coercion. However, the general destabilizing effects of IMF policies have to be analyzed together with the state structures that mediate and translate those policies into practice. Those states which have strongly penetrated civil society with a dense network of institutions and organization (such as Mexico) are better situated to enforce IMF directives despite the extremely regressive nature of the measures. The impact of the IMF measures is then as much influenced by state–civil society relations as it is by their intrinsic nature.

There are few studies which attempt to examine the structural effects of IMF programs (see Bernal 1984, and Tokman 1984). Killick et al. (1984, 228) have examined the "effects of Fund programmes on some key macroeconomic variables . . ." While not answering the questions we have raised above, they conclude that Fund programs have had a statistically insignificant effect on improving the macroeconomic variables (ibid., 264–66). IMF programs have had difficulty in reaching stabilization goals, let alone positive effects on development. Even more extraordinary is the lack of "association between Fund programmes and sustained liberalisation" (ibid., 265)! Thus, even in monetarist terms, IMF policies cannot be said to have positively improved the economic situation of recipient countries or liberalized world trade.

The implementation of IMF programs requires state actions. Of course, the state, unlike its monetarist ideal, is not some exogenous super-actor existing outside of civil society. The state on the one hand is an intermediary between foreign capital, banks, local capital, and the popular classes, and on the other hand is shaped by those same social agents.

The state can be characterized along two dimensions: the mixture of means being used for legitimation, and the state's relationship of civil society. Democratic states tend to achieve legitimation through redistributive and ideological means by constructing a consensus through institutions that regulate negotiations and compromises between antagonistic groups. Authoritarian states tend to achieve legitimation by using coercion to limit or shape dissent by some social groups. The IMF stabilization programs, with their class-selective austerity programs, severely depressed wages, income, credits, and imports, heighten social and political polarization and conflict and thus bring about increased repression. In short, IMF programs result in a severe blurring of the distinction between democratic and authoritarian regimes. Elected regimes pursuing IMF stabilization have in recent years been among the most repressive, as the cases of Peru under Belaunde, the Dominican Republic under Blanco, and Jamaica under Seaga attest. IMF agreements play an important role in delegitimizing elected regimes and increasing the level of coercion while undermining the process of securing a national consensus and the possibility of pursuing redistributive policies. The outcome is built into the class bias present in the "free market" solutions propounded by IMF ideologues.

An extremely important factor shaping the impact of IMF policies is the relationship between state and private institutions. Some states in Latin America are characterized by relatively limited linkages among institutions, while others have dense linkages—state institutions that are deeply integrated with other institutions and pervade all aspects of social life. States with dense linkages tend to be able to control and channel dissent and conflict with selective use of direct coercion or rapid changes in the redistribution of the surplus. States with weak linkages, on the other hand, are either easily destabilized or are forced to resort to more extreme measures of direct coercion or to the cementing of social compromises by relatively large expenditures of surplus. The type of linkage will mediate a state's capacity to respond to popular opposition to IMF-designed austerity programs, and the mixture of means of legitimation of a regime will determine the form that response will take.

In contemporary South America it is possible to observe two different historical patterns of response to IMF austerity packages. In some states, such as Mexico, the state has penetrated deeply throughout civil society, controlling almost all state and local governments and mass associations. Argentina under the military and Chile under Pinochet lack effective penetration of civil society: the opposition is a dominant force among labor, students, and neighborhood groups, while the military controls the state apparatus. Brazil under the military seems to be an intermediate case, with some influence through its civilian organization but still lacking the durable and dense networks of Mexico. As a result the Mexican regime was able to impose one of the harshest austerity programs in the Third World with a minimum of opposition. On the other hand, the military regimes of Chile, Argentina, and Brazil encountered mass, sustained opposition, which at least in the case of Brazil forced the regime to renegotiate its terms of agreement with the IMF. The Mexican regime's effective use of the party-state organization allowed it to combine repression with political manipulation of social groups; while in the military regimes, coercion gave way, at least in the case of Brazil and Argentina, to a change of regimes. In summary, the response of the populace cannot be gauged by the harshness of the austerity program but by the character of the state's legitimation and the density of its linkages with civil society.

In Argentina and Chile the Peronist and Allende regimes of the early 1970s attempted to appeal to a broad alliance of antagonistic classes and rejected IMF-dictated austerity programs. These alliances were cemented, not by deep linkages between the state and civil institutions, but through concessional state expenditures to class organizations. In avoiding the discipline of the IMF, the regimes proceeded to evade imposing their own financial discipline. In Chile loans and credits from the state to the bourgeoisie and petty bourgeoisie were "channeled through the leadership and organizations of the Right" (Petras 1978, 205) and contributed to the increase of imports, provoking balance of payments deficits and inflationary pressure. The social expense of concessional payments to both labor and capital became too high and too difficult to finance with the onset of the first oil shock in 1973. Competition over scarce resources threatened the accumulation process, and the class struggle intensified. In Chile inflation rose from 22.1 percent in 1971 to 508 percent in 1973, and in Argentina inflation rose from 40.1 percent in 1974 to 335 percent in 1975 (Marshall et al. 1983, 277–78). These popular regimes failed to impose their own form of austerity and control based on their own class commitments, and thus their position became untenable. The military dictatorships that seized power from them were willing and able to implement IMF-style austerity programs with all of their negative consequences for the popular classes.

The military dictatorships in Chile and Argentina were granted IMF credits in the period after the establishment of their regimes. In 1975 Argentina suffered a $1,107 million balance of payment deficit and was granted, in 1976, 260 million SDR from the IMF; similarly in 1973 Chile had a $112 million balance of payment deficit and was given 79 million SDR in IMF credits (Marshall et al. 1983, 276–78). In both Chile and

Argentina, ceilings were set on the expansion of bank credit, and in Chile interest rates were also monitored by the IMF (ibid., 279–82). In Chile and Argentina limits were set on credit to the public sector and on government expenditures (ibid., 284). In addition to these measures, balance of payments tests were established which required Chile to undertake a large devaluation (ibid., 286). The agreement between Chile and the IMF explicitly called for real wage increases and the liberalization of prices. In 1975 an indexation program, which would tie wages to inflation, was implemented. In fact, however, real wage levels dropped precipitously and did not recover their 1970 high thereafter. The IMF did not cut off funding when that criteria was missed. However, inflation was controlled by contractive "monetary and fiscal policies," which resulted in massive unemployment (ibid., 295). In Argentina wage increases were implemented at below the rate of inflation (ibid., 295).

Because the military dictatorships exercised total control over society through such means as arrests, torture, kidnapping, and assassination, implementation of IMF agreements during the late 1970s was fairly successful. In Argentina liberalization programs were implemented, and most performance targets were met to the IMF's satisfaction (ibid., 299). In Chile, while inflation and credit expansion "greatly exceeded" the IMF's ceilings, liberalization policies were implemented. Chile succeeded in reducing its balance of payments deficit, and its obligations to the Fund were repaid. We are told that "relations between the Fund and Chile since 1974 have been very good" and that Santiago was privileged to be host to IMF representatives during the five-year period following the coup (ibid., 303).

IMF Successes and the Decline of Industry, Labor, Income, and Employment

The "successful" implementation of the IMF program in Argentina and Chile was accompanied by structural changes that weakened the industrialization process. Industrial employment in Argentina dropped from 32.4 percent of nonagricultural employment in 1974 to 24.2 percent in 1981, and in Chile it sank from 24 percent in 1970–1971 to 19.1 percent in 1981 (Tokman 1984, 107). The volume of industrial production in Argentina in 1982 was 83 percent of the 1974 level, and in Chile the drop was slightly greater (ibid., 108). These declines in the manufacturing sector are especially dramatic, according to Tokman, when one considers that in the late 1960s and early 1970s this sector was growing (ibid., 108). The industrial output of other Latin American countries rose by 3.8 percent per year between 1974 and 1980 (ibid., 108–9). Since the decline of manufacturing in these countries corresponds neither to historical trends in these countries, nor to international trends, Tokman (ibid.,

109) states that it "signifies a disruption of industrial development" that was "a product of the policies pursued during this period" (ibid.).

The destruction of industry in these countries involved the liquidation of productive assets and not merely the accumulation of underutilized capacity (ibid., 110–12). In Chile bankruptcies rose from 356 per year in 1975 to 3,521 per year in 1982. In Argentina, during the same period, bankruptcies rose from 46 to 142 per year. Contrary to expectations, this did not result in increased concentration—the hardest hit were the largest firms (ibid., 111). Nor was labor moved to more productive activities. In Argentina approximately 52 percent of unemployed manufacturing workers remained unemployed or were employed or in "low-productivity" activities, while in Chile 50 percent remained unemployed and the other half entered into low-productivity activities and government make-work programs (ibid., 113). In Argentina employment in the "informal sector" (low paid, low productive services), grew 25.6 percent during the 1970s, and in Chile the growth rate was 17.9 percent (ibid., table 6). The application of IMF programs resulted in a decline in the development of the productive system. IMF regulation of capital had the effect of restructuring the relations between productive and nonproductive capital—increasing the latter at the expense of the former. At the same time it restructured the relation between the advanced capitalist countries and these Latin economies, once more increasing their dependence on foreign manufacturing imports and on the export of primary products.

The relationship between labor and capital during this period also changed. The unit cost of labor declined 47 percent in Argentina between 1974 and 1982 and declined 31 percent in Chile between 1970 and 1982 (ibid., 115). Aglietta (1979, 90) has argued that changes in the unit labor cost (which he calls the "real social wage cost") is an inverse indicator of changes in the rate of surplus-value. Since this change in the rate of surplus-value does not correspond to increases in industrial output, it could be achieved only by heightening the rate of exploitation of the working class. This is supported by the evidence reported above concerning changes in the structure of employment and wage levels.

The dismantling of a broad array of manufacturing enterprises—the deindustrialization of Chile and Argentina—totally undermines the IMF's notion that its stabilization program is a prelude to the reactivation of their economies and the structure of their development. Besides the considerable distance needed to catch up to the "potential" growth that was lost during the preceding decade, IMF programs have increased their technological lag behind the newly industrialized countries. Even at the level of reaching IMF stabilization goals, the two countries were not successful. By the 1980s economic depression was matched by inflation and a serious balance of payments crisis. The IMF programs through contractionary fiscal and monetary policies provoked a decline in "international competitive capacity." The removal of tariff and other barriers and a change in incentives encouraged the growth of financial speculation and participation in nonindustrial activities. The result was the emergence of economies which were less developed, less competitive, more dependent on new loans, and suffering from increasingly precarious fiscal and financial status.

The IMF programs, while increasing the rate of exploitation of labor in these countries, undermined industrial capitalists at the expense of finance and foreign capital. It is of little benefit to capital to pay low wages if there is no market to sell goods. The contradictory growth of finance capital, based on its parasitic relationship to productive sectors, was ultimately limited by the destruction of manufacturing in Chile and Argentina.

The dominance of financial capital was shortlived in Chile. The speculative bubble of the 1970s collapsed in 1981–1982, and almost all of Chile's major private banks faced bankruptcy. The lack of regulation—part of the free market policies of the Pinochet regime—led bankers to lend capital to themselves to take over firms, to increase their imports, and to channel funds to overseas bank accounts. The imminent collapse of the banking system forced Pinochet toward state intervention. More banks, in fact, are under state control today than was the case during the Allende period, though of course the role and nature of state intervention serve other purposes. Ironically, in the real world of existing market economies, IMF policies have had the effect of creating the very economic relations they ostensibly oppose.

The incapacity of IMF austerity programs to stabilize and reactivate the Argentinian economy led the Argntinian junta to seek a military-political success to contain the erosion of its support. The Malvinas fiasco, however, merely accelerated the junta's demise and laid the groundwork for the eventual return to an elected regime. In Chile the failure of the IMF program has led to a massive upsurge of popular protest, a return to mid-seventies style state repression (that is, torture, kidnappings, and assassinations) and even more generous outlays of IMF and collaborative bank financing. Thus the political consequences for regimes implementing unsuccessful programs vary: in the case of Argentina, democratization; in the Chilean context, polarization and intensified repression. Already in democratic Argentina the Alfonsin regime's agreement to IMF austerity programs is provoking increasing civil unrest. The lack of dense linkages with either the labor movement or the military portends difficult times for the present government. Once again Alfonsin's broad electoral base prevented his regime from implementing a progressively based austerity program—thus allowing the country to run a three- and even a four-digit rate of inflation.

Lacking the capacity to impose discipline internally, the regime has turned to the externally imposed discipline of the IMF, with the political costs that it implies.

Conclusion

The cumulative effect of IMF policies is reshaping the global economy. The role of conditionality—austerity programs tied to new credits—has led to increased flows of funds to metropolitan countries, the undermining of locally owned enterprises, and the shrinking of the local market.

IMF policies are purported to deal with specific problems (such as balance of payments) but in fact have profound effects over the whole economy. In their broadest form, IMF policies and debt crises have resulted in a reconcentration of income and productive forces on a world scale. The IMF does not act alone, however, nor is it the only force applying its particular brand of development policies. Local dominant classes also invoke instability as a rationale for economic austerity, thus justifying reduction of social expenditures and the redistribution of income toward capital. The pivotal institution affecting the introduction and implementation of IMF policies is the state: the collaboration or resistance of national forces is decisive in shaping IMF impact.

The historical impact of the IMF in stabilizing economies in Latin America is problematical. For elected regimes—such as the recent cases of Peru under Belaunde, Bolivia under Siles, Manley, and now Seaga in Jamaica—the record is abundantly clear: implementation of IMF austerity programs is inversely related to electoral success. Apart from the electoral process, the deeper meaning of austerity is found in the restructuring of the economy—its greater vulnerability to external control—and in the human cost exacted by the distintegration of the social infrastructure built in the postwar period. The primary thrust of austerity is the refocusing of the anarchy of the market onto the popular classes. The political consequences, however, are not as drastic as one might expect. The question may be asked: Can austerity invoke a revolutionary upheaval? The answer up to now has been negative. While *regime* changes and *policy* alterations have occurred under mass pressure, the movements to revise IMF policies have been hegemonized by middle class forces. Because austerity affects a broad array of classes, attention becomes focused on the IMF and its policies and is diverted from the underlying structural forces that allowed the IMF to become a significant actor in the first place.

The postwar expansion of capital resulted in the growth of the demands of both the working class and local capitalists, because it provided the space for those demands to be met. The initial success of the working class in meeting its economic goals amplified its demands and eventually threatened the relations underlying the accumulation process. The crisis that followed expansion provided the justification for austerity policies, which attempted to readjust relationships and allow the reproduction of capitalist production relations.

But this process is not automatic. The crisis continues and the deprivation of labor may have reached its limits. The continued reproduction and extension of the debt crisis-austerity process can lead to movements seeking to redefine relations to banks, the IMF, and the market. To date, the IMF functions to insure that the crisis does not lead to forced autarky and the cessation of international trade. The threat is real—the crisis of the 1930s led to the virtual end of international trade and the replacement of economic imperialism with military imperialism.

In terms of insuring the short-term liquidity of capital in international trade, the IMF has been relatively successful. As we have seen, however, the long-term impact of the IMF on development has been disastrous. The measures taken to achieve short-term liquidity have heightened long-term risks to the system by increasing inequalities and reducing the ability of the IMF to implement policies.

Calls for a new international economic order to address the long-term needs for equality, stabilization, and development have been unsuccessful. No institutional mechanisms exists by which the surplus-controlling countries could be forced or would acquiesce to reducing their advantages. The interests of international capital are being served by the transfer of the costs of global instability onto deficit countries and their popular classes: this is done limiting IMF credit to amounts merely sufficient for crisis management and selective shaping of the adjustment policies required to reduce balance of payments deficits. The Reagan administration encouraged, at least in its first years, the reduction of IMF commitments. The increase in IMF resources in 1983–1984 was combined with institutional changes limiting the access of individual countries to those resources (Wood 1985; 188). The growth in the militancy of popular classes has been countered by the increased use of the U.S. military and ideological support for repressive measures. The development of Latin American countries must depend not on hopes for an expanded international commitment to long-term stabilization and development, but on fundamental social transformation internally and more selective forms of integration with the world economy.

Bibliography

Bacha, E. 1983. "Vicissitudes of Recent Stabilization Attempts in Brazil and the IMF Alternative." In *IMF Conditionality*, edited by John Williamson. Cambridge, Mass.: MIT Press.

Bernal, R. 1982. "Transnational Banks, the International Monetary Fund and External Debt of Developing Countries." *Social and Economic Studies* 31 (4): 71–101.

———. 1984. "The IMF and Class Struggle in Jamaica, 1977–1980." *Latin American Perspectives* 11 (3): 53–82.

Bird, G. 1978. *The International Monetary System and the Less Developed Countries.* London: Macmillan.

Browne, R. 1984. "Conditionality: A New Form of Colonialism?" *Africa Report* 29 (5): 14–18.

Callaghy, T. 1984. "The Ritual Dance of the Debt Game." *Africa Report* 29 (5): 22–26.

De Larosiere, J. 1984. "Challenges Facing the World Economy and the Role of the International Monetary Fund." *Atlantic Community Quarterly* 22 (2): 139–47.

Dell, S. 1983. "Stabilization: The Political Economy of Overkill." In *IMF Conditionality,* edited by John Williamson, Cambridge, Mass.: MIT Press.

Diz, A. 1983. "Economic Performance Under Three Stand-by Arrangements: Peru 1977–80." In *IMF Conditionality,* edited by John Williamson. Cambridge, Mass.: MIT Press.

Foxley, A. 1983. *Latin American Experiments in Neoconservative Economics.* Berkeley: Univ. of California Press.

Frankel, R., and G. O'Donnell. 1979. "The 'Stabilization Programs' of the International Monetary Fund and Their Internal Impacts," In *Capitalism and the State in U.S.–Latin American Relations,* edited by R. Fagen. Stanford, Calif.: Stanford Univ. Press.

Green, R. 1983. "Political-Economic Adjustment and IMF Conditionality: Tanzania 1974–81." In *IMF Conditionality,* edited by John Williamson. Cambridge, Mass.: MIT Press.

Ground, R. 1984. "Orthodox Adjustment Programmes on Latin America: A Critical Look at Policies of the International Monetary Fund." *CEPAL* [Economic Commision for Latin America] 23: 45–82.

Gruhn, I. 1983. "The Recolonization of Africa: International Organizations on the March." *Africa Today* 30 (4): 37–48.

Helleiner, G. 1983. "The IMF and Africa in the 1980s." *Essays in International Finance,* no. 152, July. Princeton, N.J.: Princeton Univ., International Finance Div.

Killick, T. 1983. "Kenya, the IMF, and the Unsuccessful Quest for Stabilization." In *IMF Conditionality,* edited by John Williamson. Cambridge, Mass.: MIT Press.

Killick, T., et al. 1984. *The Quest for Economic Stabilisation: The IMF and the Third World.* London: Heinemann Educational Books.

Lichtensztejn, S. 1983. "IMF-Developing Countries: Conditionality and Strategy." In *IMF Conditionality,* edited by John Williamson. Cambridge, Mass.: MIT Press.

Macesich, G. 1981. *The International Monetary Economy and the Third World.* New York: Praeger.

Marshall S., J., et al. 1983. "IMF Conditionality: The Experiences of Argentina, Brazil and Chile." In *IMF Conditionality,* edited by John Williamson. Cambridge, Mass.: MIT Press.

Massad, C., and R. Zahler. 1984. "The Adjustment Process in the 1980s: The Need for a Global Approach." *CEPAL* 23: 83–105.

Moffit, M. 1983. *The World's Money: International Banking from Bretton Woods to the Brink of Insolvency.* New York: Simon & Schuster.

Paul, A. 1984. "The 'Destabilisation' Program of the IMF in Jamaica." *Inter-American Economic Affairs* 37 (2): 45–61.

Petras, J. 1978. "Reflections on the Chilean Experience: The Petty Bourgeoisie and the Working Class." In *Critical Perspectives on Imperialism and Social Class in the Third World*, edited by J. Petras. New York: Monthly Review Press.

Sharpley, J. 1983. "Economic Management and IMF Conditionality in Jamaica." In *IMF Conditionality*, edited by John Williamson. Cambridge, Mass.: MIT Press.

Thomas, C. 1982. "Guyana: The IMF-World Bank Group and the General Crisis." *Social and Economic Studies* 31 (4): 16–70.

Tokman, J. 1984. "Global Monetarism and the Destruction of Industry." *CEPAL* 23: 107–121.

Williamson, J. 1983. "The Lending Policies of the International Monetary Fund." In *IMF Conditionality*, edited by John Williamson. Cambridge, Mass.: MIT Press.

———. 1983. "The Lending Facilities of the Fund." In *IMF Conditionality*, edited by John Williamson. Cambridge, Mass.: MIT Press.

Wood, R. 1985. "The Aid Regime and International Debt: Crisis and Structural Adjustment." *Development and Change* 16: 179–212.

Statistical Appendix to Chapter 2

One of the difficulties in assessing the impact of IMF policies is the heterogeneity of IMF agreements and the differences in the degree of implementation of those programs. Table 2.1 lists the percent usage of quota by various Latin American countries between 1973 and 1984. Roughly, a percentage usage above 95–100 percent indicates a high conditionality agreement. In most cases the more usage is above 100 percent the greater is the conditionality of the agreement. The longer the percent usage remains above 100 percent the more likely the agreement has been implemented, since otherwise credit would have been cut off. Unfortunately, the lack of credit usage does not indicate a lack of an IMF agreement: many countries agree to stand-by arrangements without actually using the available credit. Table 2.2 lists high-conditionality agreements.

In table 2.3, economic indicators for Argentina, Bolivia, Brazil, Chile, Mexico, Nicaragua, Peru, and Uruguay are listed. The latest source available using indicators adjusted for inflation was 1981.

SOURCES

Iglesias, E. "A Preliminary Overview of the Latin American Economy During 1983." *CEPAL Review* 22 (1984): 7–38.

IMF Financial Statistics (published International Monetary Fund: Washington, D.C.), 1982, 1983, 1984.

United Nations, ECLA. 1983. *Economic Survey of Latin America, 1981*. Santiago, Chile: United Nations E/CEPAL/G. 1248.

Wood, R. 1985. "The Aid Regime and International Debt: Crisis and Structural Adjustment." *Development and Change* 16: 180–212.

Table 2.1.   Usage of IMF Credit as Percent of Quota

	1973	1974	1975	1976	1977	1978	1979	1980	1981	1982	1983	1984
Argentina	.00	.00	70.75	61.25	78.30	.00	.00	.00	.00	.00	100.70	100.70
Bolivia	49.19	.00	12.70	.00	.00	33.30	33.30	93.40	90.60	115.70	94.00	71.60
Brazil	.00	.00	.00	.00	.00	.00	.00	.00	.00	50.00	172.80	292.20
Chile	.00	76.27	111.90	78.73	190.30	122.80	62.60	29.60	12.80	1.70	131.40	180.50
Mexico	.00	.00	.00	112.68	113.30	42.90	19.30	.00	.00	25.00	103.30	206.60
Nicaragua	12.00	3.30	12.20	.00	7.40	5.90	128.00	75.80	41.50	34.40	26.10	13.30
Peru	.00	.00	.00	154.07	137.20	156.20	227.50	151.00	135.30	239.40	270.90	208.00
Uruguay	23.77	94.64	77.10	55.07	142.40	.00	.00	.00	.00	68.90	138.50	138.50

Source: IMF Financial Statistics.

Table 2.2. High-Conditionality Agreements, 1980–1983

	Stand-by			Extended	
	Dates	SDR		Dates	SDR
Argentina	1/83–1/84	1500.00			
Bolivia	2/80–1/81	66.38			
Brazil				3/83–2/86	4239.38
Chile	1/83–1/85	500.00			
Mexico				1/77–12/79	518.00
				1/83–10/85	3410.64
Nicaragua	5/79–12/80	34.00			
Peru	11/77–12/79	90.00		6/82–6/85	650.00
	9/78–12/80	184.00			
	8/79–12/80	285.00			
Uruguay	3/79–3/80	21.00			
	5/80–5/81	21.00			
	7/81–7/82	31.50			
	4/83–4/85	378.00			

Source: Wood 1985, 204–5.

Table 2.3. General Economic Indicators for Selected Latin American Countries

	1975	1976	1977	1978	1979	1980	1981	1982	1983
Uruguay									
Annual Growth Rates									
Gross domestic product	4.8	4.0	1.2	5.3	6.2	5.8	-.1	-8.7	-5.5
Consumer prices	66.8	39.9	57.3	46.0	83.1	42.8	29.4	20.5	62.7
Private sector wages (real)	N/A	N/A	-12.8	-4.1	-9.0	-6.3	-7.9	-.7	N/A
Rate of unemployment	N/A	12.7	11.8	10.1	8.3	7.4	6.7	11.9	15.7
External sector (millions of dollars)									
Total external debt	1,031	1,135	1,320	1,240	1,682	2,153	3,129	4,255	4,250
Peru									
Annual Growth Rates									
Gross domestic product	4.5	2.0	-.1	-.5	4.1	3.8	3.9	.4	-12.0
Consumer prices	24.0	44.7	32.4	73.7	66.7	59.7	72.7	72.9	124.9
Private sector wages (real)	N/A	8.5	-15.6	-9.9	-3.2	9.9	-2.0	1.4	N/A
Rate of unemployment	7.5	6.9	8.7	8.0	6.5	7.1	6.8	7.0	8.8
External sector (millions of dollars)									
Total external debt	3,474	3,987	8,534	9,291	9,301	9,561	8,227	9,503	10,600
Nicaragua									
Annual Growth Rates									
Gross domestic product	2.2	5.0	6.3	-7.2	-25.5	10.0	8.7	-1.4	2.0
Consumer prices	1.9	6.2	10.2	4.3	70.3	24.8	23.2	22.2	N/A
Industrial wages (real)	N/A	N/A	N/A	N/A	N/A	N/A	N/A	N/A	N/A
Rate of unemployment	N/A	8.7	13.1	14.5	22.9	17.8	16.6	20.3	N/A
External sector (millions of dollars)									
Total external debt	644	681	874	961	1,131	1,579	2,163	2,789	3,400

Mexico

Annual Growth Rates									
Gross domestic product	5.6	4.2	3.4	8.1	9.2	8.3	7.9	-.5	-4
Consumer prices	11.3	27.2	20.7	16.2	20.0	29.8	28.7	98.8	91.9
Industrial wages (real)	N/A	N/A	N/A	N/A	N/A	N/A	N/A	N/A	N/A
Rate of unemployment	7.2	6.8	8.3	6.9	5.7	4.5	4.2	6.7	12.5
External sector (millions of dollars)									
Total external debt[a]	14,449	19,600	29,894	33,946	39,685	49,349	72,007	81,350	85,000

Chile

Annual Growth Rates									
Gross domestic product	-12.9	3.5	9.9	8.2	8.3	7.8	5.7	-14.3	-.5
Consumer prices	340.7	174.3	63.5	30.3	38.9	31.2	9.5	20.7	23.7
Wages (real)	-3.3	.5	12.9	6.4	8.3	9.0	9.1	-.4	N/A
Rates of Unemployment	15	16.3	13.9	13.3	13.4	11.7	9.0	20	19.7
External sector (millions of dollars)									
Total external debt (gross)	4,854	4,720	5,201	6,664	8,484	11,084	15,542	17,153	17,600

Brazil

Annual Growth Rates									
Gross domestic product	5.7	9.0	4.7	6.0	6.4	8.0	-1.9	1.1	-5.0
Consumer prices	31.2	44.8	43.1	38.1	76.0	86.3	100.6	101.8	175.2
Industrial wages (real)	N/A	N/A	2.3	4.9	1.5	1.5	6.0	10.0	N/A
Rate of unemployment	N/A	N/A	N/A	6.8	6.4	6.2	7.9	6.3	6.8
External sector (millions of dollars)									
Total external debt[a]	21,171	25,985	32,037	43,511	49,904	53,847	65,000	75,000	83,000

(continued on next page)

Table 2.3 (continued)

	1975	1976	1977	1978	1979	1980	1981	1982	1983
Bolivia									
Annual Growth Rates									
Gross domestic product	5.1	6.1	4.2	3.4	1.8	1.2	-1.1	-9.2	-6.0
Consumer prices	6.6	5.5	10.5	13.5	45.5	23.9	25.2	296.5	249.0
Industrial wages	N/A	N/A	N/A	N/A	N/A	N/A	N/A	N/A	N/A
Rate of unemployment	N/A	N/A	N/A	4.5	6.2	7.5	9.7	N/A	12.6
External sector (millions of dollars)									
Total external debt (public)	883	1,107	1,458	1,762	1,941	2,220	2,450	2,373	2,700
Argentina									
Annual Growth Rates									
Gross domestic product	-.9	-.2	6.4	-3.4	7.1	1.1	-5.9	-5.4	2.0
Consumer prices	334.9	347.5	150.4	169.8	139.7	87.6	131.2	209.7	401.6
Industrial wages (real)	N/A	N/A	-1.5	-1.8	14.8	12.0	-10.8	-10.4	N/A
Rate of unemployment	2.6	4.5	2.8	2.8	2.0	2.3	4.5	4.7	4.9
External sector (millions of dollars)									
Total external debt	N/A	N/A	11,761	12,496	19,034	27,162	35,671	38,907	42,000

a1975–1976, public debt; 1977–1983, total debt.
Some of the data for Peru, Mexico, and Brazil includes only medium long-term debt.

Source: United Nations, ECLA, 1982, 1983, 1984; and Iglesias 1984.

3 / *Third World Industrialization: Implications for Trade Union Struggles*

JAMES PETRAS and DENNIS ENGBARTH

Introduction

Third World industrialization has become an increasingly important theme in the development literature. The shift in emphasis from underdevelopment to industrialization has been dramatic. Only a short decade ago for many writers, especially those associated with the dependency school, industrialization of the Third World was looked at as an impossibility or at best a phenomenon only possible through a radical rupture in the global capitalist system.[1] Today the intellectual trend is generally in the opposite direction. The assumption of rapid and dynamic industrialization of the Third World is assumed to be part of the new economic reality. Within this perspective some writers have elaborated a theoretical framework, arguing that a "New International Division of Labor" (NIDL) has evolved in which the Third World, specializing in labor-intensive industries, complements the high-tech production of the advanced capitalist countries.[2]

While these theorists have provided a corrective to the earlier, more dogmatic assertions of dependency theory, their view of Third World industrialization suffers from some of the same flaws and misconceptions as that of their adversaries: the tendency to project limited country experiences onto a global pattern—to extrapolate from favorable conjunctures and formulate generalizations that cut across economic cycles. In order to understand the implications of Third World industrialization for trade union struggles, it is necessary to correct several misconceptions concerning the process.

The Realities of Third World Industrialization

More precisely, the immense diversity, dynamics, and limitations of the process of industrialization in the Third World have generally been overlooked by NIDL theorists intent on tailoring the richness of this experience to fit their vision of global capital redeployment. However, the dynamics of the development process—and its implications for trade union movements—can only be comprehended by close examination of three factors: the *scope* (that is, the share of gross domestic product [GDP] accounted for by the industrial, particularly manufacturing, sector), the *depth* (degree of growth of capital goods or high technology sectors), and the *diversity* of industrialization in Third World countries and regions. Moreover, we find intensifying pressures for *differentiation* between various types of Third World development patterns (including some of the dynamic "newly industrializing countries" [NICs]) based on sharply divergent reactions to cyclical movements in the world economy, and problems arising from both the success and failure of individual developmental efforts.

THE SCOPE OF THIRD WORLD INDUSTRIALIZATION

The spread of industrialization throughout the Third World can be measured by the rapid increase in industrial and manufacturing production and employment. During the 1970s, Third World growth rates rose for a wide range of manufactured products. Manufacturing production climbed by 85.5 percent in developing economies (DEs) during the past decade, compared with a rise of only 37.7 percent in the developed market economies (DMEs), according to United Nations statistics (see table 3.1) Furthermore, while industrial and manufacturing employment declined in the DMEs, the Third World industrial workforce showed a steady growth of five percent per year over the same period (see table 3.2).

The scope of industrialization in most developing countries is, however, still quite limited. Most "middle-income economies" (defined by the World Bank as having per capita GNP over $410 in 1982) have less than 25 percent of their productive activity in manufacturing (see table 3.3). Despite impressive growth figures, Third World economies have yet to overcome the critical edge enjoyed by DMEs in the high growth of labor productivity, a disadvantage that limit their capacity to compete in international markets (see table 3.4). Thus the developing countries' share of total world manufacturing exports remained low, at 9.7 percent in 1980. (Its slow growth from 6.3 percent in 1970 provides little support for theories based on notions of *global* realignment of productive forces.) (*UN Yearbook of International Trade Statistics*, 1981, 1114)

Table 3.1. Index Numbers of Industrial Production (1975 = 100)

Branch of Activity	Developed Market Economies		Developing Market Economies	
	1970	1980	1970	1980
Manufacturing	90	122	69	134
Light manufacture	91	116	77	127
Heavy manufacture	90	125	65	140
Food and beverages	86	116	79	138
Textiles	96	109	80	111
Wearing apparel	95	102	70	113
Wood products	92	102	70	113
Paper and publishing	97	126	66	132
Chemical, petroleum, and plastic products	85	128	68	134
Nonmetallic mineral products	92	121	69	143
Basic metal industry	102	113	75	150
Metal products	88	142	55	141
Electrical machinery	85	142	52	134
Transport equipment	86	118	53	134
Mining	97	125	90	110

Source: UN Yearbook of Industrial Statistics, 1981, vol. 1. (New York 1982)

Table 3.2. Index Numbers of Industrial Employment (1975 = 100)

Branch of Activity	Developed Market Economies		Developing Market Economies	
	1970	1980	1970	1980
Manufacturing	103	99	73	122
Light manufacture	104	96	74	123
Heavy manufacture	102	101	70	121
Food and beverages	101	100	74	125
Textiles	116	84	77	109
Wearing apparel	103	94	63	146
Wood products	100	96	72	116
Paper and publishing	105	97	82	119
Chemical, petroleum, and plastic products	99	102	66	122
Nonmetallic mineral products	103	97	76	124
Basic metal industry	105	92	57	118
Metal products	101	104	70	122
Electrical machinery	—	—	—	—
Transport Equipment	—	—	—	—
Mining	109	103	88	102

Source: UN Yearbook of Industrial Statistics, 1981, vol. 1.

Table 3.3. Structure of Production: Percentage of GDP in Manufacturing

Type of Economy	1960	1982
Low income	13	14
Middle income	21	20
Oil exporting	14	17
Oil importing	22	23
Capital surplus oil exporting	—	4
Industrial market	30	24

Source: World Development Report 1984, 222–23.

Moreover, growth in manufacturing production and exports in the Third World is highly concentrated. Seven economies (Taiwan, South Korea, Hong Kong, Singapore, Brazil, India, and Mexico) accounted for 65 percent of Third World manufacturing export value in 1980, up from 55 percent for the same countries in 1965. Although a few other countries have also recorded strong export performances in recent years, the limitation of rapid manufacturing growth to a relatively small and diverse assortment of countries suggest that the critical issue may be the interaction of particular configurations of more or less "internal" factors—such as class structure, state composition and policy, and

Table 3.4. Index Numbers of Labor Productivity in Industry (1975 = 100)

Branch of Activity	Developed Market Economies		Developing Market Economies	
	1970	1979	1970	1979
Manufacturing	89	120	104	108
Light manufacture	89	116	108	105
Heavy manufacture	89	123	94	114
Food and beverage	85	112	105	105
Textiles	85	122	104	104
Wearing apparel	92	109	100	96
Wood products	94	116	108	116
Paper and publishing	95	121	114	112
Chemicals, petroleum, and plastic products	86	129	115	106
Nonmetallic mineral products	91	123	90	104
Basic metal	96	127	126	120
Metal products	89	120	85	118
Mining	97	105	99	109

Source: UN Yearbook of Industrial Statistics, 1981.

domestic resource endowments—with transformations in the world economic and political environment.

For example, the continued predominance of agriculture among many low- and lower-middle-income countries often reflects strong class linkages between primary producing classes and the state. The enduring power of traditional divisions of labor and a lack of strong public and private industrial entrepreneurial groups often inhibit domestic capital accumulation and the launching of sustained development efforts that can take advantage of shifts in the world political economy.

Not all constraints on industrialization are political or social. Limited resources, poor geographical locations, inadequate infrastructure, or the lack of basic market or productive systems (as in the case of subsistence agriculture) often impede domestic saving and private industrial investment, given better profit- and interest-earning opportunities elsewhere. Third World countries distant from the cutting edges of superpower confrontation are also far less likely to receive large grants or loans aimed at the creation of strong military allies and developmental "showcases." (Such outlays were *initially* important for poor countries like Taiwan and South Korea, but effective utilization of the opportunities for development brought about by association with a superpower is also conditioned by the capabilities of local states and entrepreneurial strata.)

Not only is the scope of Third World industrialization fairly limited, but past assumptions about the smooth ascent of Third World economies have surely been shattered by the blows delivered to many of even the most dynamic developing nations by two energy crises and a deep recession over the past decade. Average growth in industrial production among low-income oil-importing countries slowed from 6.6 percent per year in 1960–1970 to 4.2 percent from 1970 to 1982. Industrial growth among middle-income oil importers fell from 7.0 to 5.5 percent per year, while oil exporters recorded a slight improvement—from 7.4 to 7.6 percent per year over the same periods (*World Development Report* 1984, 220–21).

Overall, Third World countries suffered more from the 1980–1982 recession than from the 1973 energy crisis. Middle-income oil importers were especially hard hit, but even oil exporters proved vulnerable after the recession and world-wide energy conservation efforts led to an oil glut and the collapse of the petroleum market in 1981–1982 (see table 3.5). Contrary to most expectations, the export-led East Asian countries were the least affected by the 1980–1982 recession and have been the fastest to recover. Semi-industrialized Latin American nations such as Brazil and Mexico have suffered the most, with negative GDP growth since 1981 and dim hopes for an early recovery, given their massive debt burdens.

Intensifying differentiation among Third World countries and contin-

Table 3.5. GDP Growth Rates, 1960–1973 (averaged annual percentage change)

Country Group	1960–73	1973–79	1980	1981	1982	1983 (est.)
Developing Countries	6.3	5.2	2.5	2.4	1.9	1.0
Low income	5.6	4.8	5.9	4.8	5.2	4.7
Asia	5.9	5.2	6.3	5.2	5.6	5.1
China	8.5	5.7	6.1	5.2	5.6	5.1
India	3.6	4.3	6.9	5.7	2.9	5.4
Africa	3.5	2.1	1.3	1.2	0.5	−0.1
Middle-income oil importers	6.3	5.6	4.3	0.9	0.7	0.3
East Asia and Pacific	8.2	8.6	3.6	6.7	4.2	6.4
Middle East and N. Africa	5.2	3.0	4.2	−2.4	5.5	2.0
Sub-Saharan Africa	5.6	3.7	5.5	3.9	1.1	0.3
Southern Europe	6.7	5.0	1.5	2.3	0.7	−0.9
Latin America and Caribbean	5.6	5.0	5.8	−2.3	−0.4	−2.2
Middle-income oil exporters	6.9	4.9	−2.4	2.4	0.9	−0.7
High-income oil exporters	10.7	7.7	7.4	0.0	—	—
Industrial market economies	4.9	2.8	1.3	1.3	−0.5	2.3

Source: World Development Report 1984, 11.

ued uneven development of the scope of industrialization seem to be inevitable outcomes of these developments.

THE DEPTH OF INDUSTRIALIZATION

We can see a similar pattern when we examine the *depth* of Third World industrialization (here measured in terms of the growth of producer goods, chemicals, and transportation equipment sectors).[3] Only 12 of 55 capitalist middle- and low-income countries surveyed by the World Bank have 25 percent or more of manufacturing value-added derived from capital goods, transporation equipment, or chemical sectors (see table 3.6). Twenty countries, on the other hand, have less than 10 percent of their manufacturing value-added in these lines (see table 3.7). Industrialization for most Third World nations has apparently taken place overwhelmingly in light consumer goods industries.

Countries with strong capital goods and chemical sectors tend to be middle-income economies in Latin America or Asia; only two (India and Kenya) fall into the "low-income" bracket of World Bank statistics. The high concentration (9 of 12) of "upper-middle-income" economies (with per capita GNP over $1,500 in 1982) suggest that the deepening of industrialization may be partly related to growing internal markets and associated with increasingly differentiated class structures.

The "deepening" and "widening" (of the scope) of industrialization by Third World countries is thus clearly possible, if only for a select few.

Table 3.6. Distribution of Manufacturing Value-added, 1981 Percentages (1975 prices)

Country	Light Industries	Capital Goods/Chemicals/ Transportation Equipment
Low income		
Chad (1980)	83	0
Bangladesh	68	20
Ethiopia	54	2
Burma	45	5
Malawi	64	0
Upper Volta	81	11
Uganda	79	0
India	31	34
Rwanda (1980)	58	2
Haiti (1980)	52	1
Central African Republic (1980)	87	2
Madagascar (1980)	66	12
Sri Lanka	56	0
Togo (1980)	78	0
Ghana (1980)	28	0
Pakistan	60	23
Kenya	34	39
Lower middle income		
Liberia (1980)	22	0
Senegal (1980)	58	8
Indonesia	36	19
Zambia	38	24
Honduras (1980)	61	8
Egypt (1980)	42	24
Thailand (1980)	57	18
Philippines	51	21
Zimbabwe	38	21
Nigeria	51	23
Morocco	43	19
Cameroon (1980)	41	9
Nicaragua (1980)	67	0
Congo, People's Republic	42	7
Peru (1980)	41	21
Dominican Republic (1980)	86	6
Ecuador	41	17
Turkey	35	27
Tunisia	40	24
Columbia	47	23
Paraguay	48	14
Upper middle income		
Syria	59	8
Malaysia	39	24
South Korea	39	29
Panama	63	8

Table 3.6 (continued)

Country	Light Industries	Capital Goods/Chemicals/Transportation Equipment
Upper middle income (contd.)		
Chile	20	26
Brazil	25	37
Mexico	27	32
Algeria	40	13
Portugal	30	36
Argentina	23	36
Uruguay (1980)	49	19
South Africa	25	29
Venezuela	33	16
Greece	46	18
Israel	27	33
Singapore	8	59
Trinidad and Tobago (1980)	28	16

Note: Data for some countries were available only for 1980.
Source: World Development Report 1984, 230–31.

Yet analysis of the relatively successful experiences also shows that the deepening process is multilinear and historically conditioned by the interaction of a complex matrix of "internal" and "external" factors, a state of affairs which severely limits the utility of imposing any single strategy or explanatory theory on developing countries.

Historically, the deepening of industrialization beyond the production of consumer goods in the Third World has been associated with two broad (and not mutually exclusive) types of development strategy.

The older, larger countries (several Latin American nations) over time have been able to develop substantial capital goods and chemical industries, primarily in connection with their sizable internal markets, in successive stages of primary and secondary import substitution. Development efforts in such nations have usually featured powerful and extensive state leadership and direct involvement in the industrialization process. Significant strata of domestic capitalists have also risen, along with large volumes of direct transnational capital (TNC) investment (generally aimed at local or regional markets) and extensive state and private sector ties with Western financial capital.

More recently, small East Asian economies (South Korea, Taiwan, Singapore, and Hong Kong) have capitalized on large pools of surplus labor to develop labor-intensive, assembly-based industries producing inexpensive consumer goods for external markets. Considerable amounts of export-oriented TNC investment and tight integration with the world market are well-known features of this "export-led industrial-

Table 3.7. **Low and Middle Income Countries: Share of Manufacturing Value-added in Capital Goods, Chemicals and Transportation Equipment, 1981 (number of countries)**

Percentage	Middle Income	Low Income
more than 30%	6	2
25–29	4	0
20–24	8	2
15–19	9	0
10–14	2	2
less than 10	9	11
Total	38	17

Source: World Development Report 1984, 230–31.

ization" path. Yet, despite the free market rhetoric of their political leaders and overseas boosters, these countries have also had energetic and powerful public sector enterprise heavily involved in economic activity. The expansion of light export-oriented industries has also been accompanied by state efforts to build intermediate and upstream heavy and chemical industries, often with sizable foreign capital inputs.

Both routes have successfully promoted relatively deep industrial development in Latin American and East Asian NICs. These economies, however, now confront urgent problems of adjustment and upgrading to overcome pressures generated by both the strengths and weaknesses of their developmental paths as well as by the recent recession.

The 1980-1982 recession brutally exposed the mortal weakness of the externally financed developmental efforts of Latin American NICs. These countries, among many others in the Third World, had increasingly turned to transnational banks (TNBs) and Eurodollar funds in the mid-1970s to cover rising oil bills and the costs of massive capital goods imports required for their ambitious development projects. In several Latin American nations, the state was either unable or unwilling to obtain sufficient amounts of capital from domestic sources, perhaps due to either the economic weakness or political strength of ruling interests and inadequate levels of domestic savings from other social classes.

The sudden eruption of the second oil crisis in 1979, the subsequent recession, and contractive Western industrial policies deepened the crisis. Service ratios on external public debt alone soared (to 42.1 percent for Brazil and 29.5 percent for Mexico by 1982), sparking a flurry of debt reschedulings and raising the specter of defaults (see table 3.8). This

Table 3.8. **External Public Debt Service as Percentage of Exports of Goods and Services**

	1970	1982
Argentina	21.5	24.5
Brazil	12.5	42.1
India	20.9	7.1
Kenya	5.4	20.3
Mexico	23.6	29.5
Philippines	7.2	12.8
Singapore	0.6	0.8
South Korea	19.4	13.1

Source: *World Development Report 1984, 248–49.*

process has left many Latin American nations subordinate to the severe austerity programs of the International Monetary Fund (IMF), which may actually lead to a degree of *de-industrialization*, with disastrous effects on the masses of the local populations.

The proposed shift to "growth-oriented, export-expanding adjustment" may not provide a cure (see *World Development Report 1984,* 29 for the case in support of this switch). This prescription is based on the successes of East Asian NICs (see below), but the context of its proposed adoption in Latin America is strikingly different. Export substitution in East Asia has been a means to make maximum use of limited capital resources and technology to produce light industrial goods for overseas markets. Export earnings were then used to finance imports of raw materials, capital goods, and more advanced technology and to further expand production and employment. In contrast, the current promotion of *old* export lines in Latin America is accompanied by the IMF's stringent measures aimed at severely *contracting* employment, wages, and imports, primarily at the expense of the working classes.

The East Asian NICs have been far less substantially reliant on foreign capital. Export earnings and high rates of domestic savings (thanks to the mushrooming of smaller export-related firms and high levels of employment) have contributed to the availability of local capital resources as well as to the steady expansion and intensification of home markets. Direct foreign investment has been strategically less important for capital inputs than for the provision of production and management techniques and markets in the advanced industrial countries. While East Asian NICs have borrowed extensively on overseas capital markets to finance state-sponsored infrastructure or heavy industrial projects as well as private endeavors, huge export earnings have provided them with a far greater capability to support and pay back these funds.

Based upon these strengths, East Asian NICs were less affected by the recent recession and have bounced back quickly to record strong export and GDP growth rates in 1983 and 1984. The critical issues for the East Asian industrial nations concern problems arising from their economic success. The export competitiveness of their light industrial products has declined as growth in real wages has far surpassed increases in labor productivity. Moreover, rising protectionism in the West and a new wave of entrants into labor-intensive export lines (such as mainland China and some Southeast Asian nations) are pressuring the "four little dragons" (the four East Asian NICs).

Most East Asian NICs have thus intensified efforts to upgrade their industrial structures through promotion of more technology- and capital-intensive export lines and through liberalization of remaining barriers to imports and foreign investment. Rich domestic capital sources and high levels of scientific and technical education augur well for these efforts, but the obstacles are still formidable. In addition to the external pressures mentioned above, the East Asian NICs must confront fierce intercine competition from each other as well as from firms in developed countries (such as Japan) that are threatened by their rise.

The domestic difficulties are also daunting. A new developmentalist role for the state, on the lines of Japan's "industrial policy" may be needed to build a more advanced economic structure in the context of tighter integration with the world economy. Yet the state will face considerable opposition to any efforts to reshape the local industrial structure from bureaucratic and capitalist strata with vested interests in the previous pattern of export-led growth. Moreover, rising living standards and education levels have spurred movements for democratization of the authoritarian states and greater attention to social welfare and environmental issues. Such pressures may be heightened by the potential threat that industrial upgrading poses to the prosperity of small and medium-sized enterprises.

Labor movements in the East Asian NICs face a period of crisis and opportunity, whether industrial upgrading succeeds or fails. The shift to skill- and knowledge-intensive high-technology industries should improve the structural bargaining positions of skilled and semiskilled workers, but may also entail sizable unemployment and growing income inequality if compensating opportunities for displaced unskilled laborers are not created by faster economic growth. However, massive unemployment and sharp increases in inequality will surely result from the stagnation which would follow in the wake of the failure of industrial upgrading projects.

MOVING BEYOND THE "NEW INTERNATIONAL DIVISION OF LABOR"

New theories on the formation of new international divisions of labor through transnational capital expansion constitute an advance over the static conceptions of the dependency school. NIDL theorists have recognized the rapid progress of industrialization in the Third World and have drawn attention to the tendency of transnational capital to create new forms of world-wide intra-firm and inter-firm divisions of labor based on exploitation of cheap labor in export-oriented assembly and processing industries (notably but not exclusively in East Asia).

However, the process of industrialization has by no means been as core-centered or TNE-determined as NIDL theorists claim. One indication of more complex relationships is the continuing strong trade among industrializing Third World nations (see table 3.9) and the emergence of regional economic networks (among Japan and East and Southeast Asian nations, for example).[4]

Moreover, through neglect of socio-historical analysis of developing countries, NIDL theorists have overlooked the ability of Third World states to intervene actively in the development process. In East Asian NICs, for example, the thrust of such intervention has been to seize the opportunities offered by association with emerging international and regional specializations to build strong foundations for sustained interdependent development.

Finally, the nearly exclusive focus placed on the formation of TNE-centered subordinating divisions of labor has often led NIDL proponents to overlook the substantial degree of social transformation that has taken place in rapidly industrializing Third World nations. Failure to comprehend the dynamism of economic development has spawned a

Table 3.9. Destination of Manufactured Exports (percentage of total)

Origin	Industrial Market Economies		Developing Economies	
	1962	1981	1962	1981
Low-income economies	57	50	—	28
Middle-income economies	50	57	43	31
Oil exporters	61	57	27	37
Oil importers	48	57	46	31
Lower middle income	53	52	38	39
Upper middle income	50	58	44	31

Source: *World Development Report, 1984*, 242–43.

blindness to the implications of the differential patterns of industrializa-tion on the working class and trade union movements in the Third World. It is to this critical dimension that we now turn.

Expanding Industrializing Countries: Development versus Exploitation

Discussions of Third World industrialization have focused almost exclu-sively on the issue of "development," or more specifically on the growth of the productive forces. This one-sided concern with emphasizing economic changes perhaps was a natural reaction to the obstinant tendency among dependency theorists to deny these developmental possibilities. In the process, however, this techno-productivist bias has blinded development students to the new emerging socio-political real-ity in which the new generation of workers located within the new productive facilities increasingly perceive the basic issue as one of "exploitation" and not "development." The growth of industry, to-gether with the incorporation of labor into industrial employment, has created a new point of departure for the second generation of workers. The problems raised by segments of the working class in the newly industrialized countries is no longer employment but the *conditions* of employment: the very development of the productive forces has brought the issue of the social relations of production to the fore, at least among some layers of the industrial labor force. While it would be a mistake to attribute the emergence of new layers of class conscious workers to merely techno-productive changes, there is evidence sug-gesting that in some of the more advanced industrial countries of the Third World there is increasing discontent with the organization and type of work that were acceptable to the first wave of workers recruited to the factory system. This is particularly the case as the industrializa-tion process becomes more advanced and complex, drawing in its wake a strata of skilled workers, with greater education and qualifications that cannot so easily be replaced. In these circumstances, the push for greater worker autonomy proceeds apace.

Free Enterprise Ideology and Statist Practice

One of the most frequently misunderstood aspects of Third World industrialization has been the relationship between free enterprise ideol-ogy and statist practice. The NIDL school has simultaneously misunder-stood the relative importance of Third World states, local capital, and local markets, exaggerated the importance of multinational capital, and understated the centrality of finance capital in the industrialization of the Third World. Third World industrialization is not the product of a "redeployment strategy" designed by the metropolitan countries; nor is it the case that the external market is the main stimulus to industrial production. Finally, Third World manufacturing exports are not exclusively directed toward the metropolitan countries but, in many cases, are part of intra-Third World exchanges (see table 3.9).

The growth of industry in close association with the growth of statism is illustrated by the experience in Latin America. In the 1960s and 1970s, foreign capital financed at most 10 to 20 percent of total investments in the Third World. The three leading industrial countries, Mexico, Brazil, and Argentina, have very substantial public sectors involved in basic industry and resources. In Asia, the state in Taiwan, South Korea, and Singapore has played a pivotal role in regulating and directing the growth of private capital. Moreover, local private capital has increased its role in some countries over the past decade. The major differences in the Third World have not been over the role of the state but over the relative importance of the domestic market in stimulating growth. In the small, labor-surplus countries of Asia, more emphasis was placed on the external market, whereas in Latin America the domestic market played a larger role. Even in Asia, however, one should not exaggerate the importance of the export market: South Korea exports about 30 percent of its manufacturing products. Thus, while the NICs adopt a free enterprise ideology, in practice statism plays a much bigger role than is usually recognized. While industrial exports have been playing a larger role for most Third World countries, the market for these products has varied with the level of industrialization of the region. Among the less industrialized countries an increasing share of their exports are going to other Third World nations, while the relatively more advanced Third World countries are increasingly trading with the advanced industrial countries. Hence there is no simple pattern of "industrial redeployment" such as is suggested by the NIDL school. The growth of metropolitan protectionism and the growing number of proponents of intra-Third World trade suggest that alternate patterns of exchange may emerge.

Sources of Foreign Financing: Banking Capital and Multinational Corporations

The 1970s and 1980s there saw a dramatic shift from direct to indirect investments or commercial loans. The attractiveness to metropolitan investors of shifting to finance capital was based on the higher rates of profit, the low risk (at the time), and the relative immunity from class struggle and nationalist expropriation. Default by individual borrowers was seen as highly unlikely as it would jeopardize a country's standing with all lender countries, since loans are increasingly lent by consortiums. External financing to local state and private capital led to greater local ownership and increasing international debt. The process of international financing of Third World industrialization was concentrated in the more developed Third World countries, stimulating growth during the expansive period of the world economy and exacerbating stagnation and crises during the period of world contraction. The cyclical nature of world capitalist development and the increasing dependence of locally owned state and private capital on finance capital has created a new set of contradictions: between national productive forces (capital and labor) and the international banks and their allies in the World Bank and International Monetary Fund. The struggle between the Third World and the multinational corporations (MNCs) postulated by the NIDL school has been dwarfed in the 1980s by the struggles emerging over debt financing and interest payments—a far more serious drain on development resources.

In summary, the process of Third World industrialization is much more complex and contradictory than has been envisioned by the proponents of a new international division of labor. Both the size and scope of industrialization must be specified to determine the balance of social forces in analyzing trade union strategies. Likewise, in the expanding Third World countries, shifts in levels and types of industrialization have raised new strata, new issues that go beyond the perspectives of "development" and raise basic issues relating to the social relations of production. The real importance of statism and its paradoxical legitimation by free market ideology raises important issues regarding the relationship between state and civil society and, in particular, the need to deepen internal class analysis as the major research strategy in determining the significance of Third World countries' insertion in the world market. This is particularly important in discussing the moves from state-controlled to autonomous trade unions. Finally the linkages between locally owned industries and foreign private banking capital have in many cases created a new set of global contradictions: between the local labor force, the state, and foreign bankers. The problem of debt payments involves a new set of alliances and conflicts in which the process of extraction of economic surplus for interest payments becomes a central concern for the trade union movement.

Industrialization and Its Implications for Third World Trade Union Struggles

Third World industrialization raises concrete issues and particular points of departure for trade union struggles that are substantially different from those found in the industrialized West. Rather than bemoan these differences (or castigate Third World unions for deficiencies), it is important to explore the means by which the specificities of Third World industrialization can be turned into advantages in the trade union struggle. Drawing on the preceding discussion of Third World industrialization, we shall look at what its specific features may mean for trade union movements.

LIMITED SCOPE OF INDUSTRIALIZATION

In most Third World countries, industrialization takes place amidst a sea of rural producers, petty commodity distributors, and a multiplicity of small household manufacturing enterprises. Moreover, in many cases industrial workers' recently arrived from the countryside retain ties with their families and land in rural areas. The limited scope of industrialization, together with the concomitant small size of the industrial working class, means that trade unions must develop ties with other strata and organizations to be politically effective. "Workerist" orientations, with their exclusive focus on factory issues and organizations, will tend to isolate the workers and perhaps even make them vulnerable to repressive forces. Two other strategic groups—small farmers and peasants in the countryside, and petty producers, distributors, and the underemployed in the cities—are central to any coalition-building effort. There are specific sets of issues on which the trade unions connect with these strata: workers share with the unemployed and petty commodity producers and distributors a whole set of common demands at the point of habitation (housing, infrastructure, potable water, and so on) that may be articulated through community organizations linked to the trade unions. Communication between workers and petty urban producers is facilitated by the frequent multiple-employment practices of working class segments. The relative social and geographic proximity of workers and other urban strata facilitates the intervention of trade unions in community struggles *and* the mobilization of community support for trade union struggle. Trade union struggles divorced from the wider community demands of the nonfactory urban poor commonly result in the recruitment of strikebreakers from the mass of surplus labor.

The second strategic group, peasants and farmers, has been in some accounts counterpoised to the industrial working class because of differences in income and standard of living. Yet an earlier study has demonstrated that in agrarian regions where highly organized miners have interacted with peasants, providing legal and material support for their struggles, the miners have exercised a radicalizing influence upon the peasants' political behavior. Moreover, the frequent visiting that takes place between urban and rural areas encourages the diffusion of ideas of organization and struggle. At a more formal institutional level, issue-specific institutions involving both rural producers and trade unions—such as producer and consumer cooperatives—serve as bridges toward broader working relations.

At the ideological level, then, the limited scope of industrialization and the relatively small size of the working class make it advantageous for trade unions to elaborate an ideology of solidarity between factory enclaves and the mass of petty producers and distributors. Without *dissolving* the basic trade union organization into a heterogeneous movement, it is necessary for unions to transcend the factory setting by establishing institutions at the community level and at the intersection of rural and urban exchanges in order to muster sufficient force to constitute a national presence.

LIMITED DEPTH OF INDUSTRIALIZATION

The spread of industry across various sectors has been quite limited. The bulk of industry has been located in the consumer goods sector and within this sector in textiles, clothing, and electronics. The limited depth of industrialization—the low level of capital investment per worker—makes these industries particularly susceptible to mobility. Particularly where there is a substantial component of foreign capital, the vulnerability to capital flight requires that trade unions attach a special importance to nationalism and nationalist movements, without sacrificing their essential class perspective. More central to trade union organization in this context is the question of worker gender in this type of industrial process: within the textile, clothing, and electronics industries there is a preponderance of women at the level of mass production; while technician and maintenance jobs (along with union leadership positions) tend to be filled by males. A fundamental issue that faces the trade unions is the need to create specific institutional and cultural support structures that would allow women to play significant roles. The basic weakness of the trade unions in the textile and electronics industries is the fact that the female majority is dominated by household concerns, directed by male trade union leaders, and manipulated and exploited by alternately paternalistic and authoritarian employers. There is virtually no time, space, or energy left for union concerns—unless a major crisis (sharp reduction in salary, factory closing, mass revolt, or the like) disrupts routines and allows women workers to change their agenda of priorities and take part temporarily in the union's struggle.

The vulnerability of light industry makes it important for trade unions to develop ties with strategic trade unions, usually in the public sector, such as light and power workers and port and transport unions. While employers can usually "wait out" a strike in consumer goods sectors (or bring in strike breakers from among the surplus labor force), strikes among the usually highly organized utility and transport workers have an immediate and highly damaging effect on the economy as a whole and on the state. These unions thus provide greater leverage in bargaining for the weaker unions in consumer industries and also compensate for internal structural weaknesses.

STATISM AND THE TRADE UNIONS

One of the most salient facts concerning Third World industrial development is the permeation of society and economy by the state; whether it be in the elaboration of development agencies to promote investments, or in the expansion of patronage appointments for followers or to extend control over potentially oppositionist associations, the state is everywhere. The centrality of politics in both promoting the productive forces and determining how its product will be allocated clearly suggests that trade union struggles must be political. Who controls the state, controls the intervention of the state in society and economy (a necesary given in all Third World development). The problem, however, is that as trade unions enter into political struggle over the state they greatly increase their chances of becoming targets of repression.

The centrality of the state and its important role as broker/partner between national capital and the multinationals also suggests that the struggles against multinational capital frequently involve conflicts with domestic political collaborators. The formidable array of forces and resources at the disposal of the state and the MNC may lead trade unions to adopt a two-step approach: first to build up strength within the realm of economic and trade union issues and after a period of accumulating strength, to deepen and extend the struggle to the political terrain.

It is apparent that ubiquitous state institutions and their highly centralized structures in many Third World countries penetrate and control trade unions at the apex—the leaders of federations and confederations frequently seem to be functionaries of the ministry of labor. Thus the national or industry-wide union structure tends to be less representative and responsive to rank-and-file demands than local factory-based unions. Where centralized state control of national trade unions exists, the growth of locally controlled factory unions ("union decentralization") is a positive step toward autonomous class unionism, although there is always the danger that employers will respond by establishing their own company unions—in avoiding bureaucratic state control, the union movement risks becoming the captive of employer designs.

Perhaps the most salient issue facing trade unions is the extensive statification of economy and society. Nationalization, heralded by many as a progressive step on the way to socialism, frequently brings bureaucratization, statification, and tighter controls over trade unions. Strikes are apt to be sharply curtailed—job action against an enterprise becomes redefined as a threat to the state and to national security and may incur heavy penalties. Rather than a "progressive" step in the transition to socialism, centralized statification more often has been the first step toward the subordination of the trade unions to the one-party state, with few compensatory trade-offs. For trade unionists the issue of autonomy of organization—independence from the state—has become a general demand throughout the Third World. What have yet to be realized, however, are the necessary concomitant programmatic changes: self-administration by local producers of the social services previously administered by the state. The issue of decentralized and producer-controlled productive and distributive units is also crucial to creating legitimate space for autonomous trade union activity.

The state's subordination of trade unions is linked to and legitimated by its broader role as general dispenser of social services. The autonomy so often violated by the state is in part legitimated by workers themselves, who look to the state to intervene on their behalf in the economy and society and to provide pay-offs. What these same claimants cannot subsequently do is contain and limit the state to its "positive" role, but must also suffer its intervention in trade union life.

Finally, on the ideological plane, the trade unions are faced with the need to demystify the doctrine of national security, particularly in view of the local bourgeoisies' increasing use of it to oppress indigenous ethnic minority groups and to expand into neighboring territories. The doctrine of national security serves to mobilize popular support for centralizing state power and repression of class demands as "divisive"— thereby delegitimizing trade union aspirations. The perception of permanent crisis engendered by the constant evocation of "national enemies" thus serves dominant class interests. To the extent that trade unions are mobilized to support nationalist expansion, they increasingly sacrifice both the immediate interests and long-range goals of labor: by backing the military components of the state and supporting the ruling class in its role of "protector" of the nation, unions provide material and ideological support for their own subsequent repression once the "national crisis" subsides.

Externally and Internally Oriented Development

It is frequently acknowledged that externally and internally oriented developments are not antithetical—that both are necessary to development. There is a marked tendency, however, particularly on the part of the World Bank and the IMF, to stress export-oriented growth as a means of earning hard currency to repay loans. Where exports are used to finance debt, there is no commensurate return for labor, as *both the products* and *the earnings* go to outside forces: labor is left with fewer goods and lower wages. It is not unusual to observe rising protest among trade unionists against export growth, which both sacrifices the production of essential commodities for local consumption and deprives the economy of investment funds to develop or upgrade productive forces. The subsequent emphasis on the "home market" over the export market is a healthy response, if not exaggerated to the point of allowing higher-cost, locally owned industries to siphon off monopoly profits. The most promising approach is to combine the two markets, subordinating external growth to the expansion of the internal market. What this suggests is the importance of not merely attacking the consequences of the opposed model (austerity measures, lower wages, and so on) but formulating positive, alternative development models. To defend jobs in stagnant industries is to provide the most potent ammunition for the suppression of trade unionism: a trade union program combining industrial conversion to advanced production with expansion of internal markets must recognize the need to be competitive in the world market but attempt to ensure that competitiveness does not become an excuse for increasing inequality between owners and workers.

The current world crisis has served as an opportunity for Third World states and international capital to lower labor costs. The crisis has also presented a challenge to the current models of accumulation. The shrinking of external markets, exploitative financial arrangements, and exorbitant interest rates have converged with trade union demands to expand production for the local market, through structural changes that increase income and purchasing power for the masses. There is among the local bourgeoisie a push in the same direction, mainly as a means of preserving their precarious enterprises from foreign competition. From the trade union standpoint, in taking advantage of world crises and attempting to revitalize the internal market, it is necessary to determine which classes in that market will benefit from the shift in development strategy.

Metropolitan "Redeployment" or National Capital

Contrary to the NIDL theories, the impetus to industrialization has not been primarily a phenomenon designed by and directed from the metropolitan countries. The expansion of multinational capital, important as it has been, largely complements major inflows of capital from local, state, and private sources. Most Third World labor is employed in thousands of locally owned industries or in state enterprises. The predominance of national forces has led to a critical re-examination of the prevalent nationalist and "anti-imperialist" doctrines that have provided some of the official animus to class conflict. Nationalism as the ideology of capitalist (private or state) industrialization has thrown a veil over the worst forms of exploitation in the Third World, especially the mass of locally owned sweat shops that exploit child labor, recent women migrants, and urban slum dwellers. MNCs usually run large factories; each factory employs relatively great numbers of workers, which concentration of labor facilitates unionization. The small and medium-sized national capitalists operate in highly competitive markets, frequently extracting surplus through systematic violation of labor laws, health controls, and minimum wage restrictions. Contrary to the folklore of traditional leftists, on the shop floor there is nothing progressive about this national bourgeoisie.

Scattered attempts by trade unionists to organize labor in this sector are violently resisted not only by right-wing regimes but by supposedly progressive populist governments, who fear that a significant sector of their coalition (of small and medium-sized businesses) will be alienated and driven to the right by the extension of union militancy. The trade union movement must choose between two possible courses. The first involves an "antimonopoly strategy" focused on the organization of a small core of workers in larger enterprises and the joining of forces with sectors of business and the middle class to promote national develop-ment and ensure legality of collective bargaining. The second alterna-tive, a radical class strategy, would seek to mobilize workers and employees in a broad array of enterprises for deeper structural changes against a formidable alliance of small and large business. The former strategy maximizes allies across class boundaries but limits socioeco-nomic changes; the latter deepens the process of change but broadens the base of opposition. While proponents of the antimonopoly strategy argue that their approach does not preclude a second, more radical stage, in fact the consequences of this approach has been to consolidate a new configuration of capitalist power.

Finance Capital, Third World Industrialization, and the Debt

Trade unionists in many Third World countries are increasingly aware of the macro-processes affecting their members. The 1970s and 1980s witnessed the increasing importance of finance capital and a relative decline in direct investment. Rental income that accrued to the petro-leum-exporting countries was recycled through Western banks into loans to the Third World. The rent- and interest-collecting, oil-rich Third World countries became a new source of extraction of surplus from the rest of the Third World. The loans placed funds in the hands of Third World state and local ruling classes to invest or spend as they saw fit.

With the world economic crises, and consequent rise in interest rates and decline in export markets, debt payments became an albatross on Third World development. Both industry and labor were put through the wringer to maintain interest payments: devaluations, cutbacks in public spending and investment, reallocation of resources from domestic consumption to exports, and restructuring of credit led to massive unemployment, inflation, and wholesale bankruptcies. The IMF played a crucial role in enforcing "discipline" on the borrowers and in intervening to control many crucial aspects of economic policy. IMF policies geared to "opening the economies" and squeezing out payments led to a weakening of productive structures and the result was *the dismantling of local industry, not the redeployment of industry*. Trade unionists clearly perceived the effort by banks and the IMF to reconcentrate income, industry, employment, and markets through their debt collection policies. Sectors of the local bourgeoisie and technocrats joined with labor to attack this generalized assault on labor's standard of living and the overall productive structure. This coalition mobilized against the IMF and private banks corresponds to the global contradictions that have emerged between the West and the Third World.

Trade unionists may choose to form alliances with the local bourgeoisies to preserve the productive structure against the IMF and banks— even as they resist becoming politically subordinate to capital in the operation of the productive system. Faced with cyclical shifts in the economy and the shifting sources of exploitation, unions need the flexibility to shift coalitions according to the priority needs of their members—at the level of both the international economy and the shop floor. Given the shifting contours and problems facing the industrialization process in the Third World, there is little room for dogmatic deductive approaches that bind the labor movement to a predetermined strategy.

Technological Change and the Uneven Transformation of Labor

Among the more industrially advanced Third World countries, the movement toward technologically sophisticated industries is deepening the uneven transformation of labor. There is the emergence, on the one hand, of a skilled, educated labor force, highly organized, capable of struggling and bargaining effectively; and on the other, a growing marginalized mass of rural migrants dissociated from permanent factory employment. The increasing demand for skilled technical labor has opened new opportunities for unionization, as the state manifests greater willingness to tolerate economic bargaining for limited segments. The continuing bifurcation of labor heightens the danger of "isolation" in a dual sense: skilled workers may be divorced from a mass constituency necessary to carry out deep structural changes, while the mass of unskilled labor is likely to be isolated from a potential leadership group. Economic and skill differentiation, however, is not an insurmountable obstacle to common action. In most advanced Third World industrializing countries, there are fundamental issues that adversely affect both skilled and unskilled workers, such as authoritarian and repressive political structures, inflation, austerity policies, restrictions on autonomous organization, and excessive concessions to foreign enterprises. As multi-polar conflicts emerge, the challenge facing trade unionists is to determine whether the skilled segments of labor will become incorporated into subordinate elements of the ruling power bloc or whether they can share hegemony with the excluded masses in directing struggles against the power bloc.

Bureaucratic Collectivism, Industrialization, and Trade Unionism

In several Third World countries collectivization and nationalization have become the instruments for industrial development. While bureaucratic collectivist regimes have achieved more egalitarian norms in the distribution of goods and services, as well as higher levels of employment, and have addressed basic needs of the working class, the structure and style of rulership has engendered new sets of contradictions. The most basic is between the legal norm of "social ownership" of the means of production and the reality of bureaucratic control. The attempts to bring reality into line with legal norms is blocked by the lack of autonomy of trade unions and other forms of workers' organization. Hence, one of the basic struggles is precisely the effort to democratize the union structure—either from within or more frequently by creating parallel or unofficial union-worker organizations that serve to articulate worker demands. The very success of collectivist societies in solving basic need problems creates the basis for workers to make new demands regarding conditions of work and a greater role in management, as well as demands for greater variety and better quality in consumer goods. Skilled workers in the increasingly complex economy demand different incentive systems, modifying rigid egalitarian norms in favor of rewards linked to merit. Reforms aimed at "dirty work" move to the foreground. The old collectivist orthodoxy divorced from the new realities loses its meaning: trade unions responsive to the new generation of workers provide the new hope for revitalizing socialist ideas. Class-based trade unionism oriented toward new democratic forms of planning represents the best hope that the demise of outmoded Eastern collectivism will not be replaced by an exploitive Western version of free market economics.

Conclusion

There appears to be no direct relationship between early and advanced stages of industrialization and labor militancy. In countries like Chile, trade union militancy occurred at the turn of the nineteenth century (during the early years of manufacturing), in the 1930s (during the first stages of the factory system), in the 1970s (during the relatively advanced industrial stage of the Allende government), and in the most recent period of industrial crisis and decline (the last two years of the Pinochet regime).

A strong case can be made for the relative importance of the larger political setting in shaping conditions for trade union militancy: the advantages of an "open political climate" with its tolerance of broader social and national movements challenging the structures of society and state. On the other hand, the establishment of an authoritarian regime and the defeats of major popular social movements (including trade unions), followed by a period of rapid and intensive industrialization, results in a prolonged period of trade union quiescence. Labor activity appears to be limited to circumscribed forms of struggle controlled by "official" trade unions. Industrialization that takes place in the framework of successful capitalist "military-political struggles" and strong state structures appears to be the key to preventing the development of trade union militancy.

The manner of insertion in the world economy does not seem to be particularly useful in explaining the level of militancy and autonomy of class action of trade unions. Trade unions under regimes promoting either "internally oriented national development" or "externally oriented export growth" have suffered repression and state control. The experiences of "inward development" in the so-called "radical" African states (Guinea, Egypt under Nasser, Libya) and in Burma and Cambodia offer evidence of very limited or nonexistent space for genuine trade union development.

In the export-oriented economies of Asia (South Korea, Hong Kong, Taiwan, and the Philippines) and Latin America (Brazil, Argentina, and Chile) the situation is similar: development imperatives take precedence over the rights of trade unions to autonomous existence. In states— whether radical-nationalist or conservative-Western—where development is the transcendent goal and trade unions are a subordinate element, there is a clear tendency for the state to try to integrate trade unions into administrative structures or to intervene and control their activities.

Trade union militancy has been found in both "nationally" oriented and "export-oriented" economies where the "political constraints" of dictatorial rulership have been loosened. Militancy has accompanied both the formation and expansion phases of trade union organization.

Cooptation occurs when two processes are combined: the internal transformation of the unions (to centralized-bureaucratic control) and their vertical integration into the state apparatus. This process can occur early or late in the industrialization process, and in both internally and externally oriented development approaches. The *political option* of the trade union becomes central to maintaining its image of integrity (trade union independence and capacity to represent its members): to struggle for a political structure, state and party that will respect the autonomy of secondary associations and tolerate fundamental opposition to statist or private development programs with strong "corporatist" tendencies.

Notes

1. André Gunder Frank, *Capitalism and Underdevelopment in Latin America* (New York: Monthly Review Press, 1967).

2. Folker Frobel, Jurgen Heinrichs, and Otto Kreyer, *The New International Division of Labor* (Cambridge: Cambridge University Press, 1980).

3. The concept of "depth" is by no means a static one, nor limited in principle to the growth of capital good sectors, but varies with the development of the world economy. High technology electronics, for example, could now be included. Moreover, the capacity for industrial upgrading should be estimated through evaluation of data on educational levels, availability of trained scientific and technical personnel, research and development expenditures, and so forth. Indicators to show the quality of life (e.g., health, education, equity) should also be considered.

4. For example, South Korea boosted the share of its manufactured exports to developing countries from 17 percent to 28 percent between 1962 and 1981. World Bank, *World Development Report* (Washington, 1984), p. 243.

Bibliography

U.N. Yearbook of International Trade Statistics, Vol. 1. New York, 1981.
World Bank. *World Development Report 1984*. Washington, 1985.

4 / Reagan's Policy and the New International Economic Order: Epitaph for an Unsuccessful Movement

JAMES PETRAS

The proposal to establish a "new international economic order" (NIEO) reflected the recognition by Third World countries that the existing economic order, fashioned in the aftermath of independence, was contributing to the continued underdevelopment of the productive forces within the region and to the increasing inequality between developed and underdeveloped countries. The novelty of the proposals for a NIEO was that they transcended bilateral efforts to secure piece-meal changes, as well as collective efforts focusing on a narrow set of trade issues. The NIEO entailed a comprehensive effort by the Third World as a whole to redefine the terms and structures affecting their relations with the industrialized countries in a multiplicity of crucial areas. It is this "wholistic" perspective, as well as a broad appeal that cut across ideological boundaries, that gave special prominence to the call for a NIEO. It was precisely these same factors, however, that created the greatest opposition. The comprehensive, "systemic" nature of the changes envisioned represented major shifts in relations and economic resources between nations and ultimately classes. The suggested changes in terms of trade, interest rates, royalty and rent payments, and investment policies—all oriented toward increasing the flow of financial resources to the Third World—would adversely affect the flow of income to a multiplicity of strategic classes within the advanced countries.

The counterargument from the Third World revolved around two points: (1) an appeal to the strategic interest of the advanced countries, which would benefit in the long term from the existence of stable and expanding Third World countries linked by trade and investment ties;

and (2) moral appeals for equity based on the universal principle of human justice. The obvious weakness of the Third World position, however, was that its bargaining position and leverage were vulnerable. The capacity of Third World countries to organize and exercise effective economic pressure has been largely confined to the oil-producing countries (and even there, that power is subject to world market conditions). The thrust of the critique from the United States was that (1) "the market" was best left alone—efforts by states to tamper with its operations would undermine its rational operation; and (2) Third World countries should look "inward" toward restructuring their internal order, particularly with an eye to becoming more integrated into the world market (increasing exports, opening the door for foreign capital, and so forth) as a way of increasing growth and overcoming underdevelopment. Thus, while both sides agreed that the differences between regions were profound and that changes were necessary, there was fundamental disagreement regarding what changes should be made and how they should be brought about. Over time, the global context within which the debate over NIEO took place changed substantially—to the disadvantage of the Third World. It is to this changing context and its implications for the Third World that we now turn for discussion.

Origins of NIEO

The proposals for NIEO revolved around the general proposition that existing relations between the "North" and the "South" were "unfavorable," "exploitative," and generally counterproductive to the rapid and sustained development of the South. At least four crucial sets of relationships were targeted for change: (1) transfer of technology, (2) external financing, (3) operations of the multinational corporations (MNCs), and (4) trading relations.

Over the past decade, Third World countries have been paying a growing quantity of foreign exchange to rent technology, and to pay for brand names or for managerial services. In fact, royalties and payments represent an increasing proportion of the earnings remitted from Third World countries. Apart from the price of technology and the depletion of foreign exchange stands the issue of "appropriate technology"—the "fit" between the technology transferred and the market, labor, and skill levels of a country. Proposals within the perspective of the NIEO called for greater control by the Third World over the costs and conditions surrounding the transfer of technology.

The second point at issue was the terms of external financing. Essentially, a great number of Third World countries were experiencing balance-of-payments deficits and a lack of development funding, and were borrowing at high cost from commercial banks. The NIEO proposals entailed large-scale, long-term funding of Third World countries through outright grants or low-interest loans, as well as proposals for long grace periods prior to initial payments and debt forgiveness in certain instances. The arguments in favor of these proposals were couched in terms of the historical disadvantages engendered by Western hegemony, which created the conditions of indebtedness.

NIEO proposed changes in a third area—namely, the relationship between the Third World and the MNCs. Here, as elsewhere, there were variations among the proponents of the NIEO as to the degree to which MNC participation is compatible with Third World growth. Some political leaders prescribed a very limited role or a role qualified by such restrictive conditions that it is hard to envision any MNC participation. Others prescribed a code of conduct under which MNCs would agree to invest, innovate, and trade within the national development priorities of the host country.

Trade relations were an area of continuing contention between developed and underdeveloped countries long before the debate over the NIEO. Among the proposed changes was the issue of "fair prices" for raw materials exports (some advocated that Third World exports be indexed to the price of manufactured goods), and the lifting of barriers for exporting industrial products from Third World countries. The improvement of terms of trade and sharing of industrial markets were viewed as essential elements in financing the industrial development of Third World countries.

The historical context is crucial to understanding the emergence of the NIEO movement. Three basic propositions that require further elaboration emerge: (1) The NIEO movement appears in a historical period following a prolonged period of world economic expansion, in which most countries, North and South, experienced substantial growth. Relative differences in aggregate size of GNP between North and South may have increased, while the relative growth rates of many Third World countries may have been higher. The "militancy" of the NIEO movement thus coincides with the growth of the Third World economies—in a period when their bargaining power vis-à-vis the advanced industrial countries was stronger, and during a time when the North was perhaps more amenable to negotiations (if not concessions).

(2) The relative decline of the NIEO since the mid-1970s coincides with the deepening of economic crisis. The worsening of conditions in both the North and South apparently weakened the "reformist" impulse concerning the world economy. The disproportionately negative impact of the crisis on the Third World hurt its bargaining position and apparently lessened the internal cohesion of the region, as witnessed by the tendency of debter countries to "go it alone" in renegotiating their debts.

(3) The upsurge of support for the NIEO coincides with the period when U.S. hegemony was weakest (the early to mid-1970s). In the same period the forces for détente grew, as did noninterventionism and Third World solidarity ("the 77," OPEC, and so forth). The politice-military defeat of the United States in Indochina and the economic decline of the dollar signaled the ebbing of U.S. hegemony. The increased bargaining power of OPEC and the emergence of other commodity-producing organizations indicated the potential organizational power of Third World countries. The increasing intracapitalist rivalries between Europe, the United States, and Japan provided some leverage for Third World bargaining, as new reformist impulses surfaced in European social-democratic circles (as evidenced in the Brandt Report).

On the other side, the emergence of détente and the Helsinki Accord signaled an apparent willingness by the superpowers to negotiate their differences—to reduce the world armaments race and the imposition of military solutions on the Third World. As a consequence, social revolutions took place in Ethiopia, Angola, Iran, and Nicaragua that reinforced the radical tendencies of the movement toward a NIEO. Finally, the Third World was able to institutionalize its position through its influence in UNCTAD, UNIDO, and ECLA, thereby creating a permanent research staff with the intellectual weaponry to carry on the struggle for the NIEO and for the redistribution of wealth on a global scale.

In summary, the international conjuncture was initially favorable to the proponents of the NIEO. Their moral appeals were backed by favorable economic conditions, increased economic and political leverage, and a favorable correlation of forces worldwide.

The New Conjuncture: Economic Crisis, Reassertion of U.S. Hegemony, and the Relative Decline of NIEO

The onset of the world economic crisis of the 1970s—stagflation—had disastrous consequences for the Third World in all economic, financial, and political dimensions. The combination of the economic crisis (and the disproportionate weight that it exerted against Third World development), together with the onset of the new Cold War, ushered in a period in which the political momentum toward a NIEO was at least stalled, if not reversed.

As economic conditions worsened, the North began to turn inwards, retrenching its expansive overseas programs and increasingly drawing resources from abroad. Responding to internal protests over rising unemployment and declining industries, policy-makers began to be influenced by strong protectionist sentiments at the expense of Third World industrial exporters. By the 1980s the NIEO debate was turned on its head: the issue was no longer whether to reform the old economic order, but rather how to prevent further economic deterioration. The political and economic climate had substantially shifted away from innovative proposals and international bankers took over. Spiraling debts, dwindling markets, and the drying up of investment funds put the crunch on Third World leaders, compelling them to shift their focus to immediate financial exigencies rather than global structural changes. The period witnessed greater outflows of capital as profit remittances exceeded new investments; rising protectionism and declining markets; higher interest payments and fewer loans; rising costs for technology and a widening of the technological gap.

Those who claimed to have found a new international division of labor (NIDL), in which Third-World industrialization would lead to greater industrial exports to the North, had greatly exaggerated the scope and depth of change in the world economy. NIDL theorists' projections were based on the expansive period of the 1960s, without serious thought about the countereffects that would result from global crisis and the reaction from within the metropolitan countries. The overly optimistic assessments—amounting almost to a sense of historical necessity—regarding the development of a NIDL was related to the continuing push for a NIEO: to the degree that the Third World moved to a different plane of development (industrializing, diversifying exports, and so forth), existing global economic relations were felt to be constrictive. With the onset of the crisis and the decline of industrialization, pressures for a NIEO also receded, as Third World regimes began to shuttle back and forth between New York, London, and Zurich, seeking financial life-savers to keep their economies afloat.

The real emerging "new international division of labor" concerns the relations of creditors and debtors, with an increasing proportion of Third-World economic activity geared to financing interest and principal payments to Northern private banks. The international division of labor today is dominated by the growing control exercised by multinational banks. In alliance with the International Monetary Fund, the multinational banks have defined a new international economic order in which they dictate Third World development agendas. The banks' insistence on "conditionality for refinancing" is the main mechanism used to compel regimes seeking loans to dismantle public enterprises, open national markets, lower labor costs, and increase the outflow of interest and principal payments. Taking advantage of the crisis, the North has exploited the financial vulnerability of the South to establish more rigid and onerous conditions of exchange.

These economic constraints projected by Northern private interests are inseparable from the political constraints emerging from global policies of right wing Western regimes—principally the Reagan administration.

Reagan Policy: Epitaph for the NIEO

The previous discussion has made clear that deep-structural forces within the world capitalist system were already operating, prior to the Reagan administration, to undermine the thrust toward developing a NIEO. Nevertheless, the ascent of the Reagan administration substantially boosted precisely those forces operating against the working out of more equitable relations between the Third World and the North. In a sense the Reagan administration was both consequence and cause of the rise to influence of forces opposing the NIEO. The rising power of the banks, the need of multinational capital to reduce state and labor costs, the demand by big business to check the revolutionary forces unleashed in the 1970s—all converged on the Reagan presidency. Reagan's policies, with all their rhetorical excesses, reflected the desire of Northern capital to come to grips with what was increasingly perceived to be the unruly South. Rejecting the compromising style of President Carter—combining human rights speeches with arms increases—as too uncertain and indecisive, U.S. and Western European capital opted for the confrontational style of Ronald Reagan and his attempt to recreate the relations between North and South, East and West that existed in the 1950s.

Part of the price paid by both European and U.S. capital for the Reaganite effort to re-establish U.S. world hegemony is Washington's critical lack of understanding of the limits of U.S. power in the changed conditions of the 1980s, a point that will be taken up later.

The Reagan policy toward the Third World tries to re-focus debate away from basic socioeconomic structural disparities between North and South, toward military-political conflicts between West and East. This world-historic shift in the nature of the debate is integral to understanding the subsequent "burial" of proposals for a NIEO. Reagan's definition of the world order revolves around two interrelated axes: (1) the growing militarism of U.S. and Western European foreign policy; and (2) the growing emphasis on selectively imposing "free market" doctrines on competing countries (while restricting access to one's own country).

At first glance, the Reagan policy toward the world economy appears to be simple and straightforward in its emphasis on freeing markets and opposing nationalism. In practice, the Reagan administration has violated many of the basic principles of "market capitalism"—running huge deficits, massively increasing the military state machinery, intervening in the political and economic life of other states via the machinery of the International Monetary Fund, and establishing state quotas and tariff barriers (to limit the flow of Brazilian steel, Japanese autos, Chinese textiles, and so on). "Free-market" rhetoric and the selective but massive state intervention practiced by the Reagan administration are both tied to the aim of re-establishing U.S. world hegemony. In that context, Reagan is not disturbed by obvious contradictions and inconsistencies. His global policy is a carefully calibrated opportunism designed to maximize the strong points in the U.S. political economy—namely, military technology and highly developed financial institutions.

The notion of opportunism is central to comprehending Reagan policy because at every level, general principles of policy are proclaimed which, in practice, are severely qualified. As mentioned above, while free trade is proclaimed as the guiding principle for the Third World, statism is a major factor in U.S. economic policy. More significantly, while Washington has launched a vast program of armaments and orchestrated a new Cold War directed at the Soviet bloc, it has promoted its own sets of economic agreements with the USSR, particularly in farm-surplus trade.

This combination of dogma and opportunism is linked to the notion of polarizing the world into Western-Eastern divisions, within which the Reagan administration will be able to selectively establish the conditions for exchange between regions and within regions. The political dogmas of the new Cold War thus fit nicely with the economic opportunism of an administration intent on securing a paramount role for the United States in the world economy.

The NIEO perspective has been squeezed between the twin pressures of the economic crises and its consequences, and the Cold War and free-market policies promoted by Reagan and his supporters in Western Europe. Reagan's military definitions of regional conflicts in the Third World have enhanced the position of all those social classes and political elites within the Third World who are opposed to the NIEO—the right-wing military dictators, commercial interests, and political collaborators who depend on ties with Western banks. In addition, the promotion of formal or informal alliances with Israel and South Africa, and the latter's willingness to "conquor territory" has forced back African and Middle Eastern countries toward issues of national preservation, as opposed to reordering global relations.

All the manifestations of the new Cold War—from the installation of Cruise missles in Europe to the invasion of Grenada—are efforts to alter the balance of power between the West and the East and the North and the South—forcing the Third World to choose between East and West, rather than uniting within the South. This Cold War strategy has been accompanied by attempts to emphasize "bilateral relations" between dominant Northern countries and Third World countries—with a host of international banks and agencies (especially the International Monetary Fund and the World Bank) joining their Northern partners in negotiating agreements.

Reagan's policy toward the Third World deepened the tendencies operating against the NIEO and hastened its demise. Reagan's policy wrote the epitaph for a movement that already was in the process of being undermined.

Contradictions

While the Reagan policy may have contributed to the demise of the NIEO, Reagan's own effort to re-establish world hegemony is shot through with contradictions, which ultimately can contribute to its failure. There are several sets and subsets of contradictions, both internal and external, that now need to be noted.

INTERNAL CONTRADICTIONS

Two important contradictions are maturing within the U.S. political economy. The effort by the Reagan administration to reconstruct the imperial state apparatus through increased military spending and to promote capital accumulation through tax cuts is creating a growing budget deficit. Increases in government borrowing to overcome the deficit have resulted in higher interest rates, which in turn slow down investment and deepen the tendencies toward stagnation with inflation. The increased strength of the dollar and high interest rates, in turn, make U.S. exports less competitive, increase the trade deficit, channel funds into money markets, and weaken the process of global accumulation. Moreover, the incentives to capital have no noticeable effect in stimulating industrial growth, as the costs/benefits are too high relative to alternative areas of activity. The conditions pursued to promote capital growth become the obstacles to growth: a gap emerges between Wall Street and Reagan as the "ideal" world of the ideologues' marketplace fails to square with the practices of bankers and investors. We have the anomaly of free enterprise ideologues in search of a social base.

The second basic contradiction emerging from the Reagan strategy involves massive cuts in social programs, conditions necessary to stimulate private growth, and the frontal attacks on labor in order to make U.S. capital competitive on a world scale. These measures conflict with the social basis of the political consensus that has underpinned U.S. global expansion since World War II. Empire is now *not* a source of compensation for both labor and capital, but rather a cost to be borne by labor for capital. The difficulties that this presents to a labor movement whose leadership is deeply wedded to empire, militarism, and the Cold War are immense. The labor bureaucracy's attempt to save its organizational gains without giving up its international commitments prevents them from breaking new political ground. The labor bureaucracy's policy is aimed at convincing the Democrats to resist social cuts and to embrace the Cold War—a program as bankrupt as Reagan's. Given the international nature of U.S. capitalism, the efforts by the trade union bureaucracy to promote internal development to provide employment will find no echo among political influentials: the conditions for external development necessarily require military programs and the consequent cut in wages, both to finance expansion and to protect it. Beyond protesting the Reaganite changes that directly affect it, the labor bureaucracy lacks any global programmatic alternative of its own. The erosion of popular support and the loss of legitimacy that the Reagan administration can experience, however, could seriously weaken its efforts to modernize capital for global expansion.

EXTERNAL CONTRADICTIONS: EUROPE, JAPAN, AND THE SOVIET BLOC

The external contradictions that the Reagan administration generates have ramifications throughout the world economy. First, to a far greater degree than that of the United States, European and Japanese growth is linked to a policy of détente. The new confrontation strategy of the Reagan administration jeopardizes Western European trade links with the Soviet bloc without providing any meaningful alternatives. European opportunities for trade in the Middle East are endangered by the adventurous militarist course adopted by Israel and the United States. Furthermore, the competition between Europe and the United States over Third World markets cuts across Reagan's efforts to polarize the world in the mold of a rigid East-West confrontation.

At the same time, the pressure by Washington to increase armaments spending among its European and Japanese allies threatens to disintegrate the social consensus in Europe. Social cuts and increased arms spending are likely to provoke sharp class cleavages and resistance—far more profoundly than in the United States. Simultaneously, the economic policies of the United States—"monetarist" supply-side economics—threaten to deepen the recession: Europeans, fearful of wholesale flights of capital to the United States, have maintained high interest rates, thus blocking any efforts at industrial recovery. The conditions for U.S. recovery, then, are counterpoised to the conditions for European development. Furthermore, the labor-based social democratic parties and governments are under intense pressure to resist supporting U.S.-backed right wing dictatorships in the Third World.

Because of the growth of Soviet bloc economic and military power, the arena of U.S.-Soviet confrontation has shifted to the Third World. Washington recognizes that any *frontal* attack on the Soviet Union or established Soviet bloc countries carries a high risk of massive retaliation and mutual destruction. It is only in the Third World, where revolutionary regimes are not yet consolidated and national liberation movements still struggle, that Washington is free to exercise its military options. (This was the case in Grenada, where Reagan intervened at virtually no military cost.) Thus, while the Reagan administration's policy envisions a global confrontation, the balance of power forces this confrontation to take place in reduced spheres of the world. While Soviet military strength remains an unalterable factor in the current global power alignment, it also serves as a source of possible support for liberation movements, particularly in Africa and the Middle East. The notion that Washington can simply overwhelm its designated revolutionary adversaries and sustain its dictatorial allies by sheer material might is doomed by the fact that alternative sources of arms exist to buttress the political fortunes of the opposition. While Soviet arms shipments, either in quality or quantity, cannot match those of the United States, they are sufficient when combined with mass popular support to seriously challenge minority regimes that dominate in the Middle East and South Africa. Recognition of this military equilibrium (objective reality) probably serves to temper the more extreme versions of global confrontation within the Reagan administration. Even as they eschew negotiation and plot growth curves in arms spending, the Reaganites cannot fail to realize the need to negotiate or at least to establish boundaries within which confrontation will take place. Open-ended conflict, without a sense of place or strategic interests, as Washington must surely recognize (and as Europeans fear), would rapidly end up in nuclear confrontation. The new Cold War, then, will continue to involve "tough talk" and extensive U.S. intervention in the Third World. It will also include negotiations and demonstrate the incapacity of the United States to reverse relations of global power or to establish domination through exclusively military solutions.

If Soviet military power stands as one constraint on the global aspirations of the Reaganites, Soviet economic growth stands as another factor limiting Washington's efforts to polarize the world between East and West. Links between the Soviet Union and the West have proliferated in recent years. And as the new Cold War heated up and U.S.–Soviet relations deteriorated, the economic links between the USSR and other capitalist countries grew. The scale of economic activity in certain areas (such as energy) and the complementary nature of East–West trade (finished goods for raw materials) cannot be matched by the United States, which is more competitive with Western Europe in both what it buys and what it sells. Washington cannot provide a satisfactory substitute for dealing with the East: on the contrary, the nature of Reagan economics is to depress and constrict overall Western growth further in the short run, and to increase U.S. competitive advantages in the medium and long run. The stepped-up arms race is incompatible with West European efforts to modernize industrial plants to maintain a competitive edge and a trading relationship with the newly industrializing countries in the Third World and in Eastern Europe. The growth of Soviet markets and opportunities for trade thus serve to promote the ascendancy of economic forces in Western Europe over and against the military, especially in times of capitalist stagnation.

The economic ties between Third World countries and the Soviet Union is another factor that inhibits many countries from joining anticommunist crusades. Moreover, Washington's effort to "confront" revolutionary regimes in the Third World by isolating them economically and encouraging counterrevolutionary activity can be effectively neutralized when these same countries turn more actively toward the Soviet bloc. The confrontation strategy toward Third World revolutionary regimes is less likely to destabilize them than it is to increase their reliance on the Soviet bloc as an alternative market, source of finance and raw materials, and base of military support.

EXTERNAL CONTRADICTIONS: THE THIRD WORLD

Significant structural changes have taken place in the Third World since World War II that constrict Washington's capacity to impose its traditional simplistic formulas. The main trends in the Third World have been in the direction of diversification of the economy—increasing industrialization, diversifying trading partners, securing new sources of finance, developing local markets, joining commodity cartels, and developing regional ties. This pattern of diversification involves developing a whole series of vital relationships and linkages that cut across the East–West polarity that Washington proposes. Moreover, new classes and trading partners link together state structures that resist fitting into the new U.S. global pattern. Brazil's trade ties with Angola, the Soviet Union, and the Arab countries are a case in point. Moreover, some Third World countries will compete with the United States in pursuit of export markets, further constraining an "overidentification" with Washington's pronouncements. Argentine exports of grain to the USSR is a ready example. In addition, while many Third World countries depend on the United States, the latter also depends on the key oil-producing countries in the periphery. Political, ideological, and economic ties with some countries (Israel and South Africa) generate conflict with other countries on which the United States is dependent (Nigeria and Saudi Arabia). The image of a "recalcitrant world" that does not recognize the same dangers as the Reagan administration is a product of the voluntarist fantasies of Cold War ideologues. The deep structural changes and the historical trends of the past decades can no longer be fit into a bipolar straitjacket—and no amount of Cold War rhetoric can undo or reverse them.

In summary, the Reagan administration's attempt to impose a bipolar scheme upon a world with increasingly complex links and relations reflects the absence of a realistic understanding of the global changes within the Third World, Europe, and the Soviet Union. Romantic reactionary nostalgia for the 1950s is a poor basis to construct a foreign policy in the 1980s. At each critical point, the Reaganites attempt to "force" countries and regions with divergent economic, strategic, and political interests to conform to Washington's policy through the trumpeting of new military dangers: failing to grasp the deep structural changes that have narrowed the scope for bipolar competition, the Reaganites improvise ad hoc explanations. "Creeping pacifism" in Europe becomes a means of evading the profound and mutually beneficial economic links with the East. "Third Worldism" becomes a means of reducing the development of regional ties and the growth of commodity-producing associations to political rhetoric. These facile simplifications may be fashionable and pass for political analysis in New York or London, but they carry little weight almost everywhere else.

Part II

U.S.–Latin American Relations

5 / *"Resurgent Democracy" in Latin America: Rhetoric and Reality*

EDWARD S. HERMAN and JAMES PETRAS

From 1984 onward, Reagan administration officials and the U.S. press have spoken with frequency and enthusiasm about the "resurgence of democracy" in Latin America. According to Secretary of State George Shultz, we have been witnessing "more people voting in more elections in more countries than ever before in the history of this hemisphere." Alan Riding, writing in the *New York Times* of November 11, 1984, expressed the new vision under the byline: "A Latin Spring: Democracy in Flower."

This spate of publicity has had several notable features. One is its excellent fit to the public relations requirements of the Reagan administration, which has urgently sought means of counteracting the widespread negative responses to its Central American policies. The administration itself has sponsored elections in delicate situations (in El Salvador, Grenada, and Guatemala) as legitimizing projects, and it has asserted its devotion to democracy as an important reason for its anti-Sandinista policies.

The administration suffered setbacks in the Nicaraguan election, the Sandinista acceptance of the Contadora proposals (which required an administration rebuff to the Contadora countries and process), and the World Court's decision on the mining of Nicaraguan harbors (which necessitated a costly rejection of World Court legitimacy). It was therefore very useful to have the press join with it in celebrating a flowering of democracy in our backyard during the Reagan term, even suggesting (in the words of Alan Riding) that "Given the United States' enormous weight in the area, the administration's public preference for democracy proved influential." By inference, given the general resurgence of democracy under the Reagan leadership, any small failings—such as forcibly overthrowing the governments of one or two small backyard defectors from "democracy"—can surely be overlooked.

A second relevant characteristic of the new publicity is its superficiality and neglect of context. Exaggeration of the scope and substance of the changes has been combined with a playing down of the important exceptions and misrepresentation of the administration's role in the transformations. The news reports in question are all breezily optimistic: the democratic "contagion" is spreading, and we may expect that trend to continue into the indefinite future. The word "democracy" is used loosely and is assumed to apply in any instance where the formal machinery of elections is put in place and civilians are allowed to occupy high office. There are no detailed analyses of the economic and political conditions that underlie the retreat of the military, nor of the extent to which the military establishments may be maintaining effective power by retaining their authority in "security" matters and their control of key instrumentalities of the state. Finally, no distinction is made between nearby Central America, where political conditions have been steadily deteriorating under active U.S. intervention, and South America, where some kind of resurgence may really be occurring.

What follows is a discussion and analysis of the roots, scope, and future of resurgent democracy in Latin America.

The Roots of Resurgent Democracy: Reaganism or Economic Failure?

In the beginning, the Reagan administration openly demonstrated its support for friendly ("nontotalitarian") authoritarian military dictatorships. Now it claims to have fathered the upsurge of democratic regimes. What has happened in the interim? From whence come these born-again democrats? The fact is that the resurgence of democracy in South America took the Reaganites quite by surprise and has in fact turned out of office some of their closest and most reliable allies.[1] They are making the best of a bad situation.

It should be noted that the return to civilian rule is taking place in states which had earlier abandoned democratic institutions with U.S. assistance and approval. The overthrow of the Goulart government of Brazil was greeted enthusiastically in Washington, as was the military coup in Chile. The satisfaction of the U.S. establishment with the military regime in Argentina is best captured in David Rockefeller's pronouncement that that country finally had a government that "understands the private enterprise system." This approval of the "resurgent authoritarianism" of the 1960s and 1970s is also attested to by the enormous flow of credit, aid, and investment that the United States lavished on military regimes during their tenure of power. These regimes all put into place an economic model well geared to serve the interests of a small strata of local business and foreign capital. The army had the responsibility of keeping the masses disorganized by terror, thus assuring low wages and a no-strike environment. The military regimes provided subsidies to business, sold off public assets to the private sector at favorable prices, and promised foreign lenders that interest payments would be met. The suspension of parliamentary government assured the banking and multinational corporate community that unruly legislatures would not interfere with the freedom of business.

This system of "supply-side economics with machine guns" did not work in Latin America even on its own terms. Even before the 1980s collapse, Argentinian, Chilean, and Uruguayan rates of savings and investment never reached their pre-coup averages. Foreign capital failed to rush in to invest in industry, confining itself instead chiefly to finance, trade, and agribusiness. All three of these countries suffered from sharply increased concentration of ownership and control, denationalization, and economic stagnation, among other problems. Only in Brazil did savings and investment rates slowly overtake those of the years before the military takeover. For the entire period of military rule in Brazil up to the 1980s collapse, however, the rates of growth of the gross domestic product (GDP) were not superior to those of the preceding years of nonmilitary rule. The rapid growth during the "miracle years" of 1968–1974 was fueled by massive foreign credits, and the miracle terminated with a whimper, ending in default and increased dependence, and with none of the country's basic problems yet addressed.

The oil price increases of the 1970s were devastating blows to the fragile, dependent economies of Latin America; and the recession and interest rate increases of the early 1980s put the finishing touches on a system of growth that, in the end, involved borrowing to pay interest on previous borrowings. Real GDP in Latin America increased from $257 billion to $336 billion between 1975 and 1984, or by 31 percent.[2] In the same period the gross external debt increased from $89.4 billion to $360.2 billion, or by 302 percent; while net payments of interest and profits rose from $5.6 billion in 1975 to $37.3 billion in 1984—increasing by 566 percent. Assuming a 9 percent rate, the interest cost on a $360 billion debt would be $32.4 billion, a sizable bite out of Latin American GDP and the equivalent of some 40 percent of merchandise export earnings.

The extent of the collapse and the seriousness of the crisis are still not fully appreciated. The GDP of Latin America (exclusive of Cuba), which had increased by 4.8 percent a year in 1975–1978, and 6.1 percent in 1979–1980, fell to zero percent on average for 1981–1984. Given the continuing rapid population growth, Latin American GDP per capita *fell* an average of 2.2 percent per year in the latter period. Unemployment, already high, reached new and higher levels in the early 1980s. Despite the massive unemployment, the price level shot up from a weighted average of about 50 percent a year for 1976–1981 to 84.5 percent in 1982, 130.8 percent in 1983, and *175.4* percent in 1984.

The crisis came to a head when major Latin American debtors were unable to pay interest and principal on their loans. Once the bubble broke, foreign capital flows dropped from $37.6 billion in 1981 to only $4.4 billion in 1983. As interest and profit repatriation amounted to $27.7 billion in 1983, there was a net capital *outflow* from Latin America totalling $23.3 billion.

The inability of the Latin economies to meet their foreign debt obligations, together with the drying up of credit, threatened a wholesale collapse of the Latin American economies and the system of world credit. There ensued a massive patching-up operation under United States and IMF auspices, in which government credits were extended to the Latin debtors and the private banks were dragooned into putting up more money, while rates and terms were adjusted (mainly, stretched out) to give the debtor countries more breathing space. In their turn, however, the debtors were compelled to give policy priority to increasing their foreign exchange receipts and doing that which the creditors deemed essential for the debtors to meet their external obligations. Twelve Latin American countries signed conditionality agreements with the IMF in 1982 and 1983. These agreements required that the debtors sharply cut their social expenditures, deficits, and inflation rates, and make diligent efforts to keep wage rates and imports down and to facilitate exports.

The IMF and creditor formulas for alleviating the crisis, in short, involved placing the burden of adjustment for economic failure on the same victims who had borne the brunt of costs of the prior system of "growth." It is extremely unlikely that this new medicine will work even on its own economic terms, for reasons which we will address later. But another question, too, is whether the Latin American populations will be willing to accept the hegemony of the international banking community, devote their surpluses to paying interest on debts accumulated in the National Security State years,[3] and quietly accept IMF deflationary medicine in that service.

By 1982 the U.S.-backed military regimes that had featured export-oriented growth with open economies were effectively bankrupt. In the course of their collapse, the socioeconomic position of many important groups, including industrialists, farmers, and salaried professionals, as well as wage workers and peasants, had been undermined; and major social movements had reemerged demanding democracy and new economic policies. Huge demonstrations, general strikes, overwhelming support for civilian rule in public opinion polls all indicated that time was running out on the military establishments, which were politically isolated and divided.

It is in this context of failure of the United States and military-backed economic model that we must explain the return to civilian government. The latter, as has been shown, was by no means a preferred option that had been sought in advance by Washington and its military allies; on the contrary, it represented a strategic retreat for both. The conception of the resurgence as a triumph of Reaganism could hardly be farther from the truth. Our focus here will be on the terms of the transition and the limits imposed on civilians by the retreating generals and their U.S. allies.

Resurgent Democracy: Amalgamation of Terrorists and Democrats

In his accolades to resurgent democracy in Latin America, George Schultz and his speech writers have treated as identical very distinct sets of political experiences with totally different meanings. For Shultz, as long as elections take place in a client state, they are equated with democracy irrespective of substantive conditions that might make electoral exercises mere facades. Thus he lumps together the fairly "open" elections in Argentina, Uruguay, Brazil, Bolivia, Peru, and Ecuador with those in both the terror-ridden societies of El Salvador and Guatemala and in U.S.-occupied Honduras and Grenada.

Elections are meaningful only when they are associated with basic freedoms: when trade unions, peasant and cooperative associations, professional organizations, local opinion leaders, and ordinary citizens can meet, talk freely, put forward candidates, and make choices without constraint or fear. Such freedoms exist in the South American countries to greater or lesser degrees—they do not exist in El Salvador and Guatemala. In these "death-squad democracies," electoral counts are accompanied by civilian body counts. El Salvador lacks the most elementary freedom: the right to dissent without being assassinated. Under the two Duarte regimes and the in-between openly military governments, 50,000 Salvadoran civilians were murdered, and a large fraction of dissident trade union, university, professional, and other groups were physically eliminated. The situation in Guatemala is little different: elections are held there for a terrorized, atomized population, herded into strategic hamlets and killed by the army and death squads at rates that have averaged several thousand per year over the past decade. In El Salvador and Guatemala, despite the existence of mass movements of the left, no left candidates can qualify to run in elections (a point which does not dampen with U.S. media praise for the quality of these elections).

The terror-cum-elections format in Central America is essentially a public relations exercise for U.S. public and congressional consumption: to provide a rationale for pumping U.S. aid into these states. Reagan administration efforts to equate Central American elections with those in South America is a means of exploiting positive liberal responses to the latter, using them to provide a further electoral cover for an essentially military policy in Central America.

Resurgence in South America: The Problem of Military Power

It should be obvious that elections may not involve any shift in power if the menu of candidates is limited to an official list approved by a behind-the-scenes power elite. It is also clear that power transfers may be limited or nonexistent if "deals" are made with the restricted list of eligible civilians and/or if an institutional structure of privilege and repression is maintained intact by prior agreement with the civilians who take office.

It is noteworthy that most of the U.S. media do not raise such issues in reference to the resurgent democracies, but instead take the emergence of civilian rule at face value. It is interesting, further, to observe that this optimism and superficial assessment are operative in contemplating, say Uruguay, but not Nicaragua. In the former case, during the recent elections returning Uruguay to civilian rule, the man generally acknowledged to be the most popular political figure in the country, Wilson Ferreira Aldunate, was not allowed to run for office and was kept in jail through the election period. A second major political contender and popular candidate, General Liber Seregni, was also kept off the ballot by army fiat. The election was held under conditions negotiated with the army, whose institutional status and power remained intact and were to be adjusted, if at all, by future negotiations between the elected government and the semiautonomous institution that monopolizes the state instruments of coercion. But Uruguay is an "approved" state, and the election winner, Julio Maria Sanguinetti, was even given the blessing of the U.S. ambassador. Thus, despite the disqualification of major candidates, Urugary is represented as a truly resurgent democracy. In the words of the newspaper of record, "Still, Uruguay is resuming its democratic vocation" (New York Times, editorial, December 1, 1984).

In the case of Nicaragua, by contrast, the fact that potentially important candidates were much freer to run than in Uruguay and that the electoral environment was equally free could not offset the Nicaraguan regime's low "credibility." Jose Arturo Cruz's *voluntary* refusal to run (which was almost surely preplanned on consultation with the U.S. government to help discredit the election), together with the Sandinista domination of the army, were considered too damaging. Again quoting the newspaper of record, "Only the naive believe that Sunday's election in Nicaragua was democratic or legitimizing proof of the Sandinista's popularity" (*New York Times*, editorial, November 7, 1984).

The stress on the Sandinista link to the army as discrediting Nicaraguan democracy and the down-playing of the army's role in states like Uruguay ignore important aspects of the region's historical background. In Nicaragua the army was part of a broad-based movement that brought a popular government into power, rather than a repressive instrument of minority rule. The officers of the Nicaraguan Armed Forces emerged from the leadership of the Sandanista guerilla movement, which was largely made up of former students, peasants, salaried and wage employees, and the self-employed. The guerrilla army was closely linked with the mass popular movements of the city and the countryside. The Nicaraguan Armed Forces today include a popular militia made up predominantly of workers and peasants, trade unionists and the self-employed, and a standing army consisting of volunteers and conscripts. The fundamental political feature of the Nicaraguan Armed Forces that distinguishes them from most other Latin military organizations is their structural linkages to the mass popular organizations and their role as defenders of egalitarian redistributive policies and national sovereignty against U.S.–directed counter-revolutionary forces. In Uruguay and virtually all of the other countries undergoing resurgence, by contrast, the army has been an elite instrument whose prime function was to keep the masses under control. Upon taking power in Argentina, Brazil, Chile, Uruguay, and elsewhere, the armies sought to destroy popular organizations and to maintain tight controls over ordinary citizens. As was pointed out in church documents produced during the 1960s and 1970s (for example, "The Cry of the People," put out by bishops of the Catholic Church in Brazil in 1973), army terror was an integral element of the workings of the "development model" put in place throughout Latin America in those years. The military and death squads killed and kidnapped (disappeared) 90,000 people during this period. Almost all of the "disappeared" are presumed dead.

The armies seizing power in the name of national security used that power to advance their own interests, in the process depressing the condition of ordinary citizens. In Argentina, for example, military spending rose by 200 percent between 1972 and 1980, while public spending on education and health *fell* 50 percent and 30 percent respectively. By 1983 military spending in Argentina had risen to 8 percent of

GDP, as compared with 2.2 to 2.5 percent under prior administrations.[4] These enlargements of military outlays have been mainly income transfers, with no proportionate spinoff in military capability. In a recent analysis of Chilean military expenditures, which, like Argentina's, swallow in the vicinity of 7 to 10 percent of GDP, it's noted that a large fraction of that goes to wages, pensions, and other forms of remuneration rather than to the purchase and maintenance of weapons. Chile spends 60 to 80 percent of its military budget on remuneration, as contrasted with 20 percent for the British. Basic Chilean military pensions are five times as high as those of ordinary citizens.[5]

The armies of the resurgent democracies are not only accustomed to power and privilege; their officer corps, with minor exceptions, are ideologically hostile to democratic rule. Thus it is extremely important to note that the military is exiting from office with its personnel and institutional privileges largely intact. Ostensibly divested of authority, this repressive and powerful institution retreats and bargains for retention of its place and power. While the deals struck are not on the public record, and in some cases are even now subject to further negotiation, there is evidence that assurances have generally been given on the protection of budgets, freedom from "vendettas" based on prior human rights violations, and continuing authority (at least partial) on security matters.

The Argentinian experience represents at the moment the most enterprising and progressive effort to reduce military power in a resurgent state. It is also a favorable case, as the army retreated from direct rule by virtue of an overwhelming and massive refusal to heed its discredited representatives. Even in this instance, however, the army has merely retreated, and the success of the reform effort remains in doubt. The army retains considerable autonomy, is able to continue sporadic violent attacks on its perceived enemies,[6] and has proved to be largely beyond prosecution for its horrendous crimes. Alfonsin's procrastination and vacillation in bringing the military officials responsible for torture and disappearances to an accounting sorely tried the patience of an important part of his democratic constituency. Over 50,000 Argentines marched in Buenos Aires in mid-March of 1985 demanding that the military officials be brought to trial. Jurisdiction in most torture-disappearance cases was given to military courts, with predictable results. In mid-April, the top nine military government leaders were finally brought to civilian trials, after the military courts acquitted them. In December of 1985 when the trial was concluded, several of the top military officials were convicted. Through this symbolic gesture, Alfonsin sought to pacify the human rights groups and retain his working relations with the military establishment. The massive protest in Buenos Aires in response to Alfonsin's policy of reconciliation is in sharp contrast to the positive response it received in Washington and in the U.S. media.

The Alfonsin government has made a number of efforts to decentralize the military, reduce its financial independence, weed out hardliners in the top echelons of the military, and cut its funding. It has been a bitter struggle, with some significant successes—over two-thirds of the highest ranking army officers have resigned or retired since Alfonsin came to power. Alfonsin talked initially of a 20 percent budget cut, but shortly thereafter Defense Minister Barras spoke of merely "reallocating" military resources, and Undersecretary Cuchiara finally explained that "no spectacular savings must be expected. There will be some military cuts, but no one must think we are about to leave the nation defenceless."[7] More recently, Alfonsin has made a further attempt to slice the military budget, but a much discussed study by Paul Rogers of the Bradford University School of Peace Studies suggests that under civilian rule the country has continued with an arms build-up, not only completing the replacement of lost equipment and supplies from the Falkland Islands War, but engaging in significant further modernization and growth.[8] With more than 95 percent of the top military and judiciary in the hands of military appointees, it is difficult to see how Alfonsin can exercise durable control. While efforts are being made by civilian regimes to curtail military privileges and power in several of the resurgent democracies, their armies remain largely intact in personnel and as institutions and power centers. In an important sense, therefore, they hold these democracies hostage to their continued privileges and their demands for adherence to "sound principles." Real democratization will require further erosion of military power and status. It remains to be seen whether the new civilian governments can survive any serious threat to army or elite privilege—or to U.S. policy positions.

Resurgent Democracy: The Economic Constraints

The importance of the perseveration of the military institution is reinforced by the economic and social contradictions confronting the new civilian regimes. On the one hand, the new leaders are under tremendous pressure from the United States and the international financial community, as well as important indigenous interests, to abide by the financial rules of the game and to do that which is required to service the external debt. In negotiating the transition, new rulers made a variety of promises to adhere to these agreements and obligations. The failure to do so would be construed as a radical act (unless forced on the government by circumstances out of its control) and would be immediately followed by reprisals, including a suspension of trade credit and new funding.[9] It would thus precipitate an immediate and severe economic

crisis, which would require a major restructuring of economic relationships, internally and externally. The existing extensive structure of
relationships with the United States and the West and the continued
strength of the military institution raise the costs of repudiation and
going it alone.[10]

On the other hand, the new regimes came into existence on a wave of
popular support, with a mandate to improve the lot of the masses.
Alfonsin, for example, promised to increase the real wages of his
constituents. Such a promise, however, is incompatible with the
measures required to generate adequate export surpluses to service
foreign debt. This obligation calls for reduced public expenditures and
deficits, curtailed subsidies on consumer goods, devaluation, reduced
imports, and the acceptance of substantial unemployment. Cuts in
military expenditures would help, as would the collection of the estimated $4 billion lost annually to tax evasion. But interest payments on
the deadweight external debt will swallow 50 percent or more of export
earnings and 6 to 8 percent of GDP into the indefinite future. The
policies that will allow these transfers will surely be regressive, hitting
the very people who were the losers in the creation of the debt. The
view of many is that the foreign debt was a burden imposed by the
foreign-supported military regime without benefit to the indigenous
majority. Alfonsin, however, has clearly opted for accommodating the
international financial community. The June 1985 program, which includes devaluation, wage-price controls, a new currency unit, and sharp
budget cutbacks as part of an overall IMF package, formalizes this
commitment. It imposes an immediate 30 percent cut in real wages.

The new program will not work, partly because the Argentinian
masses will not accept without a struggle the meeting of debt service
obligations as the overriding national economic policy objective. But the
policy will also not work because it rests on false economic assumptions.
It is based on Chicago School notions that the Latin American economies
can generate adequate export surpluses by appropriate wage, price, and
exchange rate adjustments and free market conditions, including suit-
able inducements to foreign capital. But the bubble of 1960s and 1970s
growth rested on authoritarian conditions, a world boom, and a flood of
overly sanguine financial and real foreign investment. Under post-
bubble conditions, with excessive debt burdens, deflationary policies,
slow growth and political unrest, foreign capital is not interested in
investing in Latin America, it is anxious to get out. So is domestic
capital, which had already made a substantial exodus during the prior
decade or so ($60 to $70 billion in private Latin American capital was
estimated to be in offshore liquid investment in the spring of 1985). Latin
America's difficulties pose threats that make private capital look abroad,

to the United States, or to East Asia, where, as one American executive told the *Wall Street Journal*, the people "have geared themselves to boost private enterprise."[11]

In short, the course being forced upon the resurgent democracies by the IMF, and now imposed by Alfonsin, is a Catch-22 route doomed to failure. The struggle to deflate, generate export surpluses, contain imports, and encourage foreign investment is internally contradictory in the environment of the 1980s, with a predominance of mobile and risk-sensitive capital, sharp international competition among Third World producers, and growing protectionism. Argentina has bought a little time by its new austerity program and a further increment to its borrowing capacity (and to its foreign debt and debt service), but we feel confident that this program will do nothing useful to solve the crisis.

The new civilian rulers, who assume past economic obligations and who choose to follow the dictates of the IMF, will be forced to take responsibility for likely economic failures. The military regimes and their U.S. partners, having built up an impossibly large foreign debt and having allowed the festering of social and economic sores while they "developed" their own bank accounts, now move to the wings to wait.

The civilian governments now imposing the IMF-banker conditions on the already long-suffering populations will not be able to meet any popular needs and demands. On the contrary, they find themselves in the position of enforcers of further cut-backs on basic needs. Can democracy survive in such an environment? With the military machines still intact, won't the inevitable "disorder" lead to a renewal of military rule? These issues are seldom brought to the attention of the American people, particularly by a press which has increasingly echoed the Reagan line of "resurgent democracy" in Latin America.

Brazil

The new civilian government that took office in Brazil in March 1985, led by José Sarney, is an amalgam of former military collaborators, conservative state political bosses, and reformist social democrats. The process of democratization acceptable to the military, the United States, the bankers, and the multinationals necessarily resulted in a substantial conservative presence in the victorious coalition. Of 479 federal deputies, some 300 are reportedly businessmen. While the vast majority of the electorate favors basic structural reforms, the newly elected regime is honeycombed with conservative and rightist politicians whose primary goal is to preserve the distribution of income and land, limit the power of labor, and preserve relations with the IMF and the banks, while retaining leverage to bargain over specific issues.

The demise of the military regime was a product of three factors: the profound and continuing economic crisis, the growth of autonomous mass movements, and the increasing influence of the party-led opposition, particularly the Brazilian Democratic Party Movement (PMDM) and the Liberal Front Party (PFL), which joined together to form the Democratic Alliance. Between 1981 and 1984, Brazil experienced a negative growth rate, a 9 percent decline in per capita income, a 30 percent fall in workers' income, an inflation rate of between 100 and 200 percent a year, a declining capacity to import, and an external debt that had reached $101.8 billion by 1984. As the crisis deepened, capital inflows from abroad fell sharply while overseas profit and interest payments remained at high levels ($35 billion were extracted from Brazil between 1982 and 1984), creating severe balance of payments pressures. These led in turn to IMF remedies—high interest rates, reduced investment, increased exports and sharply contracted imports. Brazil's ratio of interest payments to exports ranged between 55 percent and 37 percent during the same period. The military regime's attempts to squeeze labor further, in compliance with the demands of the IMF and international bankers, led to widespread disaffection and the proliferation and growth of activist social movements: trade unions, as well as groups promoting land occupations, food-store looting, and so on. The opposition parties benefitted from this mobilization from below and rode with it into power.

The distinction between the social movements and the ruling Democratic Alliance is crucial, however, to understanding the recent unfolding of Brazilian democracy. The Sarney government is composed of "reformists" (the left wing of the PMDB) and conservatives from the PFL and the rightwing of the PMDB. Its policies—or lack thereof—reflect its attempt to conciliate the irreconcilable antagonists emerging from opposition to the military regime. Sarney himself, in a major radio-TV address, described in populist language the sharp upward redistribution of wealth and income that had occurred under the prior regime and the increase in hunger, which he labeled the most current and challenging topic in Brazil. But while urging the importance of action to meet this challenge, his speech offered no concrete proposals, and he expressed sympathy with the widespread "despair in the face of impossible solutions."

The new government's actions have been in keeping with this sense of urgency and simultaneous regret at the impossibility of solutions. Apart from an emergency food program the regime has been stymied in its attempts to make the most elementary changes. The military has not been restructured, austerity programs are still in place, Sarney's mild agrarian reform proposal is being fiercely resisted, labor's demands for quarterly adjustments to meet the over 200 percent inflation rate have been rejected, and the divisions between the regime and its popular constituency have grown. While exports and industrial production during the first half of 1985 registered substantial increases over 1984, massive disbursements for interest payments left a balance of payments deficit of $1.4 billion for the first quarter of 1985. The economic recovery of 1985, such as it is, has not benefitted the vast majority of wage and salaried workers, and the burden of foreign debt and IMF constraints stand as barriers to either major reforms *or* rapid economic expansion.

The slackened rate of growth and the IMF austerity programs have been particularly damaging to the interests of Brazilian labor.[12] Between 1980 and 1984, wages as a percentage of production costs fell from 6.1 percent to 4.2 percent, while payrolls dropped 31 percent, and employment decreased by 15 percent. In order to recoup their losses, massive and prolonged strikes were carried out by metal workers, public service employees, teachers, medical and postal workers, and even seasonal farm workers, particularly in São Paulo State (over 150,000 workers in São Paulo alone). Meanwhile, with inflation expected to surpass the 200 percent goal set by the regime, and the government unable to fend off IMF constraints on social expenditures and expansionist policies, there is little likelihood of easy relations between the regime and the militant trade unions.

Despite the generally conciliatory, pro-business orientation of the Sarney government, it is also being squeezed by the Right. The IMF has hardened its demands, insisting that the government completely eliminate the public deficit and drastically reduce the rate of inflation—proposing contractionary measures opposed by most business people and of course by labor.[13] The military has publicly opposed allowing leftists in the government. Landlords are building up private armies to resist the land reform proposals, and some hundred peasant squatters and supportive church activists have been killed already. Moreover, there are sharp divisions within the government between those who seek to retain the authoritarian labor legislation limiting strikes and those proposing reforms, those supporting the IMF proposals and those seeking to water them down, and those who favor an agrarian reform and those who staunchly oppose it. While the regime has refused to put a ceiling on interest payments to foreign banks, it has shelved plans for an emergency program against hunger—for lack of funds. The accommodation with the military is also evident in the fact that only one military officer has been formally charged with torture, though many have been accused in publicly available documents. (The one officer convicted was merely stripped of his post.) The old military officials, schools, privileges, and prerogatives remain intact, and thus the political basis for reentry of the military into political life remains real if the civilian leadership should fail to overcome the crises and control conflict, or if it strays too far from free enterprise and banker principles.

Existing through the tolerance of everyone, but sustained by no major class, the Sarney regime embodies all the weaknesses and vacillations of liberal democracy, and few of its virtues. Fearful of labor and cringing before the banks, it has demonstrated an inability to make the socioeconomic changes necessary to sustain labor support and consolidate a popular base for democracy. The division between the "political class" located in the reform party apparatus and the independent class unions threatens to undermine the unstable balance of power of the regime. The growth of class polarization outside of parliament—between armed landlords and their hit men and the land squatters, between metalworkers and employers, between state executives and public employees— points up the inability of the current liberal regime to confront the most pressing issues. The Brazilian experience once again demonstrates that class-based institutions—including elected ones—cannot be reconciled with classless conceptions of politics and "state autonomy."

Deteriorating Democracies: Peru and Bolivia

To the degree that the new civilian leaders respond to the banks, the military, and U.S. officials, they are obliged to disregard popular demands. There is a real possibility that this continuing situation can alienate electorates and create new cycles of militancy and resurgent authoritarianism (which will then confirm the view of the thoughtless cynics who see Latin America only in terms of perpetual cycles of freedom and dictatorship). Ample evidence for these concerns is found in the experiences of the early cases of democratization.

Peru and Bolivia are two of the "oldest" of the recently democratized countries. In Peru, Belaunde's accession was accompanied by the government's agreement to meet its financial obligations to its international creditors, acceptance of IMF financial and economic prescriptions, and increased military spending as an accommodation to the outgoing military regime. A policy of economic liberalization was adopted, premised on the belief that free trade would stimulate export-led growth. Large-scale overseas borrowing, greater incentives to foreign investors, and the denationalization of local state enterprises were also parts of the banker-IMF orthodoxy put in place by the new civilian regime.

These policies, combined with the recessionary and high interest rate conditions of the Reagan era, produced the worst socioeconomic crisis of the century in Peru. GDP growth came to a halt in 1982, fell by 11 percent in 1983, and then made a modest (2.3 percent) recovery in 1984. Per capita income fell by 13.3 percent between 1981 and 1984. Manufacturing output declined by almost 20 percent during the first three years of the Belaunde term. The proportion of export revenues lost to external interest payments rose from 21.8 percent in 1981 to 35.5 percent in 1984.

Unemployment and underemployment reached a staggering 63 percent of the economically active population in 1983. Far and away the most important occupation of the population of Lima is street vending (the most unstable, least productive and remunerative form of employment). Inflation rose from 73 percent in 1981 to 106 percent in 1984. Real wages of the shrinking number of employed declined steadily in this period.

Failing entirely to cope with this severe economic crisis, the governing center-right Popular Action Party (AP) plummeted in public esteem and was crushingly defeated by a semi-populist candidate in the April 1985 elections. (The AP candidate obtained only slightly more than the 5 percent required to maintain legal registration as a political party.) Deep polarities have emerged. In the interior, Sendero Luminoso, the "Maoist" guerrilla group, has gained considerable support, particularly in Ayacucho, and appears to be spreading to other provincial areas. Meanwhile the military has taken over de facto control of the areas contested with the guerrillas. Military rule has been accompanied by widespread terror, generating the worst Peruvian human rights abuses in this century (over 4,000 were killed or disappeared over the past three years and there have been many more victims of army torture). The free market economic policies and Belaunde's decision to funnel major resources to the overseas banks has surely contributed a great deal to the remilitarization of Peru. While the major political damage has been incurred by Belaunde's party and regime, there is little doubt that the democratic process in Peru has also suffered. The new APRA party leadership faces crushing problems, without the resources or borrowing capacity necessary for escape from the debt-poverty trap.

Incoming president Alan Garcia has displayed great energy and put forward progressive initiatives that have generated enthusiasm and hope in Peru. His inaugural speech promised attention to agriculture and the poor, increased local food production, greater controls over imports, foreign exchange, and prices, cutbacks on arms purchases,[14] and a new, independent foreign policy (supporting Contadora and Nicaraguan sovereignty and protecting both from the country that "considers itself to be the owner of the hemisphere"). Some of these proposals were quickly put into effect in a new anti-inflationary package that included a partial price freeze, a small devaluation, a reduced rate of interest, and an 18 percent wage increase. The programs put into place so far, however, are marginal in relation to Garcia's larger aims and the pressing needs of the Peruvian people. The internal and external constraints on major redistribution and mobilization of resources remain severe. With interest payments $450 million in arrears, and Garcia proposing sharp limits on payments to external creditors, the likelihood of substantial net credit from abroad is dim. Given APRA's history of compromise and conciliation with international capital, there must be serious question as to Garcia's capacity to follow through on his initial proposals.

Garcia's most widely publicized, and perhaps most important, action has been his declaration that Peru would put a 10 percent cap on the amount of its export revenues available for servicing Peru's foreign debt. This proposal for a ceiling based on export revenues had been put foward earlier by Celso Furtado and others, but Garcia has attempted to implement this idea for the first time. This is an important development, because it is a unilateral act rather than a bargaining solution, and because it shifts the terms of the debate from a balancing of creditor rights and debtor capacity to pay to the primacy of the latter. The Peruvian cap is a form of limited repudiation, in which the interest and principal payments are tied to exports first, contractual obligations second.[15] What gives it some degree of acceptability is that the debt is not explicitly repudiated, but is made contingent on the level of export earnings. In Peru's case, also, economic and social conditions are such that full payment in the short term was out of the question anyway, and Peru is a small debtor. Conditions were thus ideal for implementing a cap without drastic retaliation from the international financial community. International bankers are nonetheless extremely worried that Peru's initiative may provide a model that will be resorted to sooner or later by the larger debtors as their problems continue to mount. Following the initial stage of renegotiations, postponements, and stretch-outs by mutual accord, the cap may be the beginning of a major step in a process of gradual repudiation.

In Bolivia a similar pattern has emerged. The democratic regime of Siles Suazo initially attempted to honor past debts and abide by IMF formulas prescribing salary freezes, public sector austerity, and a lessening of state controls. The consequences were disastrous. Between 1981 and 1984, GDP fell by 16 percent—a staggering 24.6 percent decline on a per capita basis. Export earnings fell from about $1 billion in 1980 to $700 million in 1984. With the foreign debt steadily rising, the ratio of debt service to exports reached 57 percent in 1984. Inflation, which had been 25 percent in 1981 reached 328 percent in 1983, soared to *2,177* percent in 1984, and is over 3,000 percent in 1985. Bolivia's interest obligations on its foreign debt now amount to about $400 million a year. Its export-oriented growth has also elevated its bills for freight and insurance, adding another $200 million per year to the Bolivian balance of payments deficit. These sums, if invested in productive activities, might well have made a difference in turning the economy around.

Through massive and sustained strikes, the Bolivian labor movement forced Siles Suazo to place a temporary moratorium on debt payments in the spring of 1984 and to ease up on the IMF austerity program. Economic conditions have not improved since then, and budget deficits and inflation are wildly out of control. Brutal impoverishment—wages of employed miners are under $60 a month—provoked a two-week general strike in early March 1985 that shut down the economy. Siles responded by calling out the armed forces to break the strike. Once again Bolivia is polarized between a radical democratic socialist movement and a regime relying heavily on military repression. The environment of uncertainty, conflict, and economic deterioration has been a propitious one for military intrigues from the narco-milicos (the various factions of the military command who deal in drugs) and for right-wing politicians. It is ironic, also, that the current stalemate aided a new bid for power by ex-dictator Hugo Banzer, under whose rule the cocaine mafia became entrenched in Bolivia and the bulk of the country's $4.5 billion debt was incurred. Banzer, friend and protector of Klaus Barbie, and a major human rights violator, was an invited guest at the 1984 Republican national convention in Dallas, Texas. His bid for power was beaten back, however, by a combination of left and "old right" forces that returned to office Paz Estensoro, long-time standard-bearer of the conservative wing of the MNR, a politician without power or program. Upon ascending to the presidency, Estensoro enforced a very harsh austerity program and called out the Army to repress labor and peasant protest. The left compromise with the MNR backfired; only the U.S. banks and the Army benefited; salaries and wages have dropped an addition 30 percent since the free elections.

The negative experiences of the older redemocratized countries supports the view that the political-economic constraints accepted by the newly elected regimes allow them few opportunities for consolidating a democratic consensus. Debt moratoria and democratic restructuring of the armed forces are necessary accompaniments to political change if democracy is to be given a chance to succeed.

Similar processes of erosion are underway in the Dominican Republic and Jamaica and throughout Central America—an especially important region to consider in evaluating the impact of U.S. policy. The areas of actual resurgent democracy are, significantly, places where U.S. intervention has been relatively slight and resource commitments small in recent years. In Central America, where U.S. intervention continues on a large scale, the power of the armed forces has grown and democratic institutions are either cynically maintained facades or are in process of rapid disintegration.[16]

Resurgent Authoritarianism: The Case of Chile

Chile presents a special case in analyzing the resurgence of authoritarianism, as its dictator has been aggressively resistant to pressures for "apertura" (political opening) and has reactivated state-of-siege conditions. The U.S. response to this resistance has been illuminating. In the case of Nicaragua, the Reaganities have been vociferous in denouncing any alleged deficiencies in pluralistic freedom and quality of elections. In the case of Chile, a denial of the rudiments of pluralism and a complete refusal to hold any elections whatsoever have been met with tolerant understanding.

Washington's attitude toward Pinochet is revealing evidence of the non- (or negative) relationship between Reagan policies and the resurgence of democracy in Latin America. The Pinochet regime is a focal point of *resistance* to democratization, and the Reagan administration has provided unconditional support for this especially brutal version of authoritarianism. The reasons for this support are twofold. First, the Reaganites still *prefer* viable rightwing authoritarian regimes to genuinely democratic governments. The reasons are numerous. (a) Pinochet has been a staunch supporter of U.S. policy on almost all major international and regional issues. (b) His regime has followed the most extreme "free market" policies favoring U.S. banks, investors, and exporters. (c) He has pursued the most repressive anti-communist policy in the history of Chile, much to the satisfaction of the Reagan administration. A second reason is that in Chile the social movements seeking Pinochet's overthrow favor basic changes in socioeconomic structures and civilian-military relations. Unlike their counterparts in other countries, these social movements are calling for democracy without military vetoes and compromises with the IMF. This has placed Washington in a small dilemma. For Washington to side with Pinochet risks alignment with a dictatorship that is rapidly losing even elite support. To pressure Pinochet to lift the state of siege and to openly negotiate with the center-right risks weakening his regime and deepening the influence of the threatening democratic movements. Washington has solved the problem, as it has in the cases of South Africa, South Korea, and numerous other friendly authoritarian regimes, by means of "quiet diplomacy"; that is, gently urging nominal or modest reforms while supporting the authoritarian rulers in all essentials. A recent visit of Langhorne Motley to Chile reportedly left Pinochet "purring with satisfaction."[17] Motley expressed confidence that the government of Chile was in good hands, urged the opposition to accept Pinochet's timetable of an election for 1989 (with all "Marxist parties" excluded), and objected to any street demonstrations and mass mobilization as playing into communist hands.

Conclusion

The Reagan administration is operating on four separate tracks in Latin America. In Central America (apart from Nicaragua), where there is a mobilized population pressing for democracy and structural change, Washington has opted for the "terror with demonstration elections" formula, attempting to destroy the social movements and then promote (and publicize) elections among local loyalists that will ratify the status quo. The second track, used in South America, involves supporting elections where liberal politicians have gained hegemony over the mass movements and are willing to trade off socioeconomic policies acceptable to the banks and armed forces for political democracy. The third track may be seen in operation in Chile. There the mass movements are powerful and mobilized, as in Central America, so that the core policy is one of continued support of authoritarian rule and state terror, with a subsidiary thrust of gently urging (but not insisting upon) gradual accommodation with center-right civilian political forces. The fourth track, and the main effort in Washington's Central American policy today, is to escalate the economic, political, and military assault on Nicaragua. By neutralizing U.S. liberals and their Latin American civilian counterparts with rhetoric on "resurgent democracy," the Reagan administration hopes to obtain a free hand in securing a military victory against this dangerously vital example of social and economic (as well as political) democracy in Central America.

Washington's multi-track policy combines support for "death squad" democracy, constrained democracy, and dictatorship: there is still a substantial road ahead before we can speak of an authentic and consequential "resurgent democracy." And it will develop in spite of, not because of, the policies emanating from Washington.

Notes

1. Upon entering office the Reagan administration quickly solicited Argentine security force aid in organizing, training, and fighting with the contras and in direct participation in fighting alongside the army and death squads in El Salvador. See "A new force in Central America reported moving against left with U.S. aid," *Philadelphia Inquirer*, Feb. 5, 1982; Council on Hemispheric Affairs, "Argentina, Chile Receive Reaganites To Discuss Relations," *Washington Report on the Hemisphere*, Feb. 9, 1982.

2. These dollar figures are expressed in 1970 prices. This data and that which follows are taken from "Preliminary Overview of the Latin American Economy During 1984," *CEPAL* [Economic Commission for Latin America], Jan. 1985.

3. Dagnino Pastore, an Argentine economist and former minister of finance, has claimed that "the asset counterpart of the increased liabilities [built up during the military years] have not added significantly to the capacity of the country to generate foreign exchange." According to Pastore, the three most important uses of the borrowings, by order of importance, were: capital flight, foreign tourism, and the purchase of nontraditional imports. Jose M. Dagnino Pastore, "An Anti-Inflationary Experiment, Argentina, 1979–81," in *Symposium on Liberalization and Stabilization: Recent Experience in the Southern Cone*, 14-15 (Washington, D.C.: World Bank, May 20-21, 1982), mimeographed.

4. Looting by the Argentinian military was also common. *Latin America*

Regional Reports noted ironically that "It is evidence of the success of Videla's administration that most of his former aides are now millionaires." *Report on the Southern Cone*, Nov. 13, 1981.

5. "Chile's Bloated Defence Spending," *Latin America Regional Reports, Southern Cone*, Oct. 12, 1984.

6. According to Adolfo Perez Esquival, 216 abductions by paramilitary groups took place in Argentina in 1984. "A Latin American democrat with a passion for justice," *Guardian* [New York], Mar. 20, 1985.

7. *Latin America Regional Reports, Southern Cone*, Apr. 13, 1984.

8. See "Rearmament drive nearly completed," ibid., Feb. 1, 1985. See also "Alfonsin purges the army," ibid., Mar. 8, 1985.

9. See the discussion below of the Peruvian "cap," which amounts to an intermediate position between full repudiation and the renegotiation compromises previously arranged between leaders and Third World borrowers.

10. On the positive economics of repudiations and confiscation, see Martin Bronfenbrenner, "The Appeal of Confiscation in Economic Development," *Economic Development and Cultural Change* 3, no. 3 (Apr. 1955).

11. Everett G. Martin, "U.S. Business Firms Don't Care to Provide What Latins Need Most: Private Capital," *Wall Street Journal*, June 25, 1985.

12. Domestic capital selectively supports IMF measures, approving those restricting wage increases and social benefits, but sometimes objecting to credit restrictions and the breaking down of protectionist barriers.

13. Sarney is resisting the IMF-banker pressures, insisting that he will not allow further contractionary measures, and he has gotten a temporary respite from the IMF and banks. But Sarney has given no hint of moving toward limiting the proportion of export earnings to be paid for foreign debt service. He will probably move in this direction only under extraordinary pressure from below and a worsening of the crisis.

14. Impoverished Peru had on order 24 Mirage military aircraft at an aggregate price of $700 million.

15. In a free market, the imposition of a cap, with its implied reduction in the likelihood of full payment of interest and principal, would result in a sharp drop in the market value of the credit instrument. If holders of that instrument were obliged to sell, or keep it on the books at market rather than historic cost value, they would have to record major losses.

16. See, e.g., Phillip Berryman, *Inside Central America* (New York: Pantheon, 1985); and Cynthia Brown, ed., *With Friends Like These: The Americas Watch Report on Human Rights and U.S. Policy in Latin America* (New York: Pantheon, 1985).

17. "Motley Visit Delights Pinochet," *Latin America Weekly Review*, Mar. 1, 1985.

6 / *The United States and Canada: State Policy and Strategic Perspectives on Central America*

JAMES F. PETRAS and MORRIS H. MORLEY

United States and Central America: The Military Dimension

INTRODUCTION

One of the striking features of long-term U.S. policy toward Central America is the continuity among different administrations. From a regional perspective, it has made little difference over time whether there have been Democrats or Republicans, liberals or conservatives, in the White House. U.S. policy-makers (with brief exceptional interludes) have relied on their *military options* and *alliances with the area's armed forces* to maintain Central America within Washington's orbit. Thus fundamental continuity in policy reflects the shared strategic position of both major political parties that U.S. domination is an unalterable reality.

At particular moments, U.S. liberal administrations have *seemed* to promote a social democratic option in Central America, but the very policies and priorities pursued by Washington in effect have undermined the possibility of sustaining a reformist option—for the simple reason that social and economic changes have always been *subordinated to the strategic goal* of *defeating revolution.*

Essentially, U.S. liberals propose to carry out changes that would improve the standard of living of the masses at the cost of the local elites without adversely affecting the multinationals, their local economic partners, or the institutional position of the military and police. U.S. conservatives, on the other hand, seek to unify all sectors of the local ruling class and downplay reforms in favor of an exclusive military approach. Hence, while the former try to forge an alliance between the middle class and the military, the latter promote a power bloc in which the traditional oligarchical-military right is dominant. The liberals also support violent measures against radical, class-based organizations but hope to exclude Christian Democratic and other center-based groups from the wave of terror. The conservatives usually do not draw these fine distinctions. Instead they support each and every effort by military-controlled governments to stamp out independent organized forces in society.

While these distinctions between liberals and conservatives have surfaced in U.S. public debate, one major factor has unified them and produced similar policy consequences: an ultimate reliance on the military and police forces to establish dominance in the target country. In the case of Guatemala, for example, the policies of all administrations from Eisenhower to Reagan, whatever their initial intentions, have consolidated the repressive forces in society and, in so doing, strengthened precisely the most significant obstacles to any serious and sustained program of socioeconomic change. During the Kennedy and Carter presidencies, the White House launched major efforts to promote a social democratic option in Guatemala. Neither, however, proved capable of bringing about reforms or modifying the pattern of state-authored mass repression. The unwillingness of either Kennedy or Carter to break with the Guatemalan military, which had destroyed the social movements capable of instituting such changes (despite criticism of the armed forces' "excesses") indicated that, in their order of priorities, defeating radical social movements was paramount over and against social and economic reforms. In the process of supporting the destruction of these movements, the U.S. liberals strengthened the very groups opposed not only to the social democratic option but to all changes—thereby also undermining the "centrist" position. In sum, the differences between U.S. liberals and conservatives, while important in a specific conjunctural context, do not lead to different outcomes.

THE MILITARIZATION OF CIVIL SOCIETY

Since the 1950s, the United States has played a paramount role in financing, training, and equipping the armed forces and police constabularies of Central America. These coercive forces have, in turn, acted as powerful institutional collaborators in the pursuit of the imperial state's economic, strategic, and political goals in the region. The Alliance for Progress included a significant expansion of Washington's military program as part of the Kennedy administration's determination to prevent "another Cuba" in the hemisphere. During the late 1960s and early 1970s, large-scale U.S. military assistance, bolstered military missions, and the active participation of the Green Berets provided much of the wherewithal for the Guatemalan armed forces' brutal counterinsurgency campaign to "pacify" insurgent movements in the countryside. The Somoza National Guard, a creature of the Pentagon from its inception to its demise, received millions of dollars worth of American weapons from the Ford and Carter administrations that enabled it to wage war against a growing mass-based urban-rural polyclass opposition. Since 1981, an additional factor has reinforced the growing U.S. military presence in the region: the need of the Reagan administration to achieve a military victory in order to justify the vast armaments program that is the core of the new Cold War. El Salvador, in particular, has become the theater in which Reagan hopes to demonstrate that force, not negotiation, works—thus intertwining regional with global politics. Central America as a whole has become an arena for recouping America's worldwide supremacy through military confrontation and military victory.

The Nicaraguan revolution of July 1979 and the developing revolutionary processes in El Salvador and Guatemala initially caused the Carter administration to pressure the Guatemalan generals, through military aid cutbacks, to be more selective in their repressive policies and forge an alliance between reformist civilian and rightist military officials in El Salvador. During 1979 and 1980, however, more conservative forces in the State Department and the National Security Council, proponents of the notion that the Central American crisis was essentially part of a bipolar global conflict, emerged as the dominant voices within the foreign policy bureaucracy. Under the combined impact of this shift and the failure of the "reformist" option, the Carter White House escalated its military aid program to El Salvador and began to expand the American military commitment to Honduras. The relative decline in arms sales to the region under Carter was reversed before the end of his presidency, and this trend has been dramatically accelerated by the Reagan administration as it seeks to overthrow established governments and defeat popular movements seeking political-state power.

The Reagan military build-up in Central America has been concentrated in El Salvador and Honduras. Between 1981 and 1984, El Salvador received over $950 million in U.S. security assistance, of which approximately $400 million was in the form of congressionally authorized military aid.[1] In the process, at least 15,000 Salvadoran soldiers and officers benefited from Pentagon training expertise. (As of 1983, almost 100 Pentagon officials were stationed in El Salvador, the majority attached to the U.S. Military Assistance Advisory Group).[2] The Reagan administration's joint $483.4 million economic-military aid package for

El Salvador in 1985 envisages a majority of these requested funds being used for military activities.[3] The preferred White House-State Department rationale for the massive military involvement in El Salvador has been the desire to prevent "other Cubas" and defend Central America from a Cuban-Soviet "takeover." Reagan has even been led to describe such aid as crucial to maintaining the "strategic balance of the world".[4]

The American military presence in Honduras is equally comprehensive in terms of the allocation of resources and the scope of imperial-state activities. U.S. military assistance jumped from a combined $6.2 million in 1979 and 1980 to $58.3 million in 1983 alone.[5] Authorized congressional appropriations, however, do not provide a complete picture of the Pentagon's role in Honduras. A classified 1983 report of the House Armed Services Military Construction Subcommittee noted the construction of airstrips, houses, radar facilities, ocean piers, roads, an eleven-mile-long tank trap, and other facilities which point to a "significant additional U.S. military presence in Honduras *for an indefinite period.*"[6] Under Reagan, the number of U.S. military personnel permanently stationed in Honduras has risen to approximately 1,300, and the Central American country has been the site of continuing large-scale U.S. military exercises (for example, the 1983 and 1984 "Big Pine I & II" exercises, and the most recent April-May 1985 maneuvers) involving thousands of U.S. military personnel. The cost of the exercises has been estimated at well in excess of $100 million, which does not include the funds provided by the White House for housing, radar stations, building or improving eight airfields, and establishing a regional military training center—all necessary accompaniments to military exercises. American armed forces personnel in Honduras have also provided combat support and training for the Salvadoran army, trained thousands of local soldiers and officers, and launched aerial surveillance missions over El Salvador and Nicaragua from bases inside the country.[7] A key aspect of Honduras' interlocking military relation with Washington has been its complicity in the U.S. war against the Sandinista regime in Nicaragua. Its territory is being used as the center of operations and the most important staging area for the U.S.-financed and trained counterrevolutionary forces seeking to overthrow the elected revolutionary government in Managua. Current efforts by the Honduran military leadership to redefine the terms of its relations with the United States are not indicative of any disposition to restructure the basic relationship with Washington or shift its commitment away from the Reagan policy objective in the area.[8]

The Reagan administration's 1986 foreign aid request reflects its determination to further increase U.S. military involvement in Central America. Even though the total request for El Salvador ($483.4 million) represents only a slight increase over 1985, it is heavily weighted in terms of military assistance. Senior executive branch officials have made it clear that, in addition, supplementary military requests are on the White House agenda, especially if the direction of the military struggle begins to shift in favor of the guerrilla forces. The Honduran aid package for 1986 is similarly biased in terms of military funding, while the administration also is asking Congress for a major increase in military assistance to the repressive military junta in Guatemala—from a mere $300,000 in 1984 to $35.5 million in 1985.[9]

The single most important objective behind this massive expansion of U.S. military assistance to Central America, apart from the desire to prop up client regimes and allies, has been "to step up the pressure" on the Nicaraguan government to make political and economic concessions.[10] An official privy to the White House-National Security Council-Pentagon-CIA discussions toward the end of 1983 summarized the policy consensus: "The Sandinistas are on the ropes—keep the pressure on."[11] Total U.S. government security assistance to the three countries (El Salvador, Honduras, and Costa Rica) that border Nicaragua skyrocketed from $89.3 million in 1981 to $287.2 million in 1982 to $476.2 million in 1983 to $784.6 million in 1984.[12] Meanwhile, officially authorized CIA funding of the contras between early 1982 and the end of 1984, amounting to $150 million, significantly understates actual expenditures. Budgets have been bolstered by withdrawals from executive branch secret contingency funds, the transfer of equipment and facilities to the contras under cover of American military maneuvers in Honduras, the use of third-party surrogates (such as Israel and Argentina) to provide expertise and weapons, and White House encouragement to efforts by private organizations to raise aid for the CIA-backed forces.[13] The administration also is currently seeking to induce the Congress to release $14 million in covert action funds blocked in the spring of 1984, due less to members' objections to the contra program of economic "harassment" (mining of harbors, sabotage missions directed against communications and public utilities, and so on) than to continuing documented reports of contra atrocities, including the indiscriminate killings of unarmed Nicaraguan civilians. The administration, however, continues to seek release of the funds, in part because its ultimate objective has now become explicit: to exert pressure to extract concessions leading to a change of government in Managua. Destabilization and the removal of the Sandinistas is now the openly declared goal of Washington policymakers. In February 1985, President Reagan stated that the White House objective was to "remove" the "present structure" of the Nicaraguan government.[14]

Under Reagan, the logic of U.S. policy in Central America has outrun immediate economic interests: the logic of war (military build-ups and the mining of harbors and arming of opponents of established regimes in violation of international law) has replaced economic logic to the degree that Washington now links its global policy to a successful military resolution of the regional conflict. The prospect of a military defeat for the collaborator regime in El Salvador will almost certainly provoke direct U.S. military intervention. Senior officials of the Reagan imperial state have acknowledged the existence of contingency plans for possible use of American combat troops in El Salvador if the current regional militarization strategy fails.[15] While the strategic-military emphasis is divorced from immediate economic interests, however, it must be placed within the specific historical context of a larger effort to reconstitute the ideology of imperialism and the imperial state in the post-Vietnam era. Washington views the build-up of military power in Central America as the critical element in recreating economic opportunities on a world scale. El Salvador has been defined as the favored country in which to reassert U.S. power—to gain a military victory that would not only legitimize Reagan's regional policy but also the whole thrust of the administration's new Cold War definition of international politics.

United States and Central America: The Economic Dimension

INTRODUCTION

Although the internal politics of the Central American region have been fraught with instability, diverse sectors of U.S. capital have had no difficulty adjusting their interests over time. While the types, scope, and direction of capital flows have varied—beginning with direct investment in agro-mineral areas followed by manufacturing, financial loan capital, state and international bank capital—there has been no significant rupture or division among U.S. capitalist sectors regarding Washington's policy, or their relations with dictatorial regimes. Essentially the process of incorporating new capital to old has been an additive-accommodative one. The *absence of any rupture between the various forms of capital* reflects the complementary roles they perform, the interlocking interests they share, and their narrow socio-political bases of support in a region that requires strategic alliances with local repressive elites and dependence on the U.S. imperial state.

The emergence and consolidation of the U.S. state as an imperial state since 1945 has been the central factor enabling the massive growth of U.S. capital in Latin America and elsewhere. The U.S. imperial state can be defined as those executive bodies or agencies charged with promoting and protecting the expansion of capital across state boundaries by the multinational corporations. It exercises interrelated economic, coercive, and ideological functions which facilitate capital accumulation and reproduction on a world-wide scale.[16]

Forms of U.S. Capital Expansion

During the post-World War I period, the United States displaced England as the dominant economic power in Central America. Between 1919 and 1929, the American investment stake more then doubled to $251 million and was apparent in every important sector of the Central American economies: railroads, banking, public utilities, industries, mining, banana and rubber plantations, and so on. From the Great Depression to the Alliance for Progress years, the pattern of metropolitan capital flows served to consolidate and deepen the area's monoculture economy and agro-export dependence. Between 1950 and 1959, for instance, almost $100 million in new U.S. investments went into El Salvador, Honduras, Guatemala, and Nicaragua—most of it into public utilities, minerals, agro-exports, and the highly profitable food and raw material producing sectors.[17]

The tripling of U.S. direct investments in Central America between 1960 and 1980 was paralleled by an increasing concentration of new capital in manufacturing at the expense of agro-mining investments. In 1960, only $12 million out of a total $342 million was industrial investment; by 1980, approximately 40 percent of total U.S. investment ($417 million out of $1,033 million) was located in manufacturing, primarily in textiles, chemicals, food products, and pharmaceuticals.[18] Even in Nicaragua, where the Somoza family-dominated economy limited the growth of an internal market and placed major constraints on large-scale foreign capital flows into areas of profitable investment, there was no dearth of American multinationals operating in the industrial sectors on the eve of the Sandinista victory. The diminished proportion of new regional investments flowing into nonmanufacturing activities, at the same time, did not imply the erosion of the agro-mining export-based economy. Despite the changing investment pattern, all Central American economies still remain largely wedded to this type of development strategy based on growth "from above and outside."

Finance capital, particularly the largest U.S. private multinational banks (such as Bank of America, Citicorp, Chase Manhattan, and Wells Fargo) began to play an increasingly important role in Central America during the 1970s as the governments sought to cope with the twin problems of spiralling oil import costs and declining export markets. Between 1970 and 1981, finance capital assumed a commanding role in most countries: Gross inflows of medium- and long-term loans to Honduras increased from $29 million to $254 million, to Guatemala from

$37 million to $144 million, to El Salvador from $8 million to $182 million, and to Nicaragua from $44 million to $398 million.[19] This accelerated dependence on external sources of financing was accompanied by massive growth in these countries' external debt over this same period: from $90 million to over $1.2 billion in Honduras; from $88 million to $664 million in El Salvador; from $106 million to $684 million in Guatemala; and from $155 million to almost $2 billion in Nicaragua.[20] By 1981, U.S. private banks had $3.3 billion in loans outstanding to the Central American public and private sectors.[21]

American banking capital moved into the region's private sector on a significant scale during the 1970s. By 1979, U.S. banks had investments in 29 of the 41 private multinational banks doing business in Central America and in numerous nonfinancial enterprises such as breweries, sugar mills, and textile mills.[22] Moreover, they assumed positions of great importance within the agro-export production sectors. In Guatemala, according to a senior U.S. executive, the Bank of America is *"the* agricultural bank," second only to the government as a source of capital for those industries (coffee, sugar, cotton, beef, and so on) which account for over 80 percent of the country's export earnings.[23]

From the U.S. state, the Central American dictatorships have been the recipients of a vast program of bilateral and multilateral aid since the Alliance for Progress. Between 1962 and 1978, Washington and the so-called international banks provided the ruling classes of El Salvador, the Guatemalan oligarchy, the military-dominated regimes in Honduras, and the Somoza clan in Nicaragua with combined economic assistance totalling almost $2.4 billion.[24] Following the demise of the human rights lobby within the policy-making centers of the Carter administration in 1979, the selective temporary closure of access by the right-wing military or military-controlled regimes in Honduras, El Salvador, and Guatemala to large-scale economic assistance from these traditional sources began to be reversed. The shift in Washington's overall regional policy begun under Carter was cemented under Reagan, and was reflected in the further loosening of loan spigots by the U.S. and the "international banks" to favored regimes in Central America. During 1979 and 1980, Honduras and Guatemala received a combined total of almost $110 million in American economic assistance; over the three-year period 1981 to 1983, the figure rose to $347 million. In the case of El Salvador, Reagan has channeled economic aid to sustain a repressive state and policy at an even greater rate (and at the cost of massive loss of civilian lives): approximately $1 billion during Reagan's first term, compared with just under $61 million for 1979 and 1980. In the case of the "international banks," El Salvador again represents the most striking instance of renewed economic largesse: from $105 million in 1980 to $306 million during 1981 to 1982, levelling off slightly to total a still significant $474 million for the duration of the first Reagan term.[25]

In seeking to mobilize support for its political objectives in Central America within the "international banks," the Reagan administration has pursued a two-pronged strategy: maximum pressure to secure passage of loan requests by collaborator governments in El Salvador and Guatemala, and sustained opposition to all development aid to the revolutionary government in Nicaragua, which it defines as hostile to U.S. political-economic interests in the region. The White House has forced loan requests by El Salvador through the Inter-American Development Bank (BID) without consideration of serious operational problems or human rights violations perpetrated by the armed forces, security and police forces, and their death-squad allies. It has also secured International Monetary Fund (IMF) assistance for the regime over the objections of the Fund's technical staff—most notably in the case of a $35 million loan submission in July 1981. A subsequent Salvadoran loan request to the Fund in July 1982 for $85 million was the prelude to enormous U.S. pressure on the IMF's technical staff to secure a favorable recommendation to the IMF Board.[26]

While El Salvador was the major beneficiary of Reagan's total rejection of human rights factors as a consideration shaping U.S. voting decisions in the "international banks," White House efforts to mobilize support within these institutions for renewed aid to the Guatemalan military rulers also reflected this new general line and achieved some success. Because U.S. representatives in the BID were required by a 1976 law to vote against, or abstain on, loans to major human rights violators with the exception of loans defined as serving "basic human needs," the Reagan administration was initially constrained in pursuing its goal. For example, it reluctantly abstained on a $45 million BID loan for a hydro-electric dam project approved by the bank in late 1981. It did, however, decide to support two later Guatemalan loan submissions to the BID, and another before the IMF, on the grounds that they served "basic human needs." Congress did not oppose the executive branch position on these three loans, but it did caution against a positive U.S. vote for a proposed $18 million BID loan for a telephone project in rural Guatemala announced in December 1981. State and Treasury Department officials failed in efforts to convince a sceptical House Banking Committee to support the loan and, under the threat of a legislative vote against the total foreign aid bill, managed to convince the Guatemalan regime to withdraw its request temporarily. Following an internal military coup that deposed General Lucas Garcia in March 1982, the loan was resubmitted for BID consideration and, on this occasion, the State Department argued that since there had been a change of government, Guatemala could no longer be categorized as a major human rights offender. Finally, in October, the administration simply announced that it would not be bound by human rights considerations in deciding whether to support Guatemalan loan requests in the "international banks."[27] BID loans to Guatemala almost quadrupled between 1981 and 1982, rising from $25.5 million to $112.5 million.[28]

The Reagan administration's unremitting hostility toward the Sandinista government in Nicaragua has also been strikingly reflected in its behavior within the "international banks." Between July 1979 and January 1981, despite growing disaffection within the Carter White House over the policies of the Sandinista government, loans to Nicaragua from the World Bank and the BID totalled $175 million.[29] In the transition from Carter to Reagan, a more vigorous U.S. opposition to "international bank" loans to Managua was immediately put into practice, based on what a Treasury Department official termed the new administration's "overall political problem with the direction [of the Nicaraguan regime]."[30] In mid-1981, the U.S. government "adopted a position of opposing all development projects, both in formal votes and with delaying techniques during the preparation of projects by the technical staff [of the Banks]." This policy was successful in forcing a suspension of World Bank loans to Nicaragua and "in slowing down a number of projects in the other [international banks]."[31] In the case of the IMF, executive branch policy-makers indicated a readiness to work against any improvement in the already cool relationship between the Sandinistas and the Fund, which had its roots in an IMF decision to make available a loan to the Somoza dictatorship only weeks before its overthrow.

Nowhere has the Reagan administration more actively pursued its efforts to deny Nicaragua long-term development credits than in the Inter-American Development Bank. In November 1981, it forced Managua to withdraw a fishing sector loan request; in March 1982, Washington prevailed upon the BID Board to rebuff efforts to resubmit the fisheries loan; in mid-1983, the administration vetoed a $2.2 million road-building disbursal partly on the grounds of the Sandinista's insufficent encouragement to private enterprise within its development program. Between January 1982 and September 1983, the U.S. executive director cast negative votes on seven loan requests by Nicaragua involving a total of $84.4 million, all on the grounds of "inappropriate macroeconomic policies."[32] More recently, in early 1985, American Secretary of State George Shultz personally intervened with the president of the BID to block a vote on a $58 million loan to Nicaragua to provide the financial credits for small and medium-sized farms that had been under consideration by the BID for more than two years. Shultz expressed strong opposition to the loan on the grounds that the Managua regime was "not creditworthy" and raised the threat that approval of the loan might endanger or, as he put it, make "even more difficult" U.S. efforts to provide new financial contributions to the BID.[33] One highly placed Nicaraguan government official has estimated the cost to Nicaragua of these Reagan actions between 1981 and 1984 in terms of credits and loans denied by these "international banks" in the hundreds of millions of dollars.[34]

U.S. Policy and Capitalist Class Interests In Central America

INTRODUCTION

Historically, U.S. capitalist interests operating in Central America have worked closely with the U.S. imperial state and its repressive clients. In periods of crisis, particularly during those moments when the United States has lost the capacity to impose its will, capitalist interests develop a variety of positions relative to the regime in question—from outright opposition to accommodation. The clearest case in point has been the accommodating style of behavior displayed by the private banks and the multinationals operating in Nicaragua, a position that contrasts with the confrontationist posture adopted by Washington. The two faces of imperialism, business collaboration and opposition and the military confrontationist position, reflect not only different estimates of the durability of the regime but also different sets of strategic priorities. For Washington the regional conflict is embedded in global strategy and thus the ideological and symbolic meaning of "defeating Marxism" becomes paramount. For the bankers and multinationals the strategic issue is preventing the repudiation of the debt and the disintegration of the private sector in which they have a stake.

Thus the historical convergence of policy between the state and capital is not incompatible with the appearance of divergences in a particular conjuncture. Investment capital's flexibility is indicative of a belief that the imperatives of underdevelopment force revolutionaries to come to terms with the multinationals. The *prudent* counterrevolutionary policy adopted by business reflects the desire to support the destabilization of the regime provided there are good chances that the policy will succeed. On the other hand, these capitalists are opposed to hardline policies if they provide few prospects for success, as the eventual outcome would be to radicalize the regime. Thus divergences between capital and the state reflect a pragmatic or *opportunist position* on the part of capital which, however, may succumb to a state with strong ideological-strategic concerns—a consequence that apparently is unfolding in Nicaragua.

INVESTMENT CAPITAL AND THE REGIONAL CRISIS

The American multinational investment and banking community in Central America, and its structured organizations, has not projected a completely uniform response to the socio-political conflicts in the area either at the level of U.S. state policy or at the level of the particular economic stake of individual companies or financial institutions.

Organizations such as the American Association of Chambers of Commerce in Latin America were vociferous critics of Carter administration policy in Central America and welcomed the Reagan presidency as the harbinger of a new approach that would reverse what it viewed as Carter's "abdication of responsibility and traditional leadership in the region . . ."[35] The American Chamber of Commerce in Guatemala decried the "doctrinaire adherence to slogans" and their adverse impact on the local investment climate: "U.S. foreign investment has stopped and U.S. banks and companies are reluctant to finance trade with Guatemala." The Chamber expressed the hope that the Reagan White House would be "moved by pragmatic considerations of U.S. interests" leading to closer political and military relations between Washington and Guatemala's ruling generals.[36] But most U.S. companies and banks still continued to take a "wait and see" attitude before making new financial commitments in the region.

The strategies of multinational corporations with operations in Central America have been dictated by a number of factors, including the type and amount of investment, its size and profitability in relation to their subsidiaries around the world, whether the internal market is expanding or contracting, and so forth. Those companies with large fixed investments, for instance, have endeavored to ride out the changes in countries like Nicaragua and adapt to the new operating environment. Nonetheless, since 1979 there has been a notable absence of significant new foreign investment in all countries of the region. One involved American company official said in April 1982: "We operate on a day-to-day basis in the region."[37] At the time, another U.S. firm with region-wide investments had even gone so far as to prepare to absorb the loss of one of its subsidiaries as the cost of continuing to do business in Central America.[38] Still, a number of U.S. enterprises, taking advantage of declining competition and a strong demand for consumer products, have continued to reap high profits despite the persistence of operating problems such as restrictions on payments for imports. In some cases, the subsidiaries of U.S. multinationals in Central America earn profits that exceed those of subsidiaries in other parts of Latin America.[39]

In El Salvador, U.S. direct investment declined from $150 million in 1979 to approximately $100 million in 1980, paralleling a major expansion of the civil war and important gains achieved by the guerrila forces.[40] Even so, an American Embassy survey in February 1981 found that 82 affiliates of U.S. corporations were still in business and taking advantage of decimated labor organizations and minimal labor costs.[41] According to the American Chamber of Commerce in El Salvador, only 12 firms pulled up stakes between 1979 and late 1981.[42] The majority of factories still operating are engaged in assembly production for export, which requires limited capital, and are managed primarily by Salvadorean employees. U.S. companies surveyed in March 1982 exhibited a lack of enthusiasm for making new investments but most still looked forward to maintaining operations whatever the outcome of the internal social conflict.[43]

American investors in El Salvador expressed most concern over the shortage of foreign exchange and the prolonged (post-1978) economic recession, which was accompanied by a substantial decline in industrial and agricultural (coffee, cotton, and sugar) production, massive unemployment, the flight of capital, and negative foreign reserves. By early 1984, however, a number of U.S.–owned textile factories that had ceased operations for an extended period were reopening, and many American executives in El Salvador were declaring that the economic downturn had reached its limit and the worst was over. The manager of Citibank's branch operation projected plans for expansion after the March elections: "We are here to stay; it's a matter of adjusting to circumstances."[44] Scarce foreign exchange required to import machinery or goods and long delays in obtaining the Central Bank letters of credit needed to assure American suppliers of payment were not obstacles to many subsidiaries making what *Business Latin America* described at the time as "healthy profits for their operations in [El Salvador] . . ."[45] This renewed confidence was also reinforced by a growing belief among most executives of U.S. companies doing business in the region that Washington policies in Central America had forestalled any major political upheaval in El Salvador or Honduras, providing the basis for more stable and durable political orders.

Most international companies in Nicaragua surveyed by *Business Latin America* at the end of the first year of the Reagan administration described their relations with the Sandinista government as "good or at least reasonable."[46] A number of U.S. corporations had resumed their operations after July 1979 in a context where the new government confined its nationalization policy to properties owned by the Somoza family. The inevitable delays in obtaining foreign exchange for raw material imports and replacement parts, complaints over the inability to remit dividends, and other operating problems were offset by the "pragmatic" behavior of ministry of economic officials and the absence of any serious capital-labor conflicts. Although the number of U.S.

businesses in Nicaragua declined by about half (from 20 to 25 to approximately 12)[47] during the first four years of Sandinista rule, interviews conducted in 1981, and again in 1983, with executives of multinationals that maintained operations in the country reveal the general agreement that relations with the government were "pretty much business as usual."[48] Representatives of many foreign companies which sold to the domestic market or the state acknowledged the provision of "ample" or "fair" pricing margins and some projected future new investments ("The market is still sizeable") unless the government "decided to take over everything."[49] At the same time, not even profitable existing investments have eliminated apprehension over the ultimate political-economic direction of the Sandinistas, a concern which has been reflected in the continuing absence of significant new flows of investment capital into any sector of the economy. Still, increasingly, there is a common belief among those American corporate and banking interests with holdings or financial exposure in Nicaragua that the Sandinista regime is permanent and that, if the private sector is not abolished, economic realities will ultimately lead to a less statist-oriented economy.

While multinational executives were predicting moderation in Nicaragua's domestic policies once economic realities "hit more directly,"[50] by mid-1983 they were expressing growing unease over the thrust of the Reagan administration's policy. Some interpreted such White House economic sanctions as the virtual elimination of Nicaragua's sugar quota, the drying up of public economic assistance, and the vetoes of loan proposals in the multilateral development banks, as counterproductive to the interests of foreign capital: ". . . there is a feeling that what Reagan is doing is not for business, and that economic aid is needed down there," a corporate industry specialist on the Nicaraguan economy reported. "Businessmen are worried they will end up bearing the brunt of an invasion."[51] Washington's policy had already produced unprofitable economic fallout for U.S. multinationals: increased commercial relations between Nicaragua and competing capitalist and socialist bloc countries at the expense of American traders.

BANKING CAPITAL AND THE REGIONAL CRISIS

The reaction of the U.S. private banking community to the political and social conflicts in Central America has been threefold: to emphasize short-term lines of credit which can be increased or reduced speedily in dealings with Honduras and Guatemala; to halt virtually all cash-collateralized exposure in El Salvador; and to defer consideration of new loans to Nicaragua prior to the renegotiation of all outstanding debts.[52] Overall, there has been a greater reluctance on the part of American banks to finance the Central American private sector since the late 1970s. Between 1979 and 1982, for example, commercial bank and commodity trader lines of credit to the Guatemalan private sector fell by an estimated $760 million.[53]

The evolution of the relationship between the U.S. private multinational banking community and the Sandinista government in Nicaragua offers a number of insights into how banks behave regarding both their own investments and the convergence between bank actions and imperial-state policy. The debt renegotiation meetings between Sandinista officials and the country's major financial creditors during 1980 were instrumental in shaping American bankers' views of the Nicaraguan regime.[54]

The Somoza dictatorship had bequeathed to the Sandinistas a $1.5 billion foreign debt owed to approximately 120 American, Western European, and Japanese banks. Approximately 50 percent of the debt was held by 13 banks including Citibank (the largest claimant), Bank of America, the Royal Bank of Canada, and the First National Bank of Chicago. Representatives of these thirteen banks constituted the steering committee that negotiated with Nicaraguan officials. Within this committee, initially, there were two sharply divergent positions on how to proceed. Some banks expressed concern over a possible Nicaraguan walkout if negotiations were strung out and "would have been willing to sign anything." Others, including Citibank, which at one point argued for debt service payments equivalent to one-third of Nicaragua's 1980 export revenue, were adamant that the renegotiation process be subjected to standard commercial terms. In October 1980, an agreement was reached to reschedule $600 million (approximately 80 percent owed to U.S. banks) of Nicaragua's total debt over a two-year period. The development of a consensus within the steering committee that produced this result grew out of shifting perceptions of the Nicaraguan government's authority and intentions over the course of the negotiations. Ultimately, it became clear to these finance capitalists that Managua was determined to negotiate a settlement; that it was prepared to deal pragmatically with the U.S. financial community and to consider concessions in pursuit of its objective; that the Sandinistas were firmly in control of political-state power and, therefore, in a position to make necessary concessions; and that the enormous scope of economic devastation combined with the broad-based, cross-class opposition to the Somoza dynasty made the Nicaraguan case a unique one.

The successful restructuring of Nicaragua's foreign debt did not, however, lay the groundwork for new lines of credit to the Central American country. The same private foreign banks that authorized credit lines exceeding $150 million annually to the Somoza regime during its final years provided the current government with a paltry $11 million in new loans between July 1979 and July 1983. Meanwhile, over the same four-year period, Nicaragua made interest payments on its outstanding debt to these banks totalling $160 million.[55] Nicaraguan Central Bank President Luis Enrique Figueroa was informed by a number of American bankers that they had been pressured by the State Department to withhold loans to the Sandinista regime.[56] In late 1982, a consortium of twelve banks including the Bank of America did provide a $25 million to $30 million loan to Managua—but only in order to allow the financially strapped government to meet a $40 million interest payment on its foreign debt.[57] Some commercial banks, including Citibank, have made short-term credits available while others have refused to do so. One U.S. banker who turned down a Nicaraguan request for trade credits in January 1983 explained his decision with reference to the confrontationist policies of the Reagan White House: "We think the U.S. government is going to push Nicaragua into a default whether it's by backing exile invasions or cutting off their access to credit."[58]

American bankers continued to characterize the Nicaraguan regime's approach to its financial problems as "pragmatic," noting that until it missed a $4 million payment in March 1983, every previous foreign debt interest payment had been on time. Still, with the exception of some guaranteed, pre-export credit deals made in 1982, Nicaragua has received virtually no new bank loans since mid-1979—a situation not unrelated to the way in which U.S. policy has influenced and limited the options available to these financial institutions. Officials of these private banks contend that Washington has not applied *direct* pressure to stop credits to Managua. But as one analyst pointedly noted, "given the relatively small size of Nicaragua's debt, its economic prospects and the country's refusal to go to the International Monetary Fund for assistance, no pressure has been required."[59] Furthermore, the Sandinista regime's ability to meet its foreign debt obligations has been directly affected by such Reagan White House actions as the approximately 90 percent reduction in the Nicaraguan sugar quota (which has traditionally accounted for between $45 and $60 million in foreign exchange earnings) in May 1983. That same month, Nicaraguan finance officials informed American commercial bank lenders in New York that it could not meet a $45 million payment deadline in July due to the combined impact of flood damage totalling approximately $400 million, losses resulting from a severe drought affecting the cotton and sugar industries, and the costs (almost $60 million) incurred as a result of economic sabotage and other activities wrought by the U.S.-financed counterrevolutionary invasions in the first half of the year. They requested a suspension until July 1984.[60]

The ascendancy of Washington's military definition of its relations with the Sandinista regime means that state-to-state relations take precedence while economic relationships take second place in imperial-state priorities. Concretely this means that "private" economic enterprises and interests become instrumentalized by the imperial state, and essentially pursue the policies of that state even when such policies adversely affect private economic interests. The continuing subordination of private to state interests increasingly defines a period of preparation for "total warfare"—an open break in relations and unrelenting efforts to subvert the revolutionary regime.

Canada and Central America: The Economic Dimension

INTRODUCTION

Neither the Canadian state nor Canadian capital has the long-term deep structural ties with the Central American ruling classes that their U.S. counterparts have developed. Canadian linkages are primarily commercial, relatively recent, and largely independent of client-state patronage. The nature of the Canadian commitment is essential to an understanding of the Canadian government's capacity to disassociate itself from the most heinous regimes or policies in the region on the one hand and its willingness to trade with human rights violators (such as Guatemala) allied with the United States on the other. The economic-trade emphasis in Canada's relations with Central America, as opposed to the political-military, also explains why it is easier for Ottawa to diverge from Washington's policy when the latter attempts to impose an economic blockade on a regime such as Nicaragua. Trading with revolutionary states and American clients thus reflects the commercial influences that shape Canadian foreign policy in the region.

The other side of Canadian policy is its accommodation to U.S. policy in Central America, reflecting the opposition of Canadian capital to social revolution and the recognition that the U.S. imperial state provides an umbrella under which to operate. Insofar as Canadian capital depends on the same type of social and political conditions to reproduce itself, it benefits from this American umbrella and hence is reluctant to criticize its benefactor. Insofar as U.S. linkages with local power structures lead to monopoly advantages for U.S. capital, however, they stimulate Canadian opposition. Moreover, Canadian capital, having no vested interest in any particular set of rulers, can be more flexible in adapting to change, particularly if the alternatives do not threaten Canadian interests. The dilemma of Canadian policy revolves around its opposition both to U.S. hegemonic aspirations that may exclude Canadian economic interests and to local revolutionary movements that may expropriate Canadian and other foreign capital. Canadian policy thus moves between these two parameters—one side threatening displacement, the other expropriation. Canadian capital, as capital of a "follower nation," seeks to limit intervention without facilitating revolution, carving out political and economic space for itself.

The formulation of Canadian policy also reflects the centrality of state-to-state relations: the paramount importance which Canadian capital ascribes to its relations with the United States. The margins of independence are in the first instance restricted to symbolic utterances that evoke democratic principles, while the substantive policy of accommodation reflects the imperatives of the bilateral tie which is the cornerstone of Canadian foreign economic policy.

CANADIAN CAPITAL AND STATE POLICY

The Canadian economic presence in Central America has grown steadily over the last decade and a half. In 1980, approximately 17 percent (27 out of 152) of Canadian corporations with Latin American operations were active in Central America. Their investments totalled approximately $300 million and were located in various economic sectors: consulting services, engineering, food and food products (Guatemala); chemicals and paper products (El Salvador); and mining and petroleum (Guatemala and Honduras).[61] Guatemala appears to have been the most favored location of Canadian finance capital. In June 1981, for instance, the Bank of Nova Scotia participated in a $54 million loan to the country's Central Bank and loaned $5 million toward completion of a major hydroelectric project; some months later it reportedly participated with the Toronto Dominion Bank, the Royal Bank of Canada, and the Canadian Imperial Bank of Commerce in a $180 million syndicated loan to finance a multi-year Guatemalan government road construction program.[62] The concentration of Canadian investment capital in both extractive and manufacturing sectors, although not indicative of any clear-cut pattern, does suggest activities that parallel *and* compete with American investors in the area. To the extent that trade was assigned greater importance than investment or banking capital under the Trudeau government, the movement of Canadian finance capital into countries such as Guatemala that have emerged as important markets for Canadian exporters may reflect the interests of state policy-makers seeking to promote such trade.

In the early 1970s, Ottawa enunciated its "third option" strategy largely intended to break Canada's trade dependence on the United States. Since then it has aggressively promoted expanded trade ties with South and Central America and the Caribbean. This objective was facilitated by the establishment of two state agencies: the Canadian International Development Agency (CIDA), which administers the government's bilateral aid program for the hemisphere, and the Export

Development Corporation (EDC), which provides subsidies and other supports for Canadian traders. Although the largest trade gains during the 1970s were recorded in Latin America and the Commonwealth Caribbean, the value of Canadian exports to Central America still more than quadrupled, rising from $25.7 million in 1970 to $140.3 million in 1980.[63]

Despite official government statements decrying human rights violations in Central American countries, the commitment to trade expansion appears to have taken precedence in the actions of Ottawa policymakers. The EDC, for example, insured and guaranteed almost $9 million in exports to El Salvador and Guatemala during 1982. In the case of Guatemala, EDC loans were instrumental in the awarding of a $14 million contract by the military regime to Bombardier, Inc. of Montreal to supply locomotives and parts to Guatemala's national railways, leading to Canada's first trade surplus with Guatemala in several years.[64] Ottawa's ambiguous commitment to human rights in the context of its Guatemalan trade again arose in March 1983, when the Trudeau government co-sponsored a United Nations resolution condemning human rights violations by the country's military rulers, at the same time that Canadian Embassy officials were negotiating with Guatemalan air force representatives over the sale of De Havilland Aircraft planes. Although Canadian bilateral aid for new development projects in El Salvador and Guatemala was formally suspended in 1981, Ottawa refused to stop disbursing previously approved assistance, which resulted in the continued flow of Canadian dollars to finance a $10.3 million hydroelectric transmission line in El Salvador and a $5.5 million potable water project in Guatemala.[65]

The Trudeau government's bilateral aid program in Central America and its voting behavior within the "international banks" also mirrored some of the contradictory qualities of official policy statements. In these areas, instances of collaboration with Carter and Reagan administration objectives interacted with decisions that reflected independently developed Canadian positions. The military regime in Honduras and the revolutionary government of Nicaragua have been the largest recipients of Canadian bilateral assistance since 1980. Designated a "country focus" by the Canadian International Development Association (CIDA), Honduras, a center of U.S. military activities in Central America and counterrevolutionary operations against the Sandinista regime, received $44 million or 43.4 percent of total disbursed Canadian government aid to Central America between 1980 and 1984.[66] Efforts to promote military sales suffered a setback in late April 1983, when Ottawa was forced to cancel the sale of STOL aircraft worth approximately $30 million by the financially depressed De Havilland Aircraft, because of gross human rights violations in Honduras and pressures exerted by other hemispheric states.[67] In the case of Nicaragua, Ottawa sought simultaneously to promote trade through aid but at a level that would not unduly antagonize Washington. While official CIDA statistics show Nicaragua receiving more Canadian government assistance than Honduras during the 1980–1984 period, a significant proportion of the CIDA total included aid channeled to nongovernmental and business organizations that concentrated their activities in projects eligible for matching CIDA funds. In actuality, total disbursed bilateral aid to Nicaragua totalled $24 million or 23.4 percent of all economic assistance to the region, which was less than half the CIDA dollars that found their way to Managua as a result of undertakings by private Canadian enterprises.[68]

The sharpest area of disagreement between the United States and Canada in the "international banks" revolved around the question of economic assistance to the Sandinista government in Nicaragua—especially in the Inter-American Development Bank (BID), where Reagan White House efforts to halt all aid to Managua were opposed by a majority of the membership, including Canada. One of the more notable clashes between Washington and Ottawa concerned a $2.2 million Nicaraguan loan disbursal request in June 1983 to complete a road-building project in a coffee farming area. The initial project loan was approved by the BID Board in 1976. Construction was begun in 1978 but was delayed in 1979 due to the combined impact of the civil war and widespread flooding in that part of the country. With the passage of time, a new vote was required to extend the remaining $2.2 million of an original $18.4 million voted in 1976. Every member country except the United States supported the extension, which the American executive director ultimately vetoed on "macroeconomic" grounds. At the June meeting of the Board, Canadian representative Henry Hodder argued that there was no economic basis for rejecting the proposal and noted that the bank staff had found the loan perfectly acceptable. "Whatever the macroeconomic policies of Nicaragua may be," he declared, "it seems to us that in this particular case the benefits of completion of the road project are certainly commensurate with the cost and the macroeconomic policies of the country would seem to bear little relation to the completion of the project."[69]

Between 1980 and 1982, the Canadian government also abstained on three BID loan submissions by El Salvador that were all vigorously supported by the United States. The loans for agricultural and road construction projects totalled $86.4 million. Ottawa's abstentions were justified primarily in terms of the problems associated with implementing these kinds of projects in a situation of extreme political instability and civil war. Yet Canadian policy was not consistent on this point. Its executive director in the BID was directed to approve another 1982 loan request by El Salvador for $79 million to complete a dam project in the

Rio Lempa region, even though this was a major zone of military combat.[70] In the International Monetary Fund (IMF), Canadian actions have been similarly erratic. The Trudeau government supported a July 1981 request by El Salvador for a $36 million loan from the Fund's compensatory financing facility. Under enormous American pressure, the loan was eventually approved even though, as one Western European executive director pointed out, some of the basic conditions attaching to this type of funding were absent: "It does not establish the existence, let alone the size of the [balance of payments] shortfall, and it does not contain a staff proposal to the board."[71] While Canada aligned itself with Washington to support the first loan ever sanctioned by the IMF over the objections of its technical staff, it diverged over another loan request by El Salvador later that same year. In September, Canada opposed a $120 million Fund "standby" loan on the grounds of technical feasibility and operation problems likely to be encountered in a country engulfed by political and military conflict.

Since the advent of the Reagan administration, Ottawa's verbal expressions of concern over human rights violations by the Central American armed forces and their paramilitary allies do not appear to have played a significant role in shaping Canadian voting patterns within the "international banks." In the case of the two principal human rights violators in the region, El Salvador and Guatemala (which received a favorable Canadian vote for a $45 million BID loan to complete a hydroelectric project in late 1981), loans have been approved or opposed largely without reference to the issue of state-authored violence and repression. In August 1983, a correspondent for the *Toronto Globe and Mail*, discussing a Trudeau cabinet disagreement over whether human rights criteria should be an important factor in determining Canadian positions within the "international banks," concluded that the absence of any consistent policy "suggests[s] that Canada is tailoring its actions at the IMF to continue conforming to U.S. foreign policy interests."[73]

Canada and Central America: The Political Dimension

INTRODUCTION

While Canadian policy toward Central America displays relative autonomy from the United States, the Trudeau government's behavior nonetheless suggests that the capacity or willingness of Ottawa to develop a *consequential* position differing from that of Washington is sharply limited. The basic constraints on Canadian actions, which account for practical accommodations with White House policy, are several. First are the bilateral relations that govern foreign economic ties for Canada. Second, there is the dependence of Canadian capital on the United

States to counter revolutionary developments in the area. Third are the shared interests and activities of U.S. subsidiaries in Canada operating in Central America and American multinationals. Fourth, there are the joint banking efforts or consortiums that divide up the loan and interest market in the region.

Within these constraints, however, divergences in the trade sphere persist. Canada has developed an increasingly important stake in overseas trade: it is interested in breaking into new markets without reference to the ideology of the regime. In Central America, not only do politically tied or client governments closely linked with U.S. corporate interests provide limited opportunities for such expansion, but the political conflicts engendered by overt U.S. military intrusions also conflict with the essentially market-oriented policies of the Canadian government. At the same time, these trade policies allow Canadian exporters to displace their American counterparts when, for political reasons, the latter abandon markets. The relatively greater importance of market concerns and nondependence on client political regimes allows Ottawa to adopt a more flexible approach within the parameters of its ties with the U.S. The question of how far Canadian governments will pursue these differences is a function of how salient the Central American issue becomes for the Reagan White House. As Washington deepens its commitments to a military confrontation, allocating more and more resources and personnel, the likelihood is that Canadian policy will conflict less directly with the United States, hiding behind the commonplace rhetoric of accommodation to great power hegemony in the region.

CONFLICT AND COLLABORATION WITH U.S. POLICY

Canadian policy toward Central America under Trudeau was a contradictory mix of public criticism of and practical cooperation with U.S. actions. This reflected a determination on Ottawa's part not to allow differences over this particular issue to provoke a fundamental rupture in relations between the two countries.

The public statements of senior Canadian foreign policy officials during the Trudeau period were often at sharp variance with Reagan administation objectives in Central America: the origins of the crisis were ascribed to internal economic and social factors rather than Soviet-Cuban subversion; a cluster of ideologically diverse regimes were preferred to a region dominated by repressive and autocratic pro-United States regimes; and political negotiations, not the militarization of civil society, was seen by Ottawa as the only realistic solution to the area-wide conflict. These themes were expressed in numerous speeches and statements by Trudeau and senior cabinet ministers after Reagan moved into the White House. In March 1982, Secretary of State for External Affairs Mark MacGuigan, in a major policy statement almost identical to one given by the Prime Minister in February 1983, declared:

> Instability in Central America . . . is not a product of east–west rivalry. It is a product of poverty, the unfair distribution of wealth and social injustice . . . So when we look at Central America today, we cannot view this region exclusively through the prism of east–west rivalries because they are not at the root of the problem . . . I believe that the states in the region have the right to choose to follow whatever ideological path their people decide. I don't believe that when a country chooses a socialist or even marxist path it necessarily buys a "package" which automatically injects it into the Soviet orbit. This, I think, is where our views and those of the USA diverge. The internal systems adopted by countries of Latin America and the Caribbean, whatever these systems may be, do not in themselves pose a security threat to this hemisphere.[73]

Trudeau directly addressed the issue of American-Canadian differences over Central America at a press conference in late April 1983: "There are major divergences, beginning with the fact that we object to the interference in the internal affairs of other countries by any major power, even if that power is our friend. We certainly said that to the [United] States before . . ."[74] Opposition to big power involvement in the region's internal social struggles, and to the notion that Central America constitutes an arena of U.S.-Soviet global confrontation, was accompanied by repeated expressions of support for a political dialogue as the only alternative to an endless military operation. The Canadian government expressed its official concern at the highest levels in Washington over reports that the White House had authorized a multimillion-dollar covert action program to finance and train anti-Sandinista forces in Honduras. A Central American specialist in the Department of External Affairs emphasized Canadian opposition to this type of initiative, noting Trudeau's support for Mexican and Venezuelan efforts to promote negotiations between Nicaragua and Honduras.[75] In mid-1983, the new Secretary of State for External Affairs (and Deputy Prime Minister) Allan J. McEachen restated the basic Canadian policy in a speech at the University of Ottawa:

> The process of social change and economic progress in both El Salvador and Nicaragua cannot achieve success in a military confrontation. Canada, therefore, fully endorses the regional peace initiative sponsored by the Contadora Group . . . We also think that at an appropriate stage these talks should be supplemented by direct dialogue between the United States and Nicaragua, between the United States and Cuba, and between Nicaragua and Costa Rica.[76]

The Canadian Ambassador to the United States, Allan Gotlieb, articulated Ottawa's concern over escalating U.S. military assistance to Cen-

tral America and the apparent downgrading of the search for a diplomatic solution to the regional conflicts in a series of meetings with
Reagan administration officials in August 1983. He emphasized the
importance of a "political approach" in resolving differences with Nicaragua (also partly reflected in Canada's refusal to align itself with
Washington in opposing Sandinista loan requests to the "international
banks"), arguing that accelerated military pressure on Managua was a
"two-edged sword" that could just as easily make the revolutionary
regime more intransigent as force them to the negotiating table. He also
told State Department officials that the multidimensional U.S. military
presence in Honduras threatened to erode further the already limited
authority of the civilian regime and thus could only increase the power
of the armed forces and its leader General Gustavo Alvarez.[76]

Canadian-United States differences over Central America again came
to the forefront in April 1984, when External Affairs Minister MacEachen
resisted strong pressure from American Secretary of State George Shultz
to include El Salvador in a scheduled tour of Nicaragua, Costa Rica,
Columbia, and Honduras. The White House was particularly displeased
over the inclusion of Nicaragua on the minister's itinerary. In statements
prior to his trip, MacEachen reiterated Canadian support for Contadora
efforts to "demilitarize the area," expressed his government's opposition to "third party intervention by anyone," and responded to Reagan's
characterization of the forthcoming Nicaraguan elections as a means of
merely "rubber stamping" Sandinista control with the comment that
any evaluation of the elections should "not [be] blinded by ideological
blinders." Discussing Nicaragua, he also stated that "improvements
have taken place" since the overthrow of Somoza and that Canada was
"attempting to understand the social transformation" that was occurring.[78] Upon his return, MacEachen again criticized U.S. military involvement in the region. "We have differences," he said. "They've
become even clearer on this mining [of Nicaragua's harbors] question."[79]

The transition from Liberal to Conservative Party rule in late 1984 was
not, at least initially, accompanied by any major shift in Canadian policy
toward Central America. Addressing the United Nations in September,
the new government's External Affairs Minister, Joseph Clark, declared
that "Canada regrets the extension to Central America of East/West
confrontation and the related militarization of the area," expressed
Ottawa's continued support for the Contadora peace process and advocated direct negotiations between Washington and Managua.[80] The
commitment to Contadora and a political solution was again noted by
Clark in the course of a general review of U.S.–Canadian relations with
American Secretary of State Shultz in mid-October. Announcing a
sweeping review of Canadian foreign policy in February 1985, Clark

conceded that Washington's "unsettling" policies in Central America remained a source of disagreement between the two Western allies.[81]

Despite Canada's differences with the United States over Central America, Ottawa's unease has been conveyed primarily through "quiet diplomacy"[82] and has coexisted with instances of both public and private alignment with White House policy. The way in which "quiet diplomacy" served to mask a good deal of practical collaboration with U.S. policy in the region is well illustrated in the case of El Salvador.

In mid-1980, the Canadian Secretary of State for External Affairs, Mark MacGuigan, rationalized the Carter administration's decision to supply "nonlethal" military equipment to the Salvadoran junta on the grounds that the "so-called American aid is purely of a defensive nature."[83] Soon after Reagan's election, MacGuigan conferred with the new U.S. Secretary of State, Alexander Haig, at which time he was made privy to materials that subsequently formed the substance of the first Reagan "White Paper on El Salvador." These documents so "impressed" MacGuigan that, combined with his discussions with Haig, they had given him "reason to pause" over continued Canadian opposition to U.S. involvement in El Salvador.[84] Eventually, the External Affairs Minister announced that Washington "can at least count on our quiet acquiescence" if it decides to provide "offensive arms" to the Salvadoran regime.[85] During Reagan's 1981 visit, MacGuigan reaffirmed this position and sought to downplay Canada's role by contending that the region was not "an area of traditional Canadian interest."[86] And, according to MacGuigan, the meeting between the two heads of state produced a convergence of views on Central America: "There was no difference between the positions on our two governments."[87]

The same month, however, Secretary MacGuigan described U.S. military assistance to El Salvador as "neither desirable or necessary" and termed it a major "difference" between Ottawa and Washington. Nonetheless, he continued to give credence to the unproven and unsubstantiated assertions contained in the "White Paper," expressing opposition to "the import of huge quantities of arms from Cuba and other Communist countries through Nicaragua to El Salvador."[88] Throughout 1982 and 1983, Canadian statements critical of the "escalating military confrontation" in Central America were accompanied by declarations of support for the American military build-up in El Salvador, which officials justified by ascribing legitimacy to the existing government and exhibiting concern over recent guerrilla gains. In mid-1983, External Affairs Minister Allan J. MacEachen outlined the Canadian position: "We know that the guerrilla forces are obtaining support from abroad and we accept that the government of El Salvador has the right to seek support from other countries, such as the United States, to defend itself."[89]

Following a Trudeau-Reagan conference in April 1983, White House aides described the Canadian leader as basically sympathetic to U.S. policy in Central America: "The Prime Minister said he appreciated the reasons behind the President's policy and generally supported it."[90] Less than two months later, Trudeau told the House of Commons that he saw no reason for the U.S. to end its military activities in the region as long as other external forces were similarly involved.[91] This tacit acknowledgement of Washington's contention that Central America was an arena of U.S.–Soviet "testing of wills" was again suggested when he declared before parliament "that what the United States does in Latin America is its own business because the Spanish-speaking world is one of its spheres of influence."[92] The Canadian government, according to Secretary MacEachen, "fully appreciate[s] the dilemma that is facing the United States as it seeks to respond to these explosive events in a region of strategic importance to U.S. interests."[93] Periodic assertions of Canadian unease over the "escalating military confrontation" in the area were increasingly accompanied by criticisms of the guerrilla movement in El Salvador and statements of "dismay" over "the increasing tendency toward authoritarianism" in Nicaragua.[94] In April 1984, External Affairs Minister MacEachen informed Secretary of State Shultz that while he would not include El Salvador or exclude Nicaragua from his forthcoming Central American tour, he had recently asked the Nicaraguan Foreign Minister to tone down his government's criticisms of the United States.[95]

Canadian policy toward Central America since 1980 has evolved independently of the United States—but only to a limited degree. Ottawa's refusal to lend itself to military adventures, its consistent support for a political solution to the regional crisis, its more eclectic choice of economic partners (including Guatemala *and* Nicaragua), and its refusal to collaborate with Washington in opposing "international bank" loans to the Sandinista regime all reflect an independent stance. In the more recent period, however, a gradual shift appears to have taken place in the direction of conceding the primacy of American interests in the region, paralleled by official criticism of the internal policies of the Nicaraguan government and of the guerrilla movement in El Salvador. This developing convergence with U.S. policy is shaped largely by a concern not to allow Central America to become the occasion for a serious rift in bilateral relations. Ironically, neither an accommodative nor a conflictive Canadian policy has achieved an outcome compatible with Ottawa's objectives. From neither stance has Canadian policy influenced the course of U.S. actions. Moreover, although Canada remains critical of the American emphasis on military solutions in Central America, both countries share a common global purpose, and ultimately Canada depends on the "umbrella" provided by the imperial state that maintains the imperial system of which they are both a part.

Notes

1. See U.S. Agency for International Development, *U.S. Overseas Loans and Grants and Assistance from International Organizations, July 1, 1945–September 30, 1982* (Washington, 1982), 47; Steven R. Weisman, "Reagan Denies Aim Is Bigger Presence in Latin Countries," *New York Times*, July 27, 1983, 1, 11; Hedrick Smith, "Reagan Seeks a Fourfold Increase in Arms, Aid for Salvador Regime," *New York Times*, Feb. 18, 1984, 4; Congressional Research Service, The Library of Congress, *Major Legislation of the 98th Congress*, MLC—032, 98th Congress, no. 8, Dec. 1984 (summary issue); "U.S.–Nicaraguan Tension Grows as Congressional Deadline Nears," *Central America Bulletin* (U.S.) 4, no. 2 (Dec. 1984): 5; "U.S. Policy Towards El Salvador: Surface Successes Conceal Present and Potential Troubles," *Central America Bulletin* 4, no. 111 (Jan. 1985): 4.

2. See *Central American Bulletin* 4, no. 111 (Jan. 1985): 4; Lydia Chavez, "More Americans Sent to Salvador," *New York Times*, Feb. 27, 1984, 4.

3. See John M. Goshko, "Big Boost Proposed in Latin Aid," *Washington Post*, Feb. 5, 1985, A1, A4.

4. Quoted in Francis X. Clines, "Reagan Criticizes the Latin Debate," *New York Times*, Apr. 18, 1984, 13.

5. See U.S. Agency for International Development, op. cit., 51; Steven R. Weisman, op. cit., 1, 11.

6. Quoted in Fred Hiatt and Joanne Omang, "U.S. Buildup in Honduras Described," *Washington Post*, Feb. 1, 1984, A1 (our emphasis). Also see Joel Brinkley, "Senate Study Questions a Buildup by Pentagon in Honduras," *New York Times*, Feb. 2, 1984, 10.

7. See Fred Hiatt and Joanne Omang, op. cit., A8; Robert J. McCartney, "U.S. Is Dotting Honduras Countryside with Military Facilities," *Washington Post*, Feb. 17, 1984, A25; Richard Halloran, "G.I.s Will Train in Honduras Again," *New York Times*, Feb. 24, 1984, 4; Fred Hiatt, "Buildup: U.S. Has Steadily Amassed Troops, Counterrevolutionaries in Latin America," *Washington Post*, Apr. 15, 1984, A1, A28; Joanne Omang and Edward Cody, "Honduras Wary of U.S. Policy," *Washington Post*, Feb. 24, 1985, A1, A24; James LeMoyne, "U.S. to Hold More War Games in Honduras," *New York Times*, Mar. 27, 1985, 4.

8. See, for example, "Honduras" Strains in U.S. Strategy," *Central America Bulletin* 4, no. 4 (Feb. 1985): 1, 2, 7.

9. See John M. Goshko, op. cit., A1, A4.

10. Quoted in Hedrick Smith, "Ambiguities on Goals," *New York Times*, Apr. 11, 1984, 8.

11. Quoted in Hedrick Smith, "U.S. Policy on Nicaragua: Keep the Pressure On," *New York Times*, Dec. 1, 1983, 15. Also see Lou Cannon and Don Oberdorfer, "President Approved 'Harassment' Plan," *Washington Post*, July 13, 1984, A1, A14.

12. See "U.S.–Nicaragua Tension Grows as Congressional Deadline Nears," op. cit. (note 1), 5.

13. See "U.S. Hitmen: The Nicaraguan Contras," *Central America Bulletin* 4, no. 1 (Nov. 1984): 11–12.

14. Quote in John Goshko, "Nicaraguans Fight on the Hill," *Washington Post*, Feb. 26, 1985, A12. Also see John Lantigua, "Reagan Seeks More Anti-Rebel Funds, Sandinastas Say," *Washington Post*, Feb. 23, 1985, A13.

15. See Richard Halloran, "U.S. Said to Draw Latin Troops Plan," *New York Times*, Apr. 8, 1984, 1, 12; Doyle McManus, "U.S. Draws Contingency Plans," *Washington Post*, July 13, 1984, A27.

16. The economic apparatus includes both agencies serving particular forms of capital (e.g., Department of Agriculture) and agencies performing specific tasks that cut across the different forms of capital (e.g., Treasury and Commerce Departments) related to promoting investments, loans, and trade. The Department of the Treasury also pursues the larger objective in the multilateral development banks (e.g., World Bank, Inter-American Development Bank, and International Monetary Fund) through its responsibility for the appointment of U.S. representatives to these "international" institutions. The coercive apparatus of the imperial state includes the Department of Defense, the Central Intelligence Agency, and other specialized intelligence bodies. The ideological apparatus serves to promote the legitimacy of imperial activities directly through the U.S. Information Agency and related propaganda arms of the state or through "subcontracted" activities related to the practices of unofficial groups. The elaboration and coordination of U.S. imperial state policy is largely confined to the White House, National Security Council, and the State Department. The State Department, as well as Treasury, Defense, Commerce, Agriculture, and the Central Intelligence Agency, also play an important role in "operationalizing" the general policy positions and devising strategies to realize imperial objectives. This distinction between goals and tactics makes it possible to observe the continuities and common purposes in policy-making, on the one hand, and the differing institutional interests and bureaucratic conflicts that are consequential *within* the larger agreed-upon consensus over goals, on the other.

17. Walter LaFeber, *Inevitable Revolutions: The United States in Central America* (New York: W. W. Norton, 1983), 60–62, 127–28, and passim.

18. See U.S. Department of Commerce, Bureau of Economic Analysis, *Selected Data on U.S. Direct Investment Abroad, 1950–76* (Feb. 1982), 1–27; U.S. Department of Commerce, *Survey of Current Business* 61, no. 8 (Aug. 1981): 31, 32; U.S. Department of Commerce, *Survey of Current Business* 63, no. 8 (1983): 23, 24.

19. The World Bank, *World Development Report 1983* (New York: Oxford University Press, 1983), 176.

20. Ibid., 178.

21. Tom Barry, Beth Wood, and Deb Preusch, *Dollars and Dictatorship: A Guide to Central America* (New York: Grove Press, 1983), 9.

22. Ibid., 60.

23. Quoted in Allan Nairn, "Bank of America Asked to Explain Its Support for the Guatemalan Death Squads," *Multinational Monitor* 3, no. 3 (Mar. 1982): 15.

24. See U.S. Agency for International Development, op. cit., 47–48, 51–52, 54, 202–5.

25. See ibid., 47; Steven R. Weisman, op. cit., 1, 11; Hedrick Smith, "Reagan Seeks a Fourfold Increase in Arms Aid for Salvador Regime," op. cit., 4; James Morrell and William Jesse Biddle, *Central America: The Financial War* (Washington, D.C.: Center for International Policy, March, 1983), 8; "U.S. Policy Towards El Salvador: Surface Successes Conceal Present and Potential Troubles," op. cit., 6.

26. These two loans are discussed in James Morrell and William Jesse Biddle, op. cit., 2–4.

27. See ibid., 6–7.

28. Ibid., 8.

29. Ibid., 7.

30. Quoted in ibid.

31. Caleb Rossiter, *The Financial Hit List* (Washington, D.C.: Center for International Policy, Feb. 1984), 4.

32. See James Morrell and William Jesse Biddle, op. cit., 7, 10; "How the U.S. Uses Its Lending Vote," *Latin America Regional Reports: Mexico and Central America*, RM-84-01, Jan. 13, 1984, 2.

33. Quoted in Karen De Young, "Shultz Intervenes on Loan," *Washington Post*, Mar. 8, 1985, A1, A17.

35. Statement of R. Bruce Cuthbertson, regional vice president for Central America, Association of American Chambers of Commerce in Latin America, in U.S. Congress, House Hearings, Committee on Foreign Affairs, Subcommittee on Inter-American Affairs, *Business Perspectives on Latin America*, 97th Cong., 1st sess., Apr. 28, 1981 (Washington: U.S. Government Printing Office, 1981), 15.

36. Statement submitted by the American Chamber of Commerce in Guatemala, in op. cit., 46, 48.

37. Quoted in "Central American Elections Signal Little Improvement in MNC Working Conditions," *Business Latin America*, Apr. 14, 1982, 114.

38. See ibid.

39. See "Despite Political Woes, Central American Markets Offer Business Incentives," *Business Latin America*, Mar. 14, 1984, 83, 87.

40. On U.S. investment in El Salvador, see "El Salvador: U.S. Plants Hum Along Despite the Turmoil," *Business Week*, Apr. 13, 1981, 60.

41. See "Dozens of MNCs Brave El Salvador's Civil War to Keep Foot in Door," *Business Latin America*, Aug. 26, 1981, 270.

42. See "MNCs Successfully Adapt to Hardships of Business in War-Torn El Salvador," *Business Latin America*, Mar. 17, 1982, 83.

43. See ibid., 83–84

44. Quoted in Fred. R. Bleakley, "Americans in Business in El Salvador: Juggling Risk, Fear and Returns," *New York Times*, Mar. 25, 1984, 6F.

45. "MNCs Maintain Presence, Show Some Profits in War-Torn El Salvador," *Business Latin America*, Mar. 30, 1983, 99, 104.

46. Quoted in "Survey Finds Most MNC's Receive Fair Treatment from Sandinistas," *Business Latin America*, Aug. 12, 1981, 249–51.

47. See Joanne Kenen, "U.S. Is Still Nicaragua's Top Trading Partner," *Journal of Commerce*, May 11, 1983, 5A.

48. Kenneth N. Gilpin, "Nicaragua Outlook Worries Executives," *New York Times*, Aug. 15, 1983, D1.

49. Quoted in "Survey Finds Most MNC's Receive Fair Treatment from Sandinistas," op. cit., 249–51.

50. Quoted in "U.S. Executives Express Optimism Over Latin America Investment Climate," *Business Latin America*, Oct. 5, 1983, 315.

51. Kenneth N. Gilpin, op. cit., D7.

52. See John F. H. Purcell, "The Perception and Interests of U.S. Business in Relation to the Political Crisis in Central America," in Richard E. Feinberg, ed., *Central America: International Dimensions of the Crisis* (New York: Holmes & Meier Publishers, 1982), 115.

53. Tom Barry, Beth Wood, and Deb Preusch, op. cit., 58.

54. The discussion of the debt negotiations draws on John F. H. Purcell, op. cit., 107–8, 110–11. On the amount of the Nicaraguan debt and the proportion owed to U.S banks, see "Nicaragua: Foreign Debt Talks Run Aground," *Latin America Regional Reports: Mexico & Central America*, RM-80-07, Aug. 15, 1980, 5; Terri Shaw, "Cuba's Debt Mistakes: A Lesson for Nicaragua," *Washington Post*, Oct. 5, 1980, G1, G7.

55. See Central American Historical Institute (Georgtown University), *Update,* no. 8, Nov. 5, 1982; "U.S. Pressure on Lenders Blamed for Liquidity Crisis," *Latin American Markets (Financial Times),* no. 63, Aug. 1, 1983, 12.

56. See interview in Central American Historical Institute, op. cit.

57. Tom Barry, Beth Wood, and Deb Preusch, op. cit., 237.

58. Quoted in "Nicaragua: A Warmer Welcome for U.S. Businessmen," *Busienss Week,* Jan. 10, 1983, 43.

59. Kenneth N. Gilpin, op. cit., D7.

60. See ibid.

61. See Tim Draimin, "Canadian Foreign Policy and El Salvador," in Lisa North, *Bitter Grounds: Roots of Revolt in El Salvador* (Toronto: Behind the Lines, December 1981), 100; "Canadian Investment, Trade and Aid in Latin America," *LAWG Letter* 7, no. 1/2 (May–Aug. 1981): 15–17.

62. See The Taskforce on the Churches and Corporate Responsibility, *Canadian Economic Relations with Countries That Violate Human Rights,* A Brief to the Sub-Committee on Latin America and the Caribbean of the Standing Committee on External Affairs and National Defense, June 1, 1982, 13–14. The program was subsequently canceled by the new military junta in 1982.

63. See "Canadian Policy Review Suggests Greater Role in Regional Affairs," *Business Latin America,* Jan. 5, 1983, 4. Also see D. R. Murray, "The Bilateral Road: Canada and Latin America in the 1980's," *International Journal* 37, no. 1 (winter 1981–82): 119–20.

64. See Canadian International Development Agency, *Canadians in the Third World: Statistical Annex,* CIDA's Year in Review 1981–82 (Ottawa, 1983). Figures supplied by CIDA to Canada–Caribbean–Central American Policy Alternatives, Toronto, Ontario, published in an *AID* memo, Sept. 10, 1983.

65. See Letter of Allan J. MacEachen, external affairs minister, Mar. 1, 1983, quoted in ibid.

66. "Canada and Central America: Turner Takes Charge," *Central America Update* 4, no. 1 (July/Aug. 1984): 9.

67. "Canadian Policy: Variations on the U.S. Themes," *Central America Update* 6, no. 6 (June 1983): 34.

68. "Canada and Central America: Turner Takes Charge," op. cit., 2, 9.

69. Quoted in Caleb Rossiter, op. cit., 4. Also see "Political Veto Scuttles Loan," *Toronto Globe and Mail,* Oct. 3, 1983, B3.

70. See Michael McDowell, "El Salvador Aid 'Squandered,' Analyst Reports," *Toronto Globe and Mail,* Mar. 24, 1983, 15; James Morrell and Jesse Biddle, op. cit.; Suzanne Fournier and Arthur Moses, "Canadians Back Opposing Sides in Tropical Wars," *Toronto Globe and Mail,* Jan. 18, 1983, 14.

71. Quoted in Olivia Ward, "IMF Accused of Breaking Own Rules to Lend $85 Million to El Salvador," *Toronto Star,* Sept. 12, 1982, A17.

72. Martin Mittelstaedt, "Federal IMF Policy Called Inconsistent," *Toronto Globe and Mail,* Aug. 20, 1983, B14.

73. Quoted in R. V. Gorhan, assistant under-secretary, Bureau of Latin America and Caribbean Affairs, Department of External Affairs, Ottawa, *Canadian Policy Toward Latin America, Central America, and the Caribbean,* speech to Council on Hemispheric Affairs, New York, May 2, 1982, 10–12. Also see a speech by Secretary MacGuigan, Mar. 31, 1981, University of Toronto, quoted in Canadian Embassy, Public Affairs Division, *Central American and Canadian Foreign Policy,* Apr. 5, 1982. Trudeau's restatement is included in remarks delivered at a conference of heads of state of Caribbean Commonwealth countries in Feb. 1983. See Darryl Dean, "Canada 'Committed' to Caribbean Aid," *Miami Herald,*

Feb. 23, 1983, 7A; Charlotte Montgomery, "Canada a Friend 'for All Seasons,' Trudeau Promises," *Toronto Globe and Mail*, Feb. 21, 1983, 12.

74. Quoted in John Gray, "Trudeau Accuses U.S. of Interference in Central America," *Toronto Globe and Mail*, Apr. 23, 1983, 1.

75. "The Government has made very clear to the Government of the United States at the most senior levels its opposition to foreign intervention in Central America, including Nicaragua," letter from Secretary of State for External Affairs Allan J. MacEachen to Mr. John M. Kirk, Department of Spanish, Dalhousie University, Halifax, Nova Scotia, May 27, 1983. Prime Minister Trudeau expressed opposition to U.S. financing and training of the contras in *House of Commons, Debates*, May 2, 1983, 2506.

76. *Statement Discourse*, notes for a speech by the Hon. Allan J. MacEachen, deputy prime minister and secretary of state for external affairs, University of Ottawa, June 3, 1983.

77. See Michael Valpy, "In the U.S. Ear," *Toronto Globe and Mail*, Aug. 9, 1983, 6.

78. Quoted in Patrick Martin, "Canada Spurns Appeal by U.S. on El Salvador," *Toronto Globe and Mail*, Apr. 3, 1984 (on Telex, Canadian Embassy, Washington, D.C.).

79. Quoted in Patrick Martin, "U.S. Taking Wrong Road: MacEachen," *Toronto Globe and Mail*, Apr. 17, 1984 (on Telex, Canadian Embassy, Washington, D.C.).

80. "Canada & Central America: Clark Promises Moderating Role," *Central America Update* 6, no. 2 (Sept./Oct. 1984): 14.

81. Quoted in *Toronto Globe and Mail*, Feb. 10, 1985 (on Telex, Canadian Consulate, Sydney, Australia).

82. See, for example, Michael McDowell, "Canada Will Coax, Won't Push the U.S. on Central America," *Toronto Globe and Mail*, May 28, 1983, 15.

83. Quoted in Tim Draimin, op. cit., 102.

84. Quoted in "Less Canadian Opposition Seen to U.S. Aid for Salvador Junta," *Toronto Globe and Mail*, Feb. 5, 1981, 14.

85. Quoted in Tim Draimin, op. cit., 103.

86. Quoted in ibid., 104.

87. Quoted in ibid.

88. Speech by Secretary of State MacGuigan, Mar. 9, 1981, quoted in R. V. Gorhan, op. cit., 12–13.

89. *Statement Discourse*, op. cit.

90. Quoted in Bruce Ward, "PM's Central American Policy Rapped," *Toronto Star*, May 3, 1983, A8.

91. See "U.S. Needn't Withdraw Latin Aid, Trudeau Says," *Toronto Globe and Mail*, June 9, 1983, 14.

92. Quoted in Susan Riley, "Canada's Uneasy Stand on a Tricky Issue," *MacLean's*, Aug. 8, 1983, 22.

93. Quoted in "Canada Moves Closer to U.S. on Central America," *Christian Science Monitor*, July 18, 1983, 5.

94. Quoted in ibid., 5.

95. Quoted in Patrick Martin, op. cit.

7 / *Anticommunism in Guatemala: Washington's Alliance with Generals and Death Squads*

JAMES F. PETRAS and MORRIS H. MORLEY

Introduction: Liberal and Conservative Anticommunism

In the contemporary U.S. social formation, both liberal and conservative political, economic, and social forces have made the issue of anticommunism central to the domestic and foreign policy debate. Conflicts between political and economic nationalist regimes in the Third World and the U.S. imperial state over the conditions for capital accumulation and the nature of Third World class relations have been conceptualized by post-World War II American policy makers in terms of anticommunist ideology in order to justify an interventionist foreign policy. The utility of the notion is precisely that it allows the United States to disguise the basis of its ties to client regimes and ruling classes: economic interests are obscured and national class struggles are redefined as East–West conflicts. Foreign policy is not discussed in terms of a secure environment for multinationals to extract the economic surplus or in terms of political-strategic concerns but largely with reference to Third World allies' opposition to "communist subversion."

While the resort to anticommunist ideology has functioned to divert attention from the systemic concerns of the U.S. imperial state, it has also served to rationalize the impact of large-scale violence perpetrated by allied regimes against their own populations. In countries such as post-1954 Guatemala, the most heinous acts of pro-U.S. military rulers are subsumed within the anticommunist struggle. The requirement that liberal forces in U.S. society develop politics from the terrain of anticommunism in a context where the most reactionary groups have been, and remain, dominant has had profound consequences for liberal efforts to promote a reformist anticommunist option in the Third World. Ultimately, the liberal and conservative variants have generated similar outcomes: state-terrorist regimes, social and economic regression, massive state-centered corruption, fraudulent elections, foreign economic domination, and rulers who collaborate with U.S. regional and global objectives.

While the Kennedy and Carter administrations attempted to combine reformist policies with anticommunist ideology in Guatemala, neither reforms nor a lessening of repression was achieved. As has been noted, liberal, reformist anticommunism differs from its conservative variant in terms of programs, political allies, and the scope of regime violence, but not in terms of outcomes (see Chapter 6, page 108). In the period since World War II, the logic of U.S. liberal anticommunism has converged with the outcomes of its conservative counterpart, which have generated a continuous pattern of unrelieved repression sustained and supported by one set of imperial state policy makers after another. The Guatemalan experience offers a striking illustration of this convergence and its outcome: the persistence of one of the most brutal regimes in modern history.

Anticommunism as a Destabilizing Mechanism

Anticommunism has served as a mechanism to destabilize democratic and nationalist regimes which attempt to carry out reforms that adversely affect U.S. propertied interests. In this context, anticommunist ideology transforms a conflict between poor peasants and workers and multinationals into a confrontation between "Communist Terror and the Free World." This transformation of reality is central to gaining domestic support in the United States, because as a democracy it must secure the consent or acquiescence of the citizenry. (Anticommunist demonology is thus a necessary accompaniment of a manipulated democracy.) The use of anticommunism as a destabilizing mechanism probably offers no clearer instance than that of Guatemala during its brief decade of democratic rule beginning in the mid-1940s.

The overthrow of the brutal Ubico dictatorship in 1944 by a coalition of urban workers, dissident military officers, and sectors of the bourgeoisie created the basis for the freest election in Guatemalan history. The liberal democratic government of Juan Jose Arevalo (1945–1950) presided over a period of discrete but significant social and economic advances for the country's workers and peasants—as well as the revival of a competing political party system. The wage levels of the urban working class were increased and a labor code was enacted, giving workers the right to strike, establish trade unions, and engage in collective bargaining. Arevalo also introduced a social security system, passed a law forcing the oligarchy to lease unused land to the peasants, and at least established the conditions for social organization to take place in the countryside. The resistance of the oligarchy and the United Fruit Company, however, prevented the implementation of any changes in the highly concentrated pattern of landownership (2 percent of the population owned over 70 percent of the farm land). The landless mass of the population—mestizos and Indians—were forced to sell their labor power to maintain a precarious existence and were, therefore, at the mercy of the large landowners with ties to the coercive power of the state.

With the rise of the Cold War and the ideology of anticommunism as a driving force in American foreign policy during the Truman administration, the basis of Washington's policy toward Guatemala remained essentially economic, reflecting, above all, the enormous leverage exercised by United Fruit throughout the local economy, where its investments were valued at $60 million. Schlesinger and Kinzer provide a concise description of the company's reach:

> It functioned as a state within a state, owning Guatemala's telephone and telegraph facilities, administering its only important Atlantic harbor and monopolizing its banana exports. The company's subsidiary, the International Railways of Central America (IRCA), owned 887 miles of railroad track in Guatemala, nearly every mile in the country.[1]

The election of Colonel Jacobo Arbenz as president in 1950 accelerated the process of social and economic change in Guatemala initiated by his predecessor. The centerpiece of the Arbenz program was the agrarian reform law, which resulted in the expropriation of 1.5 million acres of uncultivated land belonging to approximately 100 plantations, including over 400,000 acres of United Fruit property—with compensation to be determined on the basis of 1952 tax declarations and paid in twenty-five year government bonds. By 1954, 100,000 families or approximately 500,000 individuals had received land, as well as access to bank credits and state technical assistance.[2] Arbenz further sought to end the dominance of United Fruit and other American companies in the public utilities and transportation sectors (docks, railways, highways, and electric power). The government also fostered the development of industrial and agricultural labor organizations, increased the minimum wage, and began to elaborate an independent foreign policy within regional and global political forums. Despite these efforts to reshape the Guatemalan society and economy, Arbenz did not seek to decisively challenge the capitalist mode of production. The goal of the agrarian reform, for instance, was not structural changes in the existing landholding pattern but increased efficiency and higher production levels on the plantations. Nonetheless, this comparatively modest challenge to American capital accumulation in Guatemala and concern over the possibility of a "revolution in the revolution" anchored in the newly mobilized workers and peasants led the Eisenhower administration to define the popular nationalism of Arbenz as a threat to U.S. regional hegemony and world stability.

U.S. policy-makers (including Secretary of State John Foster Dulles and CIA Director Allen Dulles, whose business and personal ties to United Fruit were longstanding) devised a multitrack strategy to destroy the Arbenz government and restore an optimal environment for capital accumulation and expansion. Washington placed an embargo on military assistance to Guatemala; economic and technical aid programs were withdrawn; an extensive media-propaganda campaign jointly financed by the U.S. government and United Fruit accused Arbenz of having permitted "international communism to gain a political base in the hemisphere"; and great pressure was exerted by the White House to mobilize regional support for its objective. High-ranking American officials characterized the expropriation of United Fruit lands as "discriminatory," denounced the compensation formula as unsatisfactory, and promised United Fruit executives that the restoration of the company's pre-Arbenz empire would be given the greatest priority under a new regime:

> At some point during the preparations for the invasion, a United Fruit official . . . met privately with Allen Dulles to discuss the status of United Fruit properties following Arbenz's downfall. Dulles promised that whoever was selected by the CIA as the next Guatemalan leader would not be allowed to nationalize or in any way disrupt the company's operations.[3]

Although the takeover of United Fruit lands and the proliferating labor and agricultural laws were instrumental factors in the August 1953 White House decision to overthrow Arbenz by military force, the destabilization policy was consistently rationalized in terms of the ideology of anticommunism and the need to respond to an "external threat" that might lead to Guatemala's withdrawal from the capitalist politico-economic orbit. Internal Truman administration memoranda expressing concern over the "ascending curve of Communist influence"[4] during the early months of the Arbenz presidency laid the basis for an evolving policy of diplomatic, political, and economic hostility toward the nationalist regime. By the time of the Eisenhower White House, Arbenz's "drift toward Communism" had become an established "fact" among Washington policy-makers. The notion that indigenous communist parties were agents of, or the transmission belts for, expansionist international communism was given explicit voice in relation to Guatemala in a draft paper prepared by the State Department in August 1953 for consideration by the National Security Council:

> In Guatemala Communism has achieved its strongest position in Latin America, and is now well advanced on a program which threatens impor-

tant American commercial enterprises in that country and may affect the stability of neighboring governments. Continuation of the present trend in Guatemala would ultimately endanger the unity of the Western Hemisphere against Soviet aggression, and the security of our strategic position in the Caribbean, including the Panama Canal.[5]

In October, Assistant Secretary of State for Inter-American Affairs John Moors Cabot castigated Arbenz for "openly playing the communist game" and declared that there could be no "positive cooperation" between the two countries.[6] Another high-level interdepartmental report on Guatemala (May 1953) decided that communist political influence was "far out of proportion to their small numerical strength," although it was clear that they lacked any influence within the key coercive institutions (army and police) of the state and had no ministerial representation.[7] Their influence centered largely around the leadership of some urban-based unions, the participation of individual party members in the administration of the agrarian reform, and the party's capacity to organize and mobilize popular support for the government's programs.

At the tenth Inter-American Conference of Foreign Ministers in Caracas in March 1954, the U.S. delegation led by Secretary of State Dulles steam-rolled through a declaration that "established anti-Communism as the principal criterion for legitimizing and delegitimizing governments and judging their hemispheric policies."[8] Shortly afterwards, the CIA received its "marching orders" from the White House and NSC, together with an estimated $20 million in funds, to plan and train an invasion force of Guatemalan exiles to overthrow the Arbenz regime. United Fruit and other American corporations with major economic investments in Guatemala were briefed on the project by senior administration officials on an ongoing basis until the ouster of Arbenz.

Washington's assessment of the Guatemalan situation was considered to have been confirmed by the country's decision to purchase a shipment of arms from Czechoslovakia in May 1954. This "discovery" provided a convenient pretext for unleashing Colonel Castillo Armas and his exiles training under CIA direction on a United Fruit plantation in Honduras. In early June, a senior State Department Middle America official wrote the U.S. Ambassador to Guatemala John Peurifoy: "There is 100 percent determination here, from the top down, to get rid of this stinker [Arbenz] and not stop until that is done."[9] Some days later, Secretary of State Dulles announced that Guatemala was in the grip of a "Communist-type reign of terror."[10] Before the end of June, Arbenz was overthrown, the social and economic experiment terminated, and a pro-United States, right-wing anticommunist regime installed in power.

Through the skillful use of anticommunist ideology, Truman and Eisenhower policy-makers were able to mobilize domestic support for a policy of antagonism toward Arbenz. In the process they were able to obliterate the fundamental conflict over property ownership and obscure an array of social and economic issues which created conflicts between the regime and foreign capital and provided the substantive basis for the actions leading to the downfall of the Arbenz government. As Walter LaFeber cogently points out, Washington's preoccupation with anticommunism in Guatemala, especially during 1953 and 1954, "overlook[ed] the previous seven years of growing confrontation that had centered on issues of private property and personnel for the Guatemalan agencies that exercised power over property."[11]

Anticommunism as a Legitimizing Mechanism

Anticommunism as a legitimizing mechanism has the virtue of obscuring the nature of Washington's principal allies, their methods of rule, and their policy objectives. Shielded under the vague rubric of anticommunism can be found the members of the death squads, military dictators, secret police torturers, and the like. The pursuit of anticommunist policies provides a cover for all the repressive activities as well as the massive corruption and pillage that have characterized arbitrary military rule. Washington's focus on the Communist-Anticommunist dichotomy has been central to the effort to redirect attention away from basic class and national dichotomies, thereby preventing any attempts by popularly based Third World governments to mobilize international support and solidarity. The emphasis on anticommunism also serves an important domestic function: It weakens the anti-interventionist impulse among the liberal U.S. public, thus neutralizing internal opposition to foreign policy initiatives and alliances with totalitarian client regimes. The period in Guatemala after 1954 provides us with an example of the way in which Washington used anticommunist ideology to mobilize U.S. public opinion to support its ties with successive dictatorial rulers by redefining issues in terms ("anticommunist" or "anti-subversive," instead of "economic/strategic") favorable to the creation of a bipartisan foreign policy. Moreover, the common use of anticommunism as a legitimizing mechanism by both liberals (such as Kennedy and Carter) and conservatives (like Eisenhower and Nixon) indicates that the issue of protecting the status quo in Guatemala through the aegis of the armed forces (the country's major anticommunist force) is the overriding priority for U.S. policy-makers.

Having utilized the ideology of anticommunism to justify the overthrow of Arbenz, American officials now wielded it to legitimate the rightist military regime of Colonel Carlos Castillo Armas (1954–1958). The regime terminated all efforts at social and economic reform, destroyed the newly organized workers and peasant unions, abolished the political party system, and initiated a period of repressive capitalist development "from above and outside," based on large-scale infusions of U.S. public and private capital. Castillo Armas cancelled the legal registration of 533 unions and revised the labor code to make future union organizing virtually impossible. Hundreds of labor leaders were murdered, and within a year union membership declined from 100,000 to 27,000.[12] In the political arena, Castillo Armas summarily disenfranchised the approximately 70 percent of the population who were illiterate. Meanwhile, the new regime moved quickly to recreate the conditions for optimal capital accumulation: almost all the labor legislation of the 1944–1954 period was abrogated; a new petroleum law eased restrictions on exploration by foreign companies and some of the largest U.S. oil multinationals received concession rights to begin operations; a pact negotiated directly with the military rulers restored to United Fruit all of the property expropriated by Arbenz; taxes on interest and dividends were abolished; efforts at agricultural and industrial diversification were terminated, and the traditional authority of the agro-commercial (principally coffee) oligarchy and United Fruit was restored. Under Castillo Armas, however, the period of economic growth came to an end and Guatemala experienced a reversion from balance of payments surpluses to substantial trade deficits. Nonetheless, the decisive factor shaping the Eisenhower administration response to the new regime was the reconstruction of the state and economy to serve the interests of private capital accumulation. U.S. economic assistance to Guatemala during the Castillo Armas presidency totalled $80 million, which contrasts sharply with the $600,000 authorized for the whole Arevalo-Arbenz period.[13]

The presidency of General Miguel Ydigoras Fuentes (1958–1963) witnessed no decisive break with the pro-United States policies of the previous military government. Domestically, however, Ydigoras Fuentes presided over a period of deepening class-economic inequalities and rural impoverishment in a context where there no longer existed political channels for social reform through elected leaders. Political closure and economic marginalization created the objective basis for the emergence of revolutionary politics in 1960, in the form of guerrilla movements led by U.S.-trained military officers hostile to the revival of traditional landlord dominance and to the expanded American economic and politico-military presence. These movements established a base of support precisely among those peasants and Indians most directly affected by the "rollback" of the social and agrarian reforms of the 1944–1954 period.

The rise of the guerrillas definitively resolved the tension inherent within the Alliance for Progress between the reformist anticommunist goals of the Kennedy administration and the right-wing conservative (military-oligarch) anticommunists embraced by Washington in the post-Arbenz era. The White House shifted all of its political and military support to the most reactionary elements in Guatemalan society in order to defeat the guerrilla challenge for state power. By this time, however, U.S. policy-makers were growing increasingly disenchanted with Ydigoras Fuentes' seeming incapacity to contain the guerrillas despite the fact that his regime continued to accommodate U.S. political and economic interests, and even allowed Guatemala to serve as a strategic base for American interventionary actions in the region (against Cuba in 1961, for example). His decision to allow Arevalo to return from exile and participate in the proposed December 1963 presidential elections was the last straw as far as both the country's military high command and the Kennedy White House were concerned. In March 1963, the army, supported and, indeed, encouraged by Washington, ousted Ydigoras Fuentes from office, cancelled the elections and installed former Defense Minister Colonel Enrique Peralta Azurdia as the new head of state. Peralta Azurdia immediately dissolved Congress, banned all political activities, and rigorously enforced the existing "state of seige" under which the country was already being governed.

Although the new military president was determined to prosecute the war against the guerrillas vigorously, his "nationalist" orientation soon created frictions with Washington over the scope of direct Pentagon involvement in the struggle. While he sought and accepted increased levels or U.S. military assistance, Peralta Azurdia opposed on-the-ground participation by American counterinsurgency experts in the war against the rural antagonists of the military state—contending that the Guatemalan armed forces were quite capable of defeating the guerrillas without foreign combat support. Meanwhile, this period featured a consolidation of the power of the Guatemalan military throughout the society, including the economic sphere, where it deepend its linkages to the oligarchy through large-scale property purchases. During the latter part of his rule, Peralta Azurdia moved to create the conditions for a revival of a limited form of electoral politics. A new constitution enacted in 1965 provided for restricted political party competition and laid the groundwork for the election of a "progressive" civilian Julio Cesar Mendez Montenegro as president in 1966. Paradoxically, however, the Mendez Montenegro government (1966–1970) was responsible for the disintegration of the progressive liberal political option in Guatemala, clearing the path for a period of violent military rule. A forced alliance between the ultra right-wing forces and the liberal elements represented by the new president, promoted by the United States with the cooperation of Mendez Montenegro, had devastating consequences for the mass of the Guatemalan populace.

Although the rightist military and oligarchy were wary of Mendez Montenegro's "liberalism" and doubted his capacity to eliminate the guerrilla threat, Washington believed he would be more likely than his predecessor to allow Pentagon counterinsurgency specialists to play battlefield roles in the anti-guerrilla struggle. American officials participated in discussions between the president-elect and the army high command that established the conditions under which Mendez Montenegro was allowed to take office.[14] The military would be allowed to prosecute the war without restrictions, the existing structure of command would be left intact, and the political left would be excluded from participation in the government. Mendez Montenegro's decision to foresake his liberal anticommunism under military-U.S. pressure, from the outset of his tenure in office, led directly to a period of wholesale massacres which had the practical effect of eliminating any differences between liberal and right-wing anticommunist forces in Guatemala.

During the Mendez Montenegro presidency (1966–1970), the U.S. military commitment to Guatemala expanded dramatically, not only in the form of direct assistance (equipment and supplies) and manpower (counterinsurgency experts), but also through a U.S. Office of Public Safety (OPS) program to instruct and arm the National Police—which increased in numbers from 3,000 to 11,000.[15] The OPS funding to Guatemala during this period constituted the second largest (after Brazil) program in Latin America. When the Guatemalan army launched its brutal "pacification" strategy in 1967 under the command of Colonel Carlos Arana Osorio in the Department of Zacapa, it was advised by U.S. military attaché Colonel John Webber and approximately 1,000 U.S. Green Beret Special Forces.[16] An estimated 15,000 individuals (mostly peasants) were killed in the Department of Zacapa alone over the next three years.[17] Complementing this officially sanctioned violence were even more brutal forms of repression perpetrated by extreme rightist organizations with the complicity of the regime. "With President Mendez's consent, and despite constitutional prohibitions," writes one authority, "private right-wing groups formed their own units to murder students, Indians, and labor leaders [even as the number of labor unions and rural cooperatives actually increased under Mendez Montenegro] suspected of sympathizing with the rebels."[18] More than twenty anticommunist "death squads," composed of off-duty police and retired military officers, proceeded to eliminate not only leftist and liberals but all those who in any way support programs of social change. A leading Christian Democratic official estimated that 6,000 political murders occurred during the "liberal" president's tenure.[19] The enormous amount of physical force applied by the state and its imperial sponsors partially destroyed a divided guerrilla movement, while the vigilante terrorism of the oligarchy-supported death squads created a more profound polarization in Guatemalan society.

In 1970, Colonel Carlos Arana Osario won the presidency due to a split among the liberal parties, which received a majority of the votes, and immediately launched a ferocious campaign of terror in an effort to eliminate permanently all segments of urban and rural opposition to military rule. Martial law was imposed and the right wing death squads and the security forces were literally given carte blanche to cut a swathe through the heterogeneous political antagonists of the Arana Osario presidency. Although as many as 1,000 people were murdered in the first three months of the regime, the Nixon administration looked favorably on Arana Osario's government as an important regional ally and showered it with military and economic aid. "During the height of one particularly bloody repression in 1971," according to an account of the period, "twenty-five officers and seven former U.S. policemen worked with the military."[20] In 1972, Washington dispatched $32.2 million in economic assistance, the second largest annual total ever provided the Central American country. Meanwhile, the authoritative *Amnesty International* reported that between 1970 and 1973 over 15,000 people were killed or "disappeared" by the regime.[21] The majority of the victims were peasants, but they also included large numbers of trade unionists, students, journalists, social democratic politicians, and representatives of various professional groups. The complicity of the Nixon-Ford administrations in this period of uncontrolled terror waged by the military state against its own population is attested to by the fact that between 1967 and 1976 almost all of Guatemala's foreign military assistance—$35 million worth—came from the United States.[22]

In 1974, General Kjell Laugerud, the preferred candidate of the military leadership, became president in one of the more fraudulent elections in contemporary Guatemalan history. The first two years of Laugerud's tenure saw a *relative* decline in the level of state-sponsored violence, the reinstitution of political activity, a growth in union membership from 28,000 in 1974 to approximately 80,000 in 1976 (still below the Arbenz period),[23] and the formation of rural cooperatives. In the urban centers, this controlled political "opening" led to a recomposition of the opposition forces and the emergence of a growing mass-based popular movement representing disparate political, social, and ideological forces. In the countryside, following the violent repression of the Arana Osorio period, guerrilla movements reemerged and began to concentrate on the development of labor and peasant unions. Land conflicts (the numbers of landless or near landless peasants had reached enormous proportions) and the government terrorism of the preceding years had fostered an increased militancy among the Indians and peasants and the development of linkages with the guerrillas, especially in the northern province of Quiche. The radicalization of these highland Indian communities, the growth of a broad-based urban opposition, and the renewed effectiveness of the guerrillas forced Laugerud to resort to a policy of selective assassination, beginning in 1977, to eliminate the leadership of this burgeoning opposition to military rule and repression.

The response of the Carter administration was to attempt to influence changes in the method of Laugerud's rulership that did not threaten any serious rupture in bilateral relations. While careful not to risk actions that might endanger the large U.S. economic stake in Guatemala, the Carter White House applied some pressures, primarily in the form of a cutback in military credits, to force the regime to modify the scope of its repressive policies: to be more selective in their application and to combine state control with limited social reforms. The refusal of the clientist ruling class to modify the more extreme features of its policy of terror created friction between Washington and Guatemala City and resulted in the suspension of military assistance, although previously authorized weaponry and funds continued to flow until 1980 and the flow of economic assistance was not disrupted.

Carter's effort to elaborate an anticommunist foreign policy "with a human face," like Kennedy's earlier attempt to combine counterinsurgency warfare with reformist anticommunist regimes, ultimately foundered on the existence of a hegemonic anticommunist ruling class in Guatemala opposed to any kind of social and economic change and, therefore, to the type of heterogeneous political coalition that Washington viewed as the basis for instituting reforms. In both instances, the White House sought to separate and disassociate liberal anticommunism from right-wing anticommunism in Guatamala, but its capacity to pursue this type of policy was obstructed by the military-oligarchy forces which controlled the state and by Washington's (liberal and conservative) first priority: sustaining the capitalist state against a rising guerrilla challenge.

The fraudulent election of General Romeo Lucas Garcia in 1978 signaled the total collapse of the reformist anticommunist option pursued by the Carter foreign policy-makers. Lucas Garcia instituted a reign of terror that matched the worst excesses of the earlier 1970s. Between 1979 and mid-1980, over 3,000 unarmed civilians were slaughtered by the army and the death squads, including peasants, labor organizers, religious workers and priests, lawyers, teachers, and journalists.[24] During the subsequent ten months, 76 leaders of the Christian Democratic Party and 10 officials of the Social Democratic United Revolutionary Front were murdered.[25] Meanwhile, army massacres of entire Indian villages was a not uncommon occurrence. By early 1981, "killings of people in opinion-making positions [had] decimated university faculties, student groups, moderate and left-of-center political organizations, rural cooperatives, newspaper and radio staffs, peasant leagues, unions and churches."[26] At this time, *Amnesty International* released a detailed report on Guatemala documenting in great detail the military government's role as the *only* author and practitioner of the "official" and "unofficial" terror: ". . . the selection of targets for detention and murder, and *the deployment of official forces for extra-legal operations*, can be pinpointed to secret offices in an annex of Guatemala's National Palace, under the direct control of the president of the Republic."[27]

With the advent of the Reagan presidency, the tension evident in the U.S. imperial state at certain historical moments between promoting the interests of liberal anticommunism as opposed to alignment with right-wing anticommunist regimes was unambiguously resolved as the new group of Washington policy-makers sought immediately to provide legitimacy for the Lucia Garcia regime. "It is very important to our interests in the region to re-establish relations with the Government of Guatemala," remarked a senior State Department official at the beginning of Reagan's tenure, "and we are actively pursuing ways in which to do so."[28] In May 1981, Secretary of State Haig's special emissary, General Vernon Walters, visited Guatemala, where he dismissed human rights criticisms as without foundation and expressed U.S. support for the military's efforts to defend "the constitutional institutions of this country against the ideologies that want to finish off those institutions."[29]

Emboldened by this public display of Washington's support, the repression continued apace, reaching its zenith in 1982, when the army, security forces, national police, intelligence services, and death squads working in concert or individually perpetrated several hundred documented massacres.[30] This terror "offensive" was conducted largely under the auspices of General Efrian Rios Montt, who succeeded Lucas Garcia as president following an internal military coup in March 1982. In early April, he approved a secret army plan for a major escalation of the counterinsurgency war in the countryside that "focused upon eliminating the insurgent's popular base by massacring whole communities of suspected sympathizers. . . ."[31] Indiscriminate and generalized murder became the order of the day in the months that followed. Military and paramilitary forces engaged in random executions, selective assassinations of community leaders, and massacres of whole indigenous villages suspected of guerrilla sympathies.[32] Between March and September, almost 8,000 noncombatants were killed, "disappeared," or made victims of collective holocausts.[33] Rios Montt's scorched earth policy against peasant and Indian villages was largely responsible for the flight of more than 100,000 Guatemalan refugees that have entered Mexico since January 1981, and for the situation of another one million displaced persons who remain in the country as internal refugees or in forced relocation centers ("concentration camps").[34]

Within the Reagan anticommunist Cold War schema, Rios Montt was a valued regional client. The Guatemalan military's war of annihilation, especially in the countryside, was of limited concern to Washington when contrasted with the regime's pro-capitalist orientation, its acceptance of the Reaganites' bipolar view of the world, and the nature of the local political antagonists—a guerrilla movement with a growing popular constituency. The Reagan White House exploited loopholes in Congressional restrictions on military aid to Guatemala, directly and indirectly, to bolster the firepower of the armed forces.[35] Wishing to facilitate U.S. corporate arms sales, it reclassified such items as jeeps and trucks as nonmilitary forms of assistance in order to circumvent the letter of the Foreign Assistance Act. Between December 1980 and December 1982, Bell Helicopter Company, acting under a license authorized by the White House and issued by the Commerce Department, sold Guatemala $25 million worth of civilian helicopters that were subsequently used for military purposes.[36] In January 1983, the Reagan administration formally approved export licenses for the sale of $6.3 million worth of helicopter parts. A similar determination to continue economic assistance to the Guatemalan rulers was exhibited. In October 1982, the White House declared that the United States would no longer vote against multilateral development bank loans to Guatemala on human rights grounds because, according to State Department officials, human rights in the Central American country had actually improved under Rios Montt![37] Reagan concluded a trip to Guatemala in December with a ringing declaration of support for Rios Montt, whom he described as "totally dedicated to democracy in Guatemala" and the object of "a bum rap" in regard to accusations of widespread human rights violations committed during his presidency.[38]

Defense Minister General Oscar Humberto Mejia Victores, who replaced Rios Montt in August 1983 following another army coup, has continued, although with not the same high level of intensity, the brutal policies of his predecessor. During the first four months of his rule, killings and disappearances of regime opponents were also accompanied by a massive program of arbitrary arrests that affected more than 7,000 persons in Guatemala City alone. The change in military leadership had no effect on Washington's policy and Reagan's efforts to increase the still relatively limited flow of economic and military assistance to Guatemala, even though Congress continues with some success to obstruct administration objectives. U.S. representatives in the international banks, for instance, have vigorously supported Guatemalan loan requests since the October 1982 policy shift. In September 1983, they voted in favor of loans to their right-wing anticommunist allies totaling $70.5 million.[39] The Reagan desire to normalize military and security ties was writ large in administration fiscal year 1984 security assistance proposals, which included a request for $10 million in foreign military sales credits and loan repayment guarantees for Guatemala. In February 1984, the White House lifted a two-month freeze on the sale of $2 million worth of helicopter parts, ostensibly imposed to pressure the Mejia Victores regime to improve its human rights performance, even though more than 800 persons were reported assassinated or "disappeared" during the first three months of the year.[40]

Conclusion

U.S. policy-makers bear direct responsibility for the ascent to political power of the Guatemalan military in 1954, and the policies of successive Republican and Democratic administrations have been instrumental in the armed forces' calculated escalation of military control and state-authored repression over three decades. Presidents from Truman to Reagan have opposed progressive democratic governments and movements in Guatemala. At the same time, they have lavishly financed and supported the right-wing military and military-controlled regimes receptive to U.S. corporate interests and prepared to align themselves with Washington's regional and global objectives. U.S. direct private investment in Guatemala rose from $131 million in 1960 to $186 million in 1970 to $260 million in 1980—the largest U.S. multinational commitment in Central America.[41] The ideology of anticommunism has been utilized by Washington policy-makers, time and again, to justify opposition to agrarian reform, organized worker-peasant movements, and nationalist development projects, and to legitimate the repressive policies pursued by rightist military rulers and their outcomes. Democratic and social reform programs based on parliamentary politics have been reversed, and all avenues of political expression and opposition have been blocked through the use of force and violence. Growth through national development benefitting the mass of the population has been exchanged for growth through exploitation based on state terror financed and supported by Washington, with consequent enrichment of the military-oligarchy ruling class and impoverishment of the country's landless masses.

The social consequences of U.S.-financed and supported military rule in Guatemala since 1954 have been profound: a concentration of land ownership and wealth in the hands of the army, oligarchy, and U.S. corporations; a decline in virtually every area of social welfare—education, public health, drinkable water, and access to electricity; widespread malnutrition and low life expectancy levels in rural areas; a persistent and serious infant mortality problem (35 percent of children nationwide and up to 60 percent in rural Guatemala die before the age of five); massive illiteracy; extensive unemployment and underemployment; the growth of urban slums; and a decline in the minimum wage to below the level of the Arbenz period (the purchasing power of the urban workers fell by one third between 1970 and 1980 alone).[42] Between 1950 and 1978, the share of national income obtained by the poorest 50 percent of the population declined from 9 percent to 7 percent while the top 5 percent of the population increased its share from 48 percent to 59 percent.[43]

Since the U.S.-orchestrated destabilization and overthrow of the reformist Arbenz government in 1954, every Guatemalan regime has engaged in large-scale extrajudicial execution of noncombatant civilians. In December 1983, *Amnesty International*, which has closely monitored the human rights situation in Guatemala since the early 1970s, issued a report that concluded on the following note:

> Under successive administrations, the regular security and military forces in Guatemala—as well as paramilitary groups acting under government order or with official complicity—have been responsible for massive instances of human rights violations, including "disappearances" and extrajudicial execution, directed at people from all sectors of Guatemalan society [Indians, peasants, teachers, students, trade union leaders, health services personnel, journalists, other professional groups, etc.] although there have been fluctuations in the volume of killings and "disappearances," the policies and structures responsible for these violations have remained virtually the same.[44]

In the three decades since democratic rule in Guatemala, the institutionalized terror of the rightist anticommunist regimes supported by conservative and liberal Washington administrations has claimed over 100,000 victims.

Anticommunist ideology in both its liberal and conservative guises has been the key mechanism destabilizing the emergence of independent political forces and legitimizing a succession of repressive military rulers in Guatemala for more than three decades. The notion has functioned to undermine the class analysis of class conflict and substitute fictitious world-system ideological conflicts. Every administration from Eisenhower to Reagan has employed it to mobilize domestic support for these totalitarian regimes that have shown themselves willing to accommodate U.S. economic, political, and strategic objectives throughout the Central American-Caribbean region. Moreover, anticommunist ideology has served to empty the language of Western democracy of all of its cognitive meanings: anticommunist terror and massacres have been continually associated with the defense of free institutions. Clearly, no return to a democratic foreign policy in the United States and elsewhere in the capitalist world is possible without a rejection of the ideology of anticommunism and the policies associated with it.

Notes

1. Stephen Schlesinger and Stephen Kinzer, *Bitter Fruit: The Untold Story of the American Coup in Guatemala* (New York: Doubleday, 1982), 12.

2. See Richard M. Immerman, *The CIA in Guatemala: The Foreign Policy of Intervention* (Austin: University of Texas Press, 1982), 66; Walter LaFeber, *Inevitable Revolutions: The United States in Central America* (New York: W. W. Norton, 1983), 116.

3. Schlesinger and Kinzer, op. cit., 120.

4. Quoted in LaFeber, op. cit., 114.

5. Draft policy paper prepared in the Bureau of Inter-American Affairs, Top Secret, "NSC Guatemala," Aug. 19, 1953, in U.S. Department of State, *Foreign Relations of the United States, 1952–1954, vol. 4, The American Republics* (Washington, D.C.: U.S. Government Printing Office, 1983), 1074.

6. Quoted in Schlesinger and Kinzer, op. cit., 135.

7. National intelligence estimate, Secret, "Probable Developments in Guatemala," May 19, 1953, in *Foreign Relations of the United States, 1952–1954*, op. cit., 1061. On the limited influence of the Communists within the state and governing regime, see Schlesinger and Kinzer, op. cit., 58–61; Cole Blasier, *The Hovering Giant: U.S. Responses to Revolutionary Changes in Latin America* (Pittsburgh: University of Pittsburgh Press, 1976), 227.

8. James Petras et al., "The Monroe Doctrine and U.S. Hegemony in Latin America," in James Petras, ed., *Latin America: From Dependence to Revolution* (New York: John Wiley & Sons, 1973), 257.

9. Quoted in Immerman, op. cit., 157–58.

10. Quoted in Schlesinger and Kinzer, op. cit., 11.

11. LaFeber, op. cit., 119.

12. See Schlesinger and Kinzer, op. cit., 219.

13. See ibid., 232–33.

14. See Suzanne Jonas and David Tobis, eds., *Guatemala* (Berkeley: North American Congress on Latin America, August 1974), 105.

15. See Schlesinger and Kinzer, op. cit., 247.

16. See LaFeber, op. cit., 169.

17. See Thomas P. Anderson, *Politics in Central America* (New York: Praeger Publishers, 1983), 26.

18. LaFeber, op. cit., 170.

19. See Thomas Melville and Marjorie Melville, *Guatemala: The Politics of Land Ownership* (New York: Free Press, 1971), 247–48.

20. LaFeber, op. cit., 257.

21. See Jenny Pearce, *Under the Eagle: U.S. Intervention in Central America and the Caribbean* (Boston: South End Press, 1982), 71.

22. See LaFeber, op. cit., 257.

23. See Anderson, op. cit., 29.

24. See LaFeber, op. cit., 260; Lars Schoultz, *Human Rights and United States Policy Toward Latin America* (Princeton: Princeton University Press, 1981), 352–54.

25. See Warren Hodge, "Repression Increases in Guatemala As U.S. Is Seeking To Improve Ties," *New York Times*, May 3, 1981, 3.

26. Ibid., 3.

27. "Guatemala: A Government Program of Political Murder—The Amnesty Report (Extracts)," *The New York Review of Books*, Mar. 19, 1981, 38.

28. Quoted in Hodge, op. cit., 3.

29. Quoted in Christopher Dickey, "Haig's Emissary, in Guatemala, Discounts Charges of Rights Abuse," *Washington Post*, May 14, 1981, A1.

30. See Richard Alan White, *The Morass: United States Intervention in Central America* (New York: Harper & Row, 1984), 104.

31. Ibid., 97.

32. See ibid., 100–101.

33. See Comite Pro Justicia Y Paz de Guatemala, *Human Rights in Guatemala,* Feb. 1983, 21.

34. See David B. Lawrenz, "Rearming the Guatemalan Military: 'Reagan Refugees' for Mexico and the U.S.," *COHA Memorandum* (Washington, D.C.: Council on Hemispheric Affairs, Feb. 13, 1984), "Refugees are everywhere," *Central America Report* (Guatemala City), vol. 11, no. 6 (Feb. 10, 1984): 42–43; United Nations, General Assembly, Report of the Economic and Social Council, *Situation of Human Rights in Guatemala,* 38th Sess. Agenda Item 12, A/38/485, Nov. 4, 1983, 32–34.

35. See Richard J. Meislin, "U.S. Military Aid for Guatemala Continuing Despite Official Curbs," *New York Times,* Dec. 19, 1982, 1, 18; Bruce P. Cameron and Christopher D. Ringwald, *Aid to Guatemala: Violating Human Rights* (Washington, D.C.: Center for International Policy, May 1983), 6 pp.

36. See Christopher Dickey, "Guatemala Uses U.S. "Civilian" Copters in Warfare," *Washington Post,* Jan. 23, 1982, A1, A11.

37. See Raymond Bonner, "U.S. Now Backing Guatemala Loans," *New York Times,* Oct. 10, 1982, 17. Also see Jim Morrell and William Jesse Biddle, *Central America: The Financial War* (Washington, D.C.: Center for International Policy, Mar. 1983), 6–7.

38. Quoted in Steven R. Weisman, "Reagan Denounces Threats to Peace in Latin America," *New York Times,* Dec. 5, 1982, 1.

39. See *MesoAmerica* (San Jose, Costa Rica: Institute for Central America Studies) 3, no. 5 (May 1984): 2.

40. See, for example, "Government Sanguine about Violence Problem," *Central America Report* (Guatemala City) 11, no. 7, (Feb. 17, 1984): 51–52.

41. See "Garrison Guatemala," Special issue of *NACLA, [North American Congress on Latin America] Report on the Americas,* 17, no. 1 (January-February 1983): 12.

42. See Washington Office on Latin America, "Guatemala: The Roots of Revolution," *Special Update* (Washington, D.C., Feb. 1983), 2–6; LaFeber, op. cit., 167–168, 259; Schlesinger and Kinzer, op. cit., 253–54.

43. See Washington Office on Latin America, op. cit., 2.

44. Amnesty International, *Guatemala Update: Amnesty International Human Rights Concerns in Guatemala Since the August 1983 Coup Which Brought General Oscar Humberto Mejia Victores to Power,* London, Dec. 23, 1983, 1.

8 / *Conclusion: Authoritarianism, Democracy, and the Transition to Socialism*

JAMES PETRAS

In contemporary political discourse, the real class constraints and historical issues that impinge on the relationship between democracy, authoritarianism, and socialism are frequently obscured through a lack of understanding of the historical process. (A detailed examination of the causes of this confusion is beyond the scope of the present work.) In looking at the relationship between democracy and socialism, it is necessary to proceed in terms of the specific problems and issues it poses in different historical moments and in different locations in the world economy. The construction of a general theory relating democracy to socialism divorced from specific world historical context leads to the enumeration of a set of abstract, idealized norms, which fail to provide any guide or meaning to complex and changing politico-economic realities.

This chapter will consider the issue of socialism and democracy in two contexts: the Third World and the Socialist bloc. (The problems of democracy and socialism posed in the industrialized West revolve around a different set of issues, which are less relevant to Latin American conditions.) In considering the Third World, two types of historical experience will be discussed: (a) the relevance of democratic socialism in the transition from authoritarian-military to democratic regimes; and (b) the relevance of authoritarian and democratic practices in the transition to socialism. The discussion of the Socialist bloc will examine reform strategies that offer alternatives to the dilemmas of bureaucratic centralism and will focus on the emergence of neoliberal market and technocratic alternatives to democratic socialism.

The discussion of the relationship between democracy and socialism is not only of academic interest but has important practical consequences in shaping struggles, movements, and societies in the coming period. My choice of topics reflects a concern with major contemporary developments and their possible future direction. A number of Third World countries are of particular interest—especially several in Latin America that are in the process of "redemocratizing": moving from authoritarian military dictatorship to democracy. For these countries, the relationship of democracy to socialism is a central issue, yet discussion has heretofore focused on other dichotomies: between democracy and dictatorships, civilian and military regimes, human rights abuses and civil rights, creditors and debtors. All the issues implied by these dichotomies are important and indeed have immense bearing on the democratic transition. But the larger socioeconomic context within which the transition to democracy is acted out and, more fundamentally, the political-economic order and conditions within which democracy can be consolidated need to be considered. Part of the fault lies in the new modes of liberal-socialist theorizing that have developed in the West: the priority given to political and legal structures over economic; the redefinition of the state as an arena for struggle by a multiplicity of competing class interests (apart from its Marxist vocabulary, a perspective similar to the liberal group conflict theory of the 1950s); and state permeationism as a dominant perspective of the state autonomists. The end result of this approach is to accept a narrow-scope conception of political action: the parameters and continuities of social action are given by the terms under which the military-civilian negotiated transition to democracy is executed. The method involves abstracting political structures from class relations and immediate political decisions from the controlling socioeconomic formation, the fragmentation of class action into its sectoral components, and the inflation of the parliamentary regime into an overarching reality that obscures the soicioeconomic underpinnings that sustain or undermine it.

The second topic chosen for discussion reflects the process of transition to socialism as it has been and is being attempted in Chile, Jamaica, and Nicaragua. Two sets of positions are rejected: the first sees the transition to socialism as an immediate extension and deepening of all democratic freedoms to all social actors; while the second sees the transition to socialism as a period of prolonged one-party revolutionary rulership involving democracy of a "new kind"—usually a sort of nondemocratic form of representation through state-aligned mass organizations. We reject both perspectives: for failing to specify the context and boundaries, conjuncture and political actors, within which democratic and authoritarian practices take place, and the relationship between them. More specifically, our perspective criticizes the proponents of democracy everywhere and always, for failing to develop a security policy—for failing to specify the appropriate political, military, and social policies capable of sustaining the social regime against its enemies. (Indeed the criticism can be extended to include a failure to recognize the nature and scope of the opposition and the consequences of its actions). With regard to the proponents of popular democracy, the issue of democracy is subsumed within a national-security metaphysic: the exceptional circumstances involving direct threats are extended, the number of enemies are constantly enlarged, and the emergencies become norms; democracy is deemed a luxury, impugned as a lower form of political organization, or redefined to include authoritarian centralized rulership. My contention is that specified boundaries for authoritarian practice are necessary accompaniments to the transition to socialism—just as democratic practice must create an adequate political-defensive framework before and during the process of socioeconomic transformation.

The third choice of topics reflects the major changes occuring in the socialist bloc countries and attempts to interpret the meaning of those processes using two distinct concepts: *liberalization* and *democratization*. The former describes what is the ascendant tendency within the reform movements—the implementation of changes increasing the scope of the market, the role of technocrats, and the margin for socioeconomic inequalities. The contrast between liberalization and democratization is central to understanding certain Communist countries' increasing integration into the world market and the limits of change from the point of view of democratic socialism. The growth of democratic trends within the socialist bloc is perceptible, incremental, and reversible. To the degree that liberalization both increases political space and social inequality, it creates a contradictory future in which the deepening of the democratization process could become a defining issue.

From Authoritarianism to Democracy: The Relevance of Democratic Socialism

The basic problem in the transition from an authoritarian regime to democratic rule is that the situation contains built-in constraints that severely strain the capacity of the newly elected regime to consolidate the new political institutions, leading to a new round of popular mobilization and the recurring phenomena of military authoritarianism.

Reaching agreement with the military and their U.S. backers (private and public officials), democratic politicians uphold the continuity of (1) the senior military officer corps—its schools, programs, and recruitment procedures; (2) the payment of the external debt; (3) and the existing distribution of wealth, property, and taxation. In this context "economic recovery" impels the democratic regime to extract surplus from the lower class, seek new foreign loans to finance current payments, and limit fiscal and structural reforms to a minimum. The result of the "democracy of compromise" between the right-wing authoritarian military and the liberal democratic forces is a democracy whose *socioeconomic content reflects the continuities with the previous regime.* The liberal democratic government acts as a funnel for overseas bankers. It remains a *component* within an authoritarian state structure and a broker between different competing "interest groups" (trade union officials, grain exporters, farmers, industrialists, and so on). The democratic regime's commitments to the bankers and state structures, which preclude it from providing substantial and tangible measures to meet the claims of its mass electorate, thus lead to alienation and increasing conflict. The cumulative effects of popular disaffection may cause the regime to increase the role of the military and police in the political system.

Several popularly elected regimes in Latin America illustrate the dilemmas of the liberal version of "redemocratization." Before these liberal governments assumed power, their predecessors, the U.S.-backed military regimes, were in deep crisis. Between 1975 and 1984, the gross external debt had increased by 300 percent; interests and profits had increased by 566 percent; the per capita GDP was a negative 2.2 percent per year in 1981–1984. Inflation sky-rocketed from 50 percent per year in 1976–1981 to 175 percent in 1984. As capital flows declined and interest and profit repatriation increased, net outflow from Latin America reached $23 billion.* In most countries, real income declined precipitously, from 20 to 50 percent over the decade. The military and its Washington backers had bequeathed to the democratic regimes highly polarized societies with deteriorating economies and standards of living, which were at the same time squeezed by debt. The massive capital outflows necessitated new financing and the entrance of the International Monetary Fund, with its class-selective "austerity measures" that necessitated shifting the burden of recovery onto wage and salaried earners, social programs, public owned enterprises, and the local market. The combined impact of producing large export surpluses and the continual drain of debt payments led to massive civilian popular protests throughout Latin America. The military and their U.S. backers were totally discredited. Lacking support from any significant political sector, they turned toward negotiating with civilian politicians. The eventual return to electoral systems was, however, based on the agreement by the incoming civilian regimes to honor their debt payments, to preserve military prerogatives, and to exclude radicals from power. The

---

*These dollar figures are expressed in 1970 prices and are taken from "Preliminary Overview of the Latin American Economy During 1984," *CEPAL* (Economic Commission on Latin America: Santiago 1985).

cases of two of the earliest countries in the region to democratize is instructive regarding the disastrous consequences of these compromises.

In 1981, when Fernando Belaunde became president of Peru, he immediately acceded to meeting its financial obligations while increasing military spending to accommodate the outgoing military. In addition, a program of economic liberalization (ending import and price controls, freezing wages, cutting state investment in productive activity) was adopted, in line with prescriptions emanating from Washington. These policies have produced the worst socioeconomic crises of the century. GDP fell by 11 percent in 1983 and per capita income by 13.3 percent between 1981 and 1984. Manufacturing output declined by 20 percent during the first three years of the liberal-democratic regime while unemployment and underemployment reached an unprecedented 63 percent of the economically active population. The social polarities and increasing misery resulting from "real existing liberalism" had several political consequences. First, the Sendero Luminoso ("shining path") guerrilla group gained considerable support throughout the highland interior. Secondly, the military was summoned by the Belaunde regime to repress it, resulting in the worst human rights abuses in decades (4,000 civilians killed, jailed, or "disappeared"). Thirdly, the government party liberal democrats plunged to fourth position in the recent elections, receiving about 7 percent of the vote, while the combined social democratic (46 percent) and left-socialist (21 percent) vote accounts for over two thirds of the electorate. The Peruvian experience demonstrates the inefficiency of "liberal realism," which attempts to consolidate democracy primarily through meeting the claims of the banks and the military. The recently elected social democratic APRA president, Alan Garcia, in his first pronouncements acknowledged as much when he stated that Peruvian development and reconstruction could not begin without some sort of moratorium on debt payments. There remain serious doubts, however, as to whether Garcia and the APRA regime will have the political will to follow up the presidential rhetoric with concrete measures.

The transition from military to democratic politics in Bolivia has followed a similar pattern. The democratic regime of Siles Suazo (which included liberals, social democrats, and pro-Moscow Communists) initially attempted to follow IMF prescriptions, pay past debts, and preserve military perquisites. The consequences were equally catastrophic. Per capita income fell by 25 percent between 1981 and 1984; inflation soared to 3,000 percent by 1985; while annual interest payments soared to $400 million—an amount that, if invested in Bolivia, would stimulate income, jobs, and productivity. The political consequences were massive general strikes by labor and the peasants, leading to the temporary suspension of debt payments and the increasing reliance of Siles on the military to retain political control. The political environment created by the liberal regime's policies have been propitious to the growth of new military intrigues, and a new round of military coups is likely.

The situation of the more recently elected Radical Party Government of Raul Alfonsin in Argentina is instructive concerning the pitfalls of "negotiated democracies." While Alfonsin initially talked of a 20 percent budget cut in the military, a recent study cites a continued arms build-up. As part of their "political realism," the Radicals (liberal-democratic party) attempted to avoid confronting the military establishment's role in the mass torture and disappearances by handing the investigation over to the military itself! The vehemence of the popular outcry over the military tribunal's predictable exoneration of all military officials forced Alfonsin to accept a new civilian tribunal. As the tribunal proceeds and accusations mount, the military has returned to conspiratorial plots against the regime. As the liberal regime answers to its democratic constituency, the conditions agreed to with the military unwind; to the degree that the Alfonsin government fails to heed the democratic electorate in pursuit of its agreements with the bankers and military, it increases the level of discontent. This is clearly evident in the area of economic policy. Alfonsin promised increases in income for wage and salaried groups to permit them to recover the levels of the mid-1970s. These promises, however, are not compatible with his agreement with the IMF, which requires huge export surpluses to service the foreign debt. As long as Argentina's liberal-democratic regime abides by its agreements with the international bankers, the external debt will consume 50 percent of export earnings and 6 to 8 percent of the GDP. The real decline in wages under Alfonsin has already provoked several major labor conflicts and more trouble is in store. Between the bankers and the military on the one side and the human rights, labor, and salaried groups on the other, the negotiated electoral change secured by liberal democracy is in tight straits.

Let there be no misunderstanding: redemocratization is clearly a desirable outcome. The problem is not democracy in the abstract, but the particular commitments and policies that specific politicians have undertaken in the process of assuming government and ruling. Experience has made it plain that commitments to meet the obligations of overseas bankers are not compatible with fulfilling the social claims of labor and the promises to business of economic recovery. In addition, the continuity of the military institutional structure and high military spending is a constant constraint on the implementation of any consequential policies aimed at redistribution of wealth.

Reallocating income to revitalize and modernize local productive facilities and to promote the recovery of labor's standard of living requires a new framework for politics—one that recognizes the indivisible linkage between political and legal change and the institutional and structural transformations needed to sustain popular electoral support for durable democratic institutions. Long-term legitimacy of the elected regime is derived from a moratorium on foreign debt payments, first, because the debt was contracted by a regime that seized and maintained power illegally. Assuming the debts of the illegitimate regime supports a degree of continuity and proximity that weakens the belief of the electorate in the authenticity of the democratic change. Moreover, the legitimacy of the regime is ultimately based on its effectiveness in reversing the patterns of economic relations: reallocating resources toward the domestic economy and away from the overseas bankers. The persistence of the previous pattern of outflow of payments can only lead to the erosion of the democratic regime: the political change will be seen as so much effluvia amidst the continual economic bloodletting.

The inability to consolidate democracy is linked to a "stage theory" of democracy: out of an initial "liberal democratic" stage, led and controlled by moderate forces, a true "democracy" will evolve, one that is capable of implementing socioeconomic policies to deal with fundamental problems and establishing social justice. This approach overlooks the fact that the liberal compromise is self-perpetuating. The links between the liberals and the military and between liberals and the bankers, as well as the liberals' own interest in continuing in office as "brokers" among diverse interests, determine future options of the regime and set the stage for a repetition of the authoritarian democratic cycle.

In all the newly democratizing nations, there exists a vast mass movement opposed to the existing military regimes and to the policies of the banks and the IMF. While there are important socioeconomic differences among the opposition, the great majority, particularly wage and salaried workers and employees and small business people, are in favor of shifting resources from overseas payments and military salaries and procurement to investment in locally owned productive facilities, social services, and local consumption. These social forces and their interests coincide with the pragmatic position of the region's socialist movements. The strength of the socialist forces varies from country to country. In Bolivia, for example, the labor movement is second to the military in effective power. In Peru, the left (United Left Coalition) is the second electoral force in the country. In Argentina, the situation is much more complex, as the major political opposition to the government is the Peronist movement, which retains many characteristics of authoritarian right-wing leadership. Thus, while socialist movements are better situated than current liberal regimes to carry out systematic reforms, they still confront the formidable enmity of the military, divisive internal rivalries, and, in the case of Argentina, a meager presence in a labor movement still controlled by "populist" labor bosses. Nevertheless, socialists and labor have, in some instances, been successful in pressuring liberal regimes to limit debt payments, even if none of the regimes until now has followed the socialist lead in declaring a moratorium on such payments. Even outside of government, the socialist presence has modified the conditions under which the original liberal-military transition to democracy was effected.

The formidable obstacles faced in attempting the transition from authoritarian government to genuine democracy suggest the relevance of socialism: in order to consolidate democracy and shatter the alternating democratic/authoritarian cycle, a series of measures that go beyond liberal reform politics are essential. Those measures are embodied in a democratic-socialist perspective that urges the dismantling of the authoritarian military apparatus and the reallocation of resources from international banks to the local economy.

Authoritarianism, Democracy, and the Transition to Socialism

The issue of democracy cannot be—and historically has not been—discussed independently of political and social context. Eighteenth-century democratic revolutionaries, as well as nineteenth and twentieth-century anticolonial revolutionaries, liberal democrats, and contemporary socialists have at one time or another supported varying degrees of democracy or authoritarianism according to the political context. While some writers have espoused the notion of supporting democracy everywhere and at all times, in practice this has proved to be an untenable position, leaving the way open to a number of unsatisfactory solutions that include: (1) proclaiming the principle of democracy and divorcing it from practice, (2) redefining democracy to include authoritarian practice, (3) invoking vague juridical formulas to cover immediate ad hoc expediencies and then revoking them when the situation becomes manageable, or (4) specifying a set of contextual circumstances in which democratic freedoms can be suspended for a specific time frame for particular transcendent political reasons. It is sheer demagoguery simply to wave the flag of democracy in every point and place in history—particularly in periods of large-scale, long-term changes from one social system to another. On the other hand, it is a perversion of democratic sensibility to make a virtue of historical necessities, to extend and institutionalize authoritarian practices beyond the particular context in which they were evoked and to claim that the new autocratic polity represents a higher form of political governance.

In discussing the relationship between democracy and the transition to socialism it is essential to distinguish three separate but interrelated phases of the process: establishing the *foundation* of the new social system; initiating the process of *institution-building;* and creating the sources of *participation* and legitimation. Each of these is integral to democratic development and must occur in its appropriate time: premature extension or delayed implementation of democracy can have equally disastrous results. For example, the exploitation by the opposition of democratic institutions led to military intervention and U.S. destabilization of the Allende government, preventing it from laying the foundations for a socialist transition. A not too dissimilar process occurred earlier in Guyana and later in Jamaica. On the other hand, the failure to promote democratic institutions subsequent to the foundation period has adversely affected democratic development among many of the Communist bloc countries.

The two strands of socialist transition—the libertarian and authoritarian—and the problems that they embody can best be observed in the experiences of Chile under Allende and Jamaica under Manley, on the one hand, and Cuba under Castro on the other.

In the case of Chile and Jamaica, major efforts were made to redistribute land, income, and political power through extensive nationalization and expropriation of plantations, mines, and industrial enterprises. New mass popular organizations were created and with varying degrees of effectiveness began to play an active role in making decisions affecting the workplace and community. In the international sphere, both regimes turned toward the nonaligned movement, took an active role in the struggle against imperialism, and led efforts to secure a new international economic order providing more equitable relations between industrialized and Third World countries. These structural changes at the national level and the international realignments, however, took place within a shell of institutional forces and arrangements that were fundamentally opposed to them. In both countries, the police and security forces were subject to imperial influence and funding; democratic officers and conscripts were purged or retired (in Chile the socialists participated in these forced retirements in order to pacify the right) providing the right wing with dominant control over the state apparatus. Most senior civil service bureaucrats retained their ties with their previous patrons among the foreign and domestic rich, blocking effective implementation of programs. Capitalists, bankers, and merchants, protected by the state apparatus, sent money abroad illegally, hoarded, sold on the black market, organized thugs to attack civilians—in short, violated the law with impunity—with the benign tolerance of the class-biased state. Parliamentarians and party opponents violated custom and reason by blocking any legislation permitting the basic operation of the legal system. With violence and conflict mounting, the opposition actively undermined the popularly elected regimes. The socialists failed to recognize the challenge to their democratic mandate and to meet it with appropriate measures: by strengthening democratic officers and purging rightists in order to reestablish law and order; assuming executive power and temporarily recessing parliament in order to pass essential budgetary measures; institutionalizing and providing resources for the newly elected popular workplace and community councils to implement legislation. By not restricting democratic participation among those who would destroy it (and who eventually did) and not deepening it for those who were its primary defenders, the libertarian socialists undermined the transition to socialism. It is ironic that today the major lesson drawn by many liberal-left commentators is that Allende and Manley went too far and too fast—that they should have sacrificed major sectors of their program to continue in office. This superficial interpretation overlooks the tremendous energy and support that the original changes engendered and that sustained the regime; mass movements of the increasingly class conscious and organized workers and poor cannot be turned on and off like a faucet.

The major issue was that the changes in civil society were not accompanied by structural changes in the state: the issue is less the rate or even the scope of socioeconomic change, but the coordinated shift in the organization of state power. In fact, greater changes in state power would have allowed for a more measured tempo in social transformation. The basis for real and effective pluralism existed in the mobilized social forces of the new state. The failure of Allende and Manley to secure the foundations of this state to facilitate the gradual socialist transition—their continuation of the politics of capitalist pluralism when the bourgeois itself had adopted a more intransigent authoritarian mode of class warfare—was fatal. Moreover, the growing hostility and confrontation with the United States should have prompted these regimes to decrease their dependence on U.S. financial and commercial networks. It is not good revolutionary strategy to retain vulnerability while increasing militancy.

In the case of Cuba, the process of socialist transition was dominated by confrontation with the United States. The period of direct military intervention required a suspension of civil liberties, the centralization of political power, and the close coordination of civil associations by the state. Having successfully defended the revolution from imperial attack, the rulers of Cuba made these temporary measures into permanent features of the society: state-party interlock became a characteristic of Cuban socialism. The exceptional and necessary conditions that originally evoked centralization and authoritarian control were turned into "virtues" and built into the basic conception of socialism. The exclusion of imperialist and capitalist restorationists was extended to limit democratic debate among socialists over issues of forms of representation, economic development strategies, the market, economic planning, and so on. The result has been the stabilization of an egalitarian but authoritarian political system. Its unresponsiveness led in the 1970s to some constructive but limited reforms, with the introduction of competitive municipal elections.

The libertarian and authoritarian trends embodied in these three experiences illustrate the problem of establishing the boundaries between democratic and authoritarian practices in the transition to socialism.

In order to develop a perspective on the problem of the interrelationships of democratic and authoritarian practices, it is essential to analyze each one of the phases in democratic development to establish the conditions and therefore the boundaries that determine the utility of each practice.

Establishing Foundations: The Authoritarian Imperatives

It is common knowledge that privileged property groups have not voluntarily allowed themselves to be divested of their property. Nor have military rulers and the police apparatuses peacefully abandoned lucrative political offices to democratic regimes intent on dismantling the repressive machinery and prosecuting the criminal and corrupt amongst them. A further problem is that the United States (and to a lesser degree Europe) has not readily conceded to having client regimes displaced by insurgent democratic movements intent on developing a nonaligned policy. In our time revolutions that are profoundly social, democratic, and national in content have occurred only in the Third World, and they have occurred in contexts of intense social, political, and continuing military confrontation against a coalition of domestic military and civilian elites and their U.S. backers. The conditions under which the political transformations occur favor the emergence of politico-military structures, organization, and discipline. The implantation of the new social regime reflects two processes: the mobilization of the beneficiaries of the transformation and displacement of its adversaries. In short, the *transformation process* is a military-political struggle in which *resistance* and *repression* are the two major activities around which the two conflicting sides mobilize. Political victory establishes the basis for *foundation-building:* the establishment of a new productive system, social order, and constitution establishing the institutions and procedures within which participation will occur. The process of foundation-building involves profound political and social polarization, intense conflict, and frequent resort to force because the displaced forces and the newly established democratic regime share no common set of values, interests, or political framework to resolve their differences. For the new regime, authoritarian measures are the order of the day and continue to operate as long as the political survival of the regime is in question. The foundations of the new society are based in part on the restrictions imposed by the continuing conflict. The original authoritarian measures can be modified to accommodate all those forces that share the common political and social perspective embodied in the founding of the new society. It is almost inevitable that the removal or modification of the original authoritarian measures introduced will evoke conflict among socialists. Among those who have acquired a niche in the new apparatuses and those who are comfortable with the ease of issuing edicts instead of responding in debates, the authoritarian impulse will live on and thrive. The main challenge for socialists in the aftermath of defeating the imperial and restorationist forces is the rapid and effective abolition of the exceptional measures and the institutionalization of democracy. While this is neither an automatic nor an easy matter, it is central to any process worthy of being called a "transition to socialism."

The codification of the revolutionary transformation embodied in the new constitution defines the new structures of authority and representation. The openness of the channels for participation and the effectiveness of the operation of the new institutional order are dependent on the degree of military security—as national survival dominates all other political realities. Continual military confrontation, particularly the conflict between an aspiring revolutionary democratic regime and an interventionist world power, requires the subordination of civilian economy to the military, democratic institutions to military mobilization. The continuation of authoritarian measures is a direct result of the military conflict, which defines the scope and form of democratic participation. The conditions under which military definitions of political reality can be considered legitimate must from the beginning be defined as *exceptional circumstances*. Furthermore, the *suspension of democratic rights should be clearly admitted* and defined as reflecting a specific situation. These conditions are necessary in order to prepare the groundwork for democratic rulership immediately upon the lifting of the military emergency.

Institutionalizing the revolution at a time of military confrontation presents special problems. The imperatives of the military context define the relations between leaders and followers in centralist terms. Military forms of rulership, the acquisition of supplies through requisitions, conscriptions of labor power for defense purposes, and the mobilization of transport lead to a strengthening of central authority rather than democratic give-and-take between leaders and followers. The organizational structure of society is largely made up of institutions for defense rather than representative political organizations. Where the latter do exist their energy and time tend to be absorbed by defense issues.

Yet for all the difficulties that military security necessarily imposes on an emerging democratic regime, it is absolutely essential that *political boundaries be established and respected;* boundaries that clearly distinguish between those political and social forces defending the old regime and those backing the new regime and new foundations, and between those who defend the country from the military aggression of the great power and those who do not. Boundaries serve basically two essential functions—restricting participation of those who would destroy the new regime and permitting it to those who accept the new regime but may differ on policy, institutional practices, and so on. Boundaries are crucial in the process of democratization in recognizing differentiation of interests in the post-transformation period and in avoiding amalgamation—the lumping together of democratic critics with the enemies of democracy. *Pluralism*—the toleration and affirmation of different viewpoints and interests within the new social system—is thus built upon the establishment of the new foundation, its institutionalization, and codification.

With the end of military confrontation and politico-military warfare, civil society should begin to gain ascendency over military-defense organizations. The basic problem in socialist transition is precisely the difficulty of this process of conversion from the period of foundation-building and defense, with its authoritarian structures, to the institutionalization of democratic pluralism. The differences between the American Revolution and the contemporary social revolutions in the Third World are not reflected in the initial periods of authoritarianism—in both situations very similar repressive processes were employed against internal enemies. Rather the difference is in the process of *conversion* and the *establishment of boundaries:* the American revolutionary leadership recognized the time-limited nature of repressive measures and more or less delineated the group to be excluded from effective participation (to be sure, numerous nonloyalists, including women, blacks, Indians, and immigrants, were also excluded from full participation). Within the new boundaries (an independent republican nation-state based on private property), full participation was granted to debate and discuss the policies of the new regime. In contrast, in the post-revolutionary period the socialist regimes operate with "elastic" boundaries: post-revolutionary policy critics are compounded with counterrevolutionaries; the period of authoritarian rule is extended beyond the period of foundation and defense and becomes the norm rather than the exception. The differences in context between a period of struggle for survival and a period of peaceful development, between foundation-making and institutionalization, are conflated: the language of politics is violated and the imagery of permanent war is evoked. The *politics of amalgamation* is introduced: dissent and debate in the post-revolutionary period are subsumed with the military activities of the counterrevolution, serving as a pretext for continuous repressive measures.

Thus twentieth-century socialist revolutions have exhibited two basic weaknesses: an inability to convert the movements of transformation into institutional configurations independent of central authority; and an inability to consolidate the transformations and establish boundaries for the free play of politics, combining a unitary government with pluralist participation. The ideology justifying this aberrant behavior is the abstract generalized conception of the revolutionary classes and their social interest. By conceiving of *the* working class and *the* peasantry and of their historic interest, their specific sets of immediate interests are obscured. Abstraction and historicism serve to justify monolithism.

In fact the passage from authoritarianism rooted in the imperatives of foundation-building and defense to the institutionalization of pluralist democracy is blocked at several points. In the process of foundation-building, the agencies to establish the foundations are restricted to a limited group within the leadership that substitutes itself for the organized participation of social forces. This substitution legitimates the leadership (who become the "founding fathers") but denies participation to the presumed beneficiaries/protagonists of the transformation process. An elected constitutional convention is a more appropriate means for defining the basic features of the new social system than reliance on a leadership clique. The process of institutionalization may be similarly blocked. The absence of autonomous civilian institutions, the incorporation and predominance of military-defense institutions from the previous period, centralized control of institutions by the state rather than by the protagonists of change, and the blurring of roles and actors in the previous authoritarian military with new institutional functions all reinforce the extension of authoritarianism into the new institutional process.

Purposeful blurring of boundaries is the hallmark of authoritarian government: blurring of the boundaries between phases, actions, and actors. Clarity in identifying specific context and immediate objectives undermines the authoritarian impulse toward amalgamation and provides the basis for moving from constraints to free expession. The democratic socialist conception envisions the proliferation of autonomous civilian organizations, the subordination and diminution of the role of military-defense organizations, societal control and direction of the new institutions independent of the state, the demobilization of the military, and the dismantling of the repressive structures. These measures create favorable conditions for the emergence of a pluralistic socialistic state.

Pluralism, Democracy, and the Socialist Transition

The term "pluralism" has been used and abused in many different contexts in discussing the issues of socialism and democracy. Pluralism refers to the existence of a variety of competing interests, ideas, and policies among different political forces each seeking to influence the decision-making process. Many conservative and liberal ideologies, however, associate pluralism with a *specific* set of socioeconomic interests in a *given* social order, with a *particular* distribution of political power. For liberals and conservatives the presence of capitalist property-owning groups defending property interests and profits, through private control of the media and political machinery reflecting the unequal distribution of economic resources, defines the minimum conditions for discussing "pluralist politics." Unfortunately many socialists agree with this view and commit two opposing types of errors. Authoritarian socialists accept the capitalist conception of pluralism, using it as an excuse to repress all expression ("If that's pluralism we are against it"). Libertarian socialists concede the conservative-liberal conception and permit propertied groups to dominate strategic sectors of the economy and society and thus to exploit their position to destroy democracy. The authoritarian response, by failing to distinguish between the notion of a plurality of interests within collectivist society and the ideologically loaded capitalist conception of pluralism, contributes to the homogenization of society and the installation of a monolithic political regime. In the authoritarian setting, political conflict is transferred to a series of interest groups located in the bureaucratic interstices of society. The socialist adaptation of the liberal conception of pluralism has led to several efforts to incorporate capitalist cooperation in the transition to socialism. Chile under Allende and Jamaica under Manley made efforts to induce private capital to cooperate in the economic development of the country. In both cases, private interests responded by arranging massive illegal and legal transfers of capital, running down plant and equipment, and working in tandem with international capital and the imperial state to destabilize and erode the popular base of the democratic-socialist regime. Subsequent to the downfall of the socialist regime, the self-styled conservative upholders of pluralist democracy supported a military dictatorship in Chile and an authoritarian conservative parliamentary regime in Jamaica.

A more realistic conception of socialist pluralism is evidenced in the efforts of the Nicaraguan government to fashion a political framework for socialist transition. The transformation of the state apparatus, the initiation of dynamic public and cooperative sectors, and the rapid growth of autonomous (or semiautonomous) mass organizations have provided the foundations within which an electoral process involving a broad range of competing social groups, interests, and programs can compete. Most important, the democratic civilian organizations are debating issues and programs during a period of military-defense emergency and infusing the process of institution-building and foundation-making with the pluralist ethos. The reaction of counterrevolutionaries has taken two forms: (1) to ally and subordinate themselves to the policy of the U.S. imperial state as armed mercenaries, and (2) to penetrate the political arena in order to weaken the foundations and institutional framework upon which the new social order rests. Their strategy is to manipulate the notion of pluralism to include bourgeois control of the strategic institutions of political decision-making (the media and the state) and economic development (public enterprises). Unwilling to accept the new social and political parameters of pluralist participation, the bulk of the Nicaraguan bourgeoisie has rejected participation and begun to run down production, thus creating the conditions they claim to have sought to avoid, namely an economy with a growing public sector. The Nicaraguan experience with pluralism and socialism highlights several issues: (1) that democracy and socialism are possible in the process of institution-building even during periods of military defense; (2) that the boundaries between dissent and armed subversion can be drawn effectively, thus preserving political freedoms while defending the new social foundations of the regime; (3) that the fundamental issue for capital is neither political participation nor economic opportunities (assured by the Sandinista government) but political power, and specifically the balance of power in the state; and (4) that the antidemocratic, antieconomic behavior of the private sector cannot be separated from an analysis of the international political-economic context in which it operates. The massive and direct intervention of the U.S. imperial state, providing subsidies to cushion economic losses as well as alternative sites for investors to relocate their operations, sustains the willingness of the private sector to risk rejecting the pluralist rules of the game. For the Sandinistas the alternative to socialist pluralism is to follow the path of the southern European socialists: to share political power with the bourgeoisie in order to obtain economic cooperation and in the process lose political control and popular support without securing any substantial increase in economic production or social improvement in the lives of the poor.

Given this international setting and the behavior of the capitalist class, socialist transitional strategies must fashion a notion of pluralism that does not count on capitalist cooperation if the democratic process is to be preserved. If individuals or groups of domestic capitalists happen to agree to abide by the rules of the game, the pluralist system can accommodate them. Depending on how the United States–Contra–

Nicaragua war proceeds, the pendulum may swing toward more authoritarian or democratic practices; while the exigencies of survival are
paramount and may evoke centralized and authoritarian measures, the
principle that these are exceptional measures as opposed to the norm of
autonomous democratic institutions should be upheld. The issue is not
the particular measure that the revolutionary regime takes at a particular
moment in time but the direction toward which it is moving.

Neoliberalism: Bureaucratic Centralism as an Alternative to Democratic Socialism

The current impasse in the development and expansion of productive
forces in the Socialist bloc countries has led in some countries to a
number of significant reforms and new policy initiatives. These changes
are having far-reaching effects on the economic structure, social order,
and perhaps political system. Reforms include the emergence of clearly
expressed alternative economic programs defining new mixes of private, public, and cooperative ownership; wide discretionary powers for
local managers above and beyond those previously delegated by central
planners; proposals to introduce participation and discussion by workers' assemblies at the workshop level concerning managerial decisions,
production targets, and conditions of work; and the increasing influence
of local municipal authorities and their capacity to shape the governance
of local communities. These reforms all suggest that the "totalitarian"
image of socialist society is no longer valid in capturing the growing
proliferation of "semi-autonomous" interest groups, decision-making
centers, and levels of power. There appears to be a two-tiered system of
power: at the highest levels, control of decisions of international importance and those relating to the general direction of society is concentrated among a small elite; while at the middle and lower levels there are
increasing numbers of interest groups, embodying a variety of social,
regional, sectoral, and ethnic interests competing for power.

Critical to defining the nature of current developments in the socialist
countries is the level of analysis that one chooses to focus on. The level
of reform at the *micro* level suggests substantial movements toward a
greater degree of participation, debate, and discussion; while at the
macro level, discussion and participation are limited to a select group of
actors, some of whom favor and others oppose the process of "decom-
pression"—the liberalization of political and economic life.

The micro-processes that evidence changes toward new forms of
participation involve the workplace and local government. At the workplace, greater responsibility for production, working conditions and
discipline, payments, product selection, and introduction of new technology has begun to emerge. At the municipal level, local authorities are

assuming greater authority and responsibility for health services, education, and other public services. The proximity of local authorities to their immediate constituency and the growth of civic awareness have led to increased citizen criticisms and claims in the arena of municipal politics.

While these micro changes in the workplace and municipal government represent an important new departure and open new vistas for a democratization process, they need to be located within the macro framework. Changes at the micro level reflect policy formulated at the national level: the micro level is where dissent and disagreements are possible. While the local organs may propose, it is the national elite that disposes. Although the boundaries of power, authority, and decision-making may be in flux—and one may say that at the local level they have been enlarged—the general direction is still for the political directorate to control the spheres of decision-making.

The process of enlarging decision-making among local authorities has resulted in part from the impasse of over-centralization and in part from the growth of local capacities for assuming responsibility. Basically it reflects the delegation of power by the central authorities to local units, which can implement policies and decisions more efficiently at that level. While the initiative may have originated at the top, however, the assumption of responsibility and autonomy of action has created a momentum of its own. This had led to the growth of rather complex relations with the center, including a certain degree of bargaining with the central authorities. The reversal of these processes is a real possibility, yet increasingly unlikely when the shifts result in more effective operations.

Shifts toward decentralized decisions and local authority have a tendency to consolidate and create new coalitions. These alliances embody new orientations among the working class, intelligentsia, and segments of the party. New concerns among workers and managers with improving performance, rewarding skills, and upgrading employment categories (rejection of "dirty work") coincide with the central authorities' concern with the growth of discontent at the workplace. In this regard the predominance of liberal party officials allows for the implementation of concessions to deflect conflict and to increase the sources of information to allow for the efficient operation of an increasingly more complex technological society.

In summary, at the middle levels, interest differentiation and interest group politics are increasingly competing with, displacing, and operating through the long-standing authoritarian bureaucratic structures. Competing social groups—intellectuals, technocrats, political cadres, and new generations of young workers—become the sources and embodiments of these pre-democratic movements and groupings. They are both "in" the system, sharing its gains in material well-being and belief in its ideological foundation, and "outside" it, retaining a belief in the need for continuing reform and redefinition of the relationship between an all-inclusive state, individualism, and the autonomy of social organization.

A major motif in some socialist bloc countries is "reform"—and the major trend within the reform currents is liberalization. For historical-structural reasons, as well as for reasons relating to the present ideological conjuncture, liberalization has been far more significant in defining the content and direction of the reforms than the democratic tendency. In this regard it is important to recognize the very distinct characteristics of the two tendencies and not to confuse them. Liberalization essentially involves measures to open the economic system to greater private initiative and responsiveness to market demands and needs. It encourages and promotes wage and income differentials, attacking the statist-egalitarian-employment security syndrome as inefficient and a constraint on modernization. Democratization involves measures taken to increase popular decision-making and involvement in the processes in which societies decide on basic priorities and public policies.

Several contradictory developments within the collectivist countries have contributed to the emergence of reform politics. Dynamic growth in broad areas of the economy has created the basis for intensive forms of development. Yet the needs of intensive expansion (new technology, overseas markets, complex organization, greater flows of information, a more flexible and responsible management and labor force, and the increasing demand for quality goods) are incompatible with a rigid bureaucratic centralist system organized for control and the meeting of quantitative targets with a semi-skilled or unskilled labor force. While the contradictions of dynamic growth created the conditions for reform, the particular direction of reform (liberal-market as opposed to democratic-socialist planning) was the result of political decisions and the particular mobilization of bias embodied in the new social forces gaining hegemony in socialist societies. Liberalization is par excellence the ideology of upwardly mobile skilled professionals ("collectivist yuppies"). Managers, intellectuals, and technocrats favor the shift to decentralized market policies because they provide greater opportunities, mobility, economic rewards, and social authority, as well as more consumer goods and increased economic rationality. Liberalization allows the party leadership to maintain political power and prerogatives while decentralizing economic decision-making and responsibility. The hope is that reform will lead to gradual depoliticization of socioeconomic issues implicit in the partial separation of political and economic spheres. Over the medium run this is seen as a way of allowing the state to appear as a "neutral" arbiter between conflicting interests, in a fashion not too dissimilar from the role ascribed to the state (by its ideologists) in capitalist society. With the introduction of liberal reforms, the political elite hope to shift the focus to the operation of the market and to meeting consumer needs. In this perspective the managerial strata become responsible for socioeconomic claims, while the party's control over political decisions, organization, and structure are not affected. The separation of the political and economic spheres results in the growth of liberal economics and in modified form the continuation of authoritarian politics. These precise structural advantages are the important reason why the regimes' efforts at self-reform take the form of liberalization rather than democratization. A second basic reason is that there are significant strata, especially among intellectuals, skilled workers in growth industries, and farmers in fertile regions adjacent to major metropolitan areas, who ultimately benefit from the replacement of bureaucratic-egalitarianism by the market mechanism. Substantial social groups who developed their skills and received higher educational training within the centralized collectivist framework now feel that it has outlived its usefulness. For them "state socialism" was a period of primitive accumulation creating the basis for "market socialism"—with greater individual mobility through the extension of market opportunities.

Democratization emerging from a movement of working class solidarity represents a top-to-bottom shift in power in contrast to the intra-elite power-sharing characeristic of liberalization processes. While liberalization optimizes market behavior, democratization increases the participation of labor in the planning process. While both liberals and democrats may favor decentralization, liberals favor devolving power from the party to the new technocratic-managerial elite, while democrats favor increasing the role of self-management councils in setting planning and development priorities. While prior to the initiation of reform, liberals and democratic socialists share a common platform of opposition to the bureaucratic authoritarian system, with the introduction of reforms, the convergence gives way. When liberal reforms threaten segments of the working class on particular issues (such as job security), opponents of reforms among unreconstructed bureaucratic centralists can occasionally pick up some support from labor.

Liberalization gives a major impetus to the economy in terms of opportunities for a greater degree of personal choice of consumer goods and services, as well as after-hours employment, and thus creates a broad basis of legitimacy. Deeper integration into the market, however, and the growing inequalities that accompany the introduction of the new economic mechanisms create new sources of discontent among young unemployed workers (not able to secure employment in cost-efficient firms) and in regions with underdeveloped or backward enterprises (such as textiles, mines, and farming in infertile zones). Moreover, over-exuberant insertion into the world market (especially through excessive dependence on overseas borrowing and misplaced zeal in importing capital goods that have few prospects of generating export earnings) can lead to severe payments crises and even submission to IMF prescriptions. Market-induced crises can further polarize market-socialist societies. Thus, while the democratization process is substantially weaker than the liberalization trend, the socioeconomic consequences engendered by the latter may provide the basis for the revival of democratic socialism. This is not a matter of wishful thinking. The liberal reforms are producing a degree of relaxation of central controls, experimentation with limited forms of worker co-participation, and more pragmatic criteria for evaluating the success or failure of the new economic mechanisms. The "liberal shell" may provide both the political space and the contradictions that will hasten the democratization process.

Chinese Neoliberalism: The Technocratic Alternative to Socialist Democracy

The current Chinese leadership has skillfully adapted the language of Western modernization doctrine, with all its classless rhetoric, to a neoliberal development strategy. The neoliberalism espoused by the regime and celebrated by the West speaks of a "flexible system," yet fails to specify the conditions that might allow all social groups within the country an equal share of the benefits. In fact the regime is militantly and inflexibly opposed to any discussion or practice that smacks of egalitarianism. The new boundaries and priorities that define the parameters within which the new flexibility operates are not specified. In particular, as the regime moves away from centralized planned egalitarianism, it is creating new rigidities imposed by the differential impact of the market on various classes, economic sectors, regions, types of households, and so on. The uneven distribution of favorable economic location, high soil fertility, and access to state credit and overseas capital affect the capacity of different groups to seize opportunities and bend the flexibility of the system to their favor.

Down-playing and little by little discarding notions of class struggle, neoliberal policy-makers have adopted a technocratic theory of social change and economic development. They have combined an exaggerated emphasis on increasing production, through maximizing income differentials, with new management techniques and work processes in a major redefinition of workplace relations. The result has been a greater degree of managerial control over employment and the terms of employment. As central planning gives way to the market and as managerial and entreprenual authority extends over the economy, labor incomes increase at the expense of employment security. The evolution of managerial authority toward greater influence within a market-based economy is in conflict with the central ideological foundations of the social system, which explicitly define the workers as the owners of the means of production. By making the future development of economy and society depend upon the productivity and efficiency of a new manager-dominated system, the regime undermines the previous ideological basis for challenging the new system. The new regime has fashioned a "pragmatic" ideology to legitimate the new forms of workplace organization. It claims practice (pragmatism) not "theory" is its criterion for truth. Measures of "success"—are basically the immediate impact of policy on production in particular social settings. Regime ideologists omit discussion of the effects of current policy on the long-term, large-scale institutional developments that provide support for local level short-term private activity. The massive infrastructure developments sustaining current activity were based on long-term, large-scale collective activity. The demobilization and individualization of agrarian units weakens the capacity to sustain these activities. Unless the state assumes the activities organized by the collective units, the infrastructure will deteriorate and ultimately affect the local/private producers: private affluence differentially distributed cannot coincide for long with the poverty of public sector activity. The restricted perspective and short-term results that characterize "pragmatic" policy-making prevents it from taking account of the long- to middle-terms effect of increasing social inequality and its potential for political and social polarization. The structural changes in the internal organization of the social order, which are accompanied by increasingly initmate relations between local upwardly mobile groups and overseas counterparts in multinational banks and corporations, can lead to the fragmentation of the society and economy. Externally integrated dynamic sectors increasingly obtain a disproportionate share of national income, while underdeveloped local enterprises vegetate at the margin of the economy.

The centrality of the market can lead to dramatic short-term increases in economic productivity; but to the degree that the market and the enterprise determine the allocation of economic resources and the terms for upward social mobility, political institutions (state, party, and ideology) will become increasingly auxiliary or marginal to the operation of society. The dissolution of political control over the economy and society can lead to market and class determinants based on income, economic power, and control.

The earlier bureaucratic, centrally planned economy and its ultra-voluntarist ideological accompaniment contributed to the rise of "pragmatism" in several ways. First, the bureaucratic centralists separated the long-range goal of a classless society from a policy of gradual and visible improvement in the availability of goods. Secondly, they equated increasing consumption with "bourgeoisefication," adopting a "market" or circulationist concept of class—(rather than defining it in terms of productive relations). Thirdly, they made virtues out of necessities: the austerity and constraints that necessarily accompany initial accumulation, revolutionary warfare, economic boycotts, and foreign intervention were translated into a false vision of socialism. The Maoists failed to separate the different phases of revolution, capitalist development, and external relations. This led them to conflate all phases and promote a policy of permanent mobilization, in which political realities were falsified or exaggerated to sustain the ideology. The result was the separation of the ideology from reality, and the subsequent manipulation of ideology as a "mobilizing tool." Permanent mobilization of the labor force against vague or fictitious political opponents and in the absence of any tangible material improvements led to political and perhaps physical exhaustion. De-politicization or privatization was accompanied by an almost exclusive focus on immediate tangible material improvements. The "devaluation" of ideology led to the transfer of loyalties to those political leaders and policies that promised tangible results.

The conflation of the different phases of the revolution led to the notion of permanent class struggle. While Mao did make a distinction between contradictions (nonviolent) among the people under socialism as opposed to the contradiction of capitalism, in practice he followed a different approach, engaging in massive and violent struggles against rich peasants, "capitalist roaders" (party members), and other elements of post-revolutionary society. The technique of amalgamating all differing perspectives into a pejorative counterrevolutionary category was intended to mobilize the negative feelings of the labor force toward new adversaries. These campaigns were orchestrated to maximize state-centered economic accumulation and to eliminate political-factional opponents. The result was disruption of the productive process and social organization and disorientation among the labor force—as previously respected comrades were castigated and removed from office. Thus the notion of "permanent revolution" came to lack any positive reinforcement: neither increased political control by labor, nor increasing improvement in income. Constant mobilization against subjectively defined enemies without concrete and clear positive consequences leads to cynicism and withdrawal from politics. The conflicts over development strategies in the post-revolutionary period were of a qualitatively different sort to those that appeared in the earlier revolutionary period. The foundation of the new economy and the new state provided the basis for a *new socialist pluralism,* in which differences were unavoidable and open debates necessary to sustain political and social commitments. *The incapacity of the Chinese leaders to recognize the new foundations as a boundary within which debate, discussion, and controversy could flourish led to the extension and deepening of the existing military-political monolithic conception of political organization.*

Likewise the failure of the Maoists to recognize that the transformation and initial accumulation phases were sharply delineated from development meant that the expropriation process was allowed to continue and eventually extended to nonexploitative groups that could and should have played a major role in the development process. The campaigns directed at landlords, money lenders, and military warlords—legitimate objects of expropriation—were replaced by violent attacks on moderately prosperous or wealthy peasants, small traders, artisans, and so on; all of whom were dubbed "kulaks." The failure to distinguish phases and forms of capitalist production—and the use of crude market criteria to categorize groups—led to the substitution of the state and individual political will (ultra-voluntarism) for social forces better placed to organize the productive forces. The failure to distinguish between initial accumulation and normal accumulation (temporal sequences) and between landlords and propertied peasants (locations in the productive process) reflects the ill-informed application of a notion of undifferentiated capitalism to all market activity.

Finally, the failure to periodicize and understand the changing nature of the international environment led to a one-dimensional foreign policy. During the civil war and Korean War and in their immediate aftermath, China *was* threatened militarily and boycotted economically. To sustain the economy in the *context of external hostility,* Mao initiated a policy of self-reliance and made a virtue of sacrifice and austerity. In the face of imminent and visible threats, Mao described the United States as a "paper tiger," a useful notion to sustain morale and mobilize mass support. Yet with the weakening of the United States during Vietnam and the crumbling of the boycott as Europe and Japan sought to tap the seemingly vast Chinese market, the Chinese leadership was slow to revise its relationship to the world market. Austerity and self-reliance, which began as necessities became a principle of socialism. The market, which could have been selectively exploited to provide needed technological advances, was rejected as a source of capitalist contamination. From being frozen out of the market by U.S. directives, to being kept out by Maoist command, the Chinese failed to develop a policy toward the market that could have increased consumption and production and avoided the continual pressure to accumulate at the expense of labor force consumption. The basic flaw in the Maoist conception of socialism was the idea that a social system is defined by its relation to the world economy. Participation in the world market became equated with capitalism. Socialism was defined by its withdrawal from the market. The consequences of this profoundly erroneous conception were negative, as the market could and does provide the means for a collectivist society to develop productive forces without having to repeat all the stages of development and to produce locally at high cost all the goods one needs. If the Chinese leadership, following Marx, had defined the social system by its social-relation of production, it would have recognized that collectively owned property could be strengthened as well as endangered by participation in the world market. The two sides of market participation include appropriation of capital or penetration by capital, and linkages between corporations and public enterprises that lead to local adaptations and growth or increasing subordination. Dangers from market participation can be obviated to the degree that internal relations are anchored in an ideological-institutional framework that mediates between socialist production and world market exchanges. The key element of this framework is the approximation of practice (working class democracy) with theory.

In summary, the Maoists indiscriminate use of Marxist ideology to describe very disparate aspects and phases of economic and political development led to its loss of any cognitive value and political relevance to development. Ideology became the subjective expression of a voluntarist elite increasingly divorced from the everyday interests of the masses.

Applying their neoliberal agenda in an ideological vacuum, the contemporary Chinese pragmatists short-circuit debate by acting first and theorizing later. By appealing to labor's immediate interest in material improvement they have recognized a vital aspect of Chinese reality that previous leaders down-played or ignored. The Chinese leadership's appeal to "facts" and empiricism is attractive to a people who were subjected to constant mobilization in ill-defined campaigns against nebulous adversaries, with no visible material payoffs. The "facts" in question are concrete: opportunities for greater income by self-induced efforts. This ahistorical, asocial, apolitical, amoral approach does not seem to the population to be another ideological deception: one can count one's chickens, pigs, tractors, or television sets. People work to raise their standard of living. They struggle to obtain work, control the conditions of work, and to improve their income. The previous regime's tortuous construction of a socio-historical reality based on real and fictitious objects of struggle and sacrifice was largely divorced from the day-to-day productive-economic activity that is characteristic of post-revolutionary China. The current regime has re-cast the world in imagery more relevant to the producers: instead of the history of struggle it emphasizes the present of increasing consumption; instead of international conflict it stresses increasing international exchanges; instead of intra-elite conflicts it emphasizes national development.

Focusing on peace and progress through hard work and education, the regime has left out any discussion of the consequences of this arrangement for social equality and political power and failed to specify any mechanism to ensure social justice. In the face of an emerging pattern of polarized development, in which opportunities are becoming increasingly unequal, the regime postulates at best a vague diffusion or trickle-down effect from the rich to the poor. To the extent that it has discussed equality, it has equated it with the austerity and poverty of the previous period, thus bypassing discussion that might combine growth and equity, liberalization and democracy.

In countering "theory" with "practice," the current Chinese leadership has created a false dichotomy. It argues for the transformation of China through a coalition of wealthy farmers, technocrats, managers of growth industries, foreign capital, and national party leaders. Through these social and political agencies the regime is stimulating the diffusion and application of new technology and reinforcing the tendencies toward new forms of private concentrated capital accumulation. The policy of deliberately favoring the "strong" is epitomized by the regime's "get rich" slogans, yet not all agrarian or industrial classes are in a position to accumulate and expand, least of all at the same rate.

Nor is it clear that "practice" was absent from the previous regime: its practice, however, was to observe a different set of facts than those observed by the current regime and to act on them in a different manner. The alliance between the old cadre/political bureaucracy and the poorest layers of the labor force was linked to a system that preserved the political prerogatives of the party machine in exchange for maintaining minimum standards and security for all. Socialism was conceived of as an authoritarian-egalitarian system in which free expression and individual mobility had no place. The current regime's conception reflects the entrepreneurial aspirations and upward mobility proclivities of substantial sectors of the agrarian and educated population. Its neoliberal approach is oriented toward promoting growth through individual and household accumulation and differential economic rewards. The attempt by the regime to deny the "practice" of its predecessors is a means of avoiding any serious discussion of earlier policies, particularly those aspects that present potential areas for debate (such as the positive results of large-scale collective efforts, job security, and food subsidies).

The style of debate presented by the current regime—self-evident truths, bland assertions of success, revision of history including distortions of the past and evasions of the present—is celebrated in the West, which is eager to document China's move toward dismantling the collective system of production.[1] Marked by ambiguity and an unwillingness to recognize multiple dimensions and layers of social reality, the notion of "practice" that is central to the current regime is associated with a *single dimension:* growing production, increasing goods, and affluent individuals. In both texture and substance, it is reminiscent of late nineteenth-century Western economic dogma. Qualitative aspects of production relations are subsumed in quantitative indicators of growth: the growth of managerial autonomy and enterprise earnings are emphasized, while labor's subordination to the market and the managerial ethos is ignored. The growth of consumer goods and their availability to a broader public are emphasized, while improvement of social services and particularly the disparities in access to these goods and services are rarely considered. The upwardly mobile new affluent classes are presented as social models. Liberalization is creating new areas of power, privilege, and status differentiation. The Chinese Horatio Algers, like their counterparts in earlier U.S. history, are a powerful myth that probably does attract and energize vast groups of the poor, who seek to emulate their path to affluence and success. The resultant individualism and rampant competitiveness lead to social fragmentation, while the absence of large-scale collective units could create serious problems in the maintenance and expansion of essential power grids, dams, rural infrastructure, and natural resource development, most of which are far out of reach of private groups or household units.

Finally, class conflicts at the local level and expressions of sporadic individual resentments by those who are displaced, bypassed, and marginalized—those who have lost relative to the upwardly mobile groups—represent a new reality that will only increase with time. The "pragmatists" may believe that trickle-down economic development benefits everyone, but historical experience throughout the world argues otherwise. The blanket condemnation of egalitarianism as a remnant of the "Maoist," "dogmatic" past and the trumpeting of the virtues of entrepreneurship cannot obscure some troubling new developments. For example, increased earnings of some farmers and merchants are creating pressure on salaries of urban wage earners; increasing dependence on the market is producing a highly differentiated peasantry; and cutbacks in state subsidies are adversely affecting low-income families.[2] Wealth in family households can only expand by extending production and exploiting nonhousehold labor. The deepening of the current tendencies in the economy will produce new class formations, and in time new class conflicts of a more extensive and entrenched character may occur.

Conclusion

The struggle for socialism and democracy are inextricably linked. As we have argued earlier, the consolidation of democracy requires the conscious intervention and mobilization of socialist forces. The problems of redemocratization in the Third World cannot be solved through electoral contests that are premised on the continuation of military power and the dominance of development agendas by international banks. The problems in the existing socialist countries are no less acute. The experiments by the state bureaucrats and their technocratic advisors with "market socialism" may gain them some popular support and breathing space, but new class differences and economic problems (unemployment, inflation, and debt) threaten to ignite a new round of social conflicts. One experiment that has yet to be tried (and that likely will not be introduced from above) is democratic planning through a labor-elected parliament. Historical development over past decades has demonstrated the enormous vitality of the struggle for socialist democracy, a history which has been little studied. (For example, no social history of the Chilean social movements and their experience with direct democracy during the Allende years has yet been written.) In the contemporary context, the most singular event is the Sandinista effort to combine social transformation and free elections under wartime conditions.

The theory and practice of democratic socialism embodied in the Sandinista experience of defense and political pluralism provide socialist theorists and activists with a wealth of new ideas concerning the opportunities for transcending existing liberal and Stalinist versions of authoritarian politics. It is precisely the attractiveness and relevance of revolutionary democratic socialism to millions—East and West—which has precipitated both Washington's sustained aggressive military and economic campaign to destroy it, and Moscow's effort to coopt it.

Notes

1. Christopher Wren of the *N.Y. Times* writes: "*People's Daily*, the Party newspaper, has assured readers that getting rich and buying consumer goods is not decadent if it makes life more pleasant" *N.Y. Times*, December 17, 1984, A10.

2. For a perceptive journalistic account of these developments, see Orville Schell, "The Wind of Wanting to Go It Alone," *New Yorker*, January 23, 1984, 43–85.

A report on the growing inequalities and emerging conflict appeared in the *New York Times* in late 1985: "Another issue that has caused considerable party friction, the shift away from subsidized food prices toward a system where values are set in the marketplace, has shown signs of causing widespread restiveness among the 200 million Chinese who do not live off the land. The transition has meant higher living costs in urban areas at a time when there was a lot of grumbling about the new prosperity of the peasants." The same article also reports the largest one year drop in grain production since the revolution and an unprecedented 11 percent rate of inflation for 1985, outcomes at least in part resulting from the free market policies promoted by the regime. See John Burns, "China Grain Crop Dips; Setback Seen for Policy," *New York Times*, Dec. 23, 1985, 4.

Index